The Therapeutic F
in the Clinical Co

The Therapeutic Frame in the Clinical Context examines some of the key issues inherent in the intimate and very often intense therapeutic relationship.

Contributors from diverse backgrounds address specific aspects of the therapeutic frame. How does a client feel about unexpectedly meeting her psychotherapist's son or daughter? How does a psychotherapist or counsellor practise within a 'frameless', often intrusive, environment in acute hospital wards? How does a counsellor manage the frame in the face of a life-threatening illness? How does a psychotherapist create a secure frame within a GP practice?

Using a wealth of examples from clinical practice, *The Therapeutic Frame in the Clinical Context* examines these issues and more, in a range of settings including the NHS, private practice, and the workplace, and provides valuable guidelines from a range of theoretical perspectives, including psychoanalytical, existential, humanistic and Jungian.

Maria Luca is a Consultant Psychotherapist and Clinical Supervisor in the NHS and in a private practice. She is the Director of the MA in Psychotherapy and Counselling, Regent's College, London.

The Therapeutic Frame in the Clinical Context

Integrative perspectives

Edited by Maria Luca

Brunner-Routledge
Taylor & Francis Group

HOVE AND NEW YORK

First published 2004
by Brunner-Routledge
27 Church Road, Hove, East Sussex BN3 2FA

Simultaneously published in the USA and Canada
by Brunner-Routledge
270 Madison Avenue, New York, NY 10016

Brunner-Routledge is an imprint of the Taylor & Francis Group

Typeset in Times New Roman by
Keystroke, Jacaranda Lodge, Wolverhampton
Printed and bound in Great Britain by
MPG Books Ltd, Bodmin, Cornwall
Paperback cover design by Hybert Design

British Library Cataloguing in Publication Data
A catalogue record for this book is available
from the British Library

Library of Congress Cataloging-in-Publication Data
The therapeutic frame in the clinical context : integrative
perspectives / edited by Maria Luca.
        p. cm.
Includes bibliographical references and index.
ISBN 1-58391-976-7 (hbk. : alk. paper) — ISBN 1-58391-977-5 (pbk. : alk. paper)
1. Psychotherapist and patient. 2. Psychotherapy—Practice. 3. Psychotherapy.
I. Luca, Maria, 1956– II. Title.

RC480.8.T455 2004
616.89′14—dc22   2004005657

ISBN 1-58391-976-7 (Hbk)
ISBN 1-58391-977-5 (Pbk)

Dedicated to my mother and father, Andriana
and Kyriakos Luca

Contents

Contributors

John Beveridge is a UKCP registered, attachment-based, analytical psychotherapist, who lives and works in private practice in London. He teaches Object Relations and Dissociation at the Centre for Attachment-Based Analytical Psychotherapy, London.

Anne Brockbank is a registered BACP practitioner, working from a humanistic person-centred stance within an integrative framework. She has worked as a counsellor for over twenty years in a variety of settings and she sees her private clients in a central London location. Her work includes trauma, bereavement and relationship issues, as well as depression and anxiety. Anne is also a qualified and experienced supervisor, and she subscribes to the BACP Code of Ethics for trainers, supervisors and counsellors and holds personal indemnity insurance. Anne is co-author, with Ian McGill, of *Facilitating Reflective Learning in Higher Education* published in 1998 by the Open University Press, and co-editor, with Ian McGill and Nic Beech, of *Reflective Learning in Practice* for Gower, published in 2002, as well as co-authoring a further edition, with Ian McGill, of *The Action Learning Handbook* published in 2003 by Kogan Page.

Stefano Ferraiolo is a UKCP registered psychotherapist and a business mentor, currently working in the public sector within the NHS and in private practice. He is currently engaged in researching on the subject of how synergies between business and psychoanalysis could support the development of individuals and senior managers within organisations. He is a part-time academic lecturer.

Deborah Killeen is a psychotherapist working in the NHS in both primary and secondary care. She trained at Regent's College School of Psychotherapy and Counselling in London and works from an integrative perspective. After graduating with a Photography and Film degree in 1989 she has worked in the media for fourteen years and currently combines part-time work for BBC Television with psychotherapy.

Maria Luca is a psychotherapist and clinical consultant in private practice and in the NHS. She is the Director of the MA in Psychotherapy and Counselling at the School of Psychotherapy and Counselling, Regent's College, London. She was book review editor for the European Journal of PCH and has published articles in professional journals, including: 'Containment of the Sexualized and Erotized Transference', in the *Journal of Clinical Psychoanalysis* (2003), 'Surviving Terror in the Clinical Encounter', in *The Psychotherapy Review* (2000), 'The Unsayable in Hysteria', in *The Psychotherapy Review* (2000), 'Pandora's Box: The shadow of femininity in the treatment of psychosomatic distress', in *Psychodynamic Counselling* (1999). She has lectured widely in the UK and in Greece. She is currently working towards a Ph.D.

Greg Madison is an existential analyst and focusing-oriented therapist living in London. Greg developed and managed the first Psychotherapy Support Team at Kings College Hospital, London, and now offers consultancy to other hospitals. He is a clinical supervisor and psychotherapist in various institutional and private settings, and a member of visiting faculty at the School of Psychotherapy and Counselling at Regent's College, London, and The Focusing Institute, New York. Greg has authored articles and book chapters on existential and experiential approaches to psychotherapy.

James Pollard is a psychotherapist in private practice in London and Cambridge. He is a training therapist and supervisor for the Centre for Attachment-based Psychoanalytic Psychotherapy (CAPP). He is the Chair of the United Kingdom Council for Psychotherapy. He has taught on a wide range of courses for the CAPP training and was for some years the Chair of CAPP. He is an Associate Member of the Cambridge Society for Psychotherapy.

Andrea Sabbadini is a chartered psychologist and a member of the British Psychoanalytical Society. A former director of the Arbours Training Programme in Psychotherapy, he currently lectures at UCL and at Regent's College. He has published in the leading professional journals and edited *Time in Psychoanalysis* (1979) and *Even Paranoids Have Enemies* (1998). He is also the founding editor of *Psychoanalysis* *and History*, the book review editor of *The International Journal of Psychoanalysis* and the chairman of the European Psychoanalytic Film Festival.

Paul Smith-Pickard, M.Ed., MA, is a UKCP registered psychotherapist working in the NHS and in private practice from an existential perspective. His first degree was in Fine Art, and he considers this to have been an excellent foundation for a creative attitude towards the art of psychotherapy. He is on the visiting faculty of both the SPC at Regent's College and the NSPC at Schiller International University, London, and is currently engaged with doctoral research into the phenomenology of encounter in psychotherapy. He is the Chair-elect of the Society for Existential Analysis.

Paola F. Valerio graduated from Edinburgh University. She trained with the Jungian section of the British Association of Psychotherapists where she is a training advisor for final year students and a member of the Training Committee. She worked as part of the Guys and Maudsley NHS Trust and has published book reviews and articles in journals, and a chapter in the book *Love and Hate in the Transference* (edited by David Mann). She has set up a small research project, as part of doctoral research, in collaboration with psychologists within a NHS Trust, looking at the efficacy of groups for woman survivors of child sexual abuse.

Nick Zinovieff worked for many years as a psychiatric social worker and has a particular interest in large groups and the dynamics of institutions. He is UKCP registered. Though the original influence on his psychotherapy practice was psychoanalytical, he completed his training in the existential-phenomenological tradition in the first Advanced Diploma in Existential Psychotherapy group at the School of Psychotherapy and Counselling at Regent's College. He works now in general and private practice and is a clinical supervisor at the SPC at Regent's College and the New School of Psychotherapy and Counselling.

Foreword

This book gives life and passion to a fundamental yet neglected topic. The metaphor of the 'frame' – first proposed by Milner in 1952, and derived from the way in which the boundary around a painting marks it out from its surroundings – is used to denote diverse phenomena in psychotherapy, such as rules, procedures, and various kinds of limits on the permitted behaviour of both patient and therapist. Many of these aspects of the frame are concerned with distinguishing the therapeutic setting and activity from other forms of personal encounter. A well-maintained frame, in terms of a disciplined and consistent stance on the part of the therapist, has often been regarded as crucial in psychoanalytic work because of the importance of preserving a clear view of the transference. Thus, as well as attending to time boundaries, the therapist is concerned to restrict his or her comments largely to interpretations of unconscious conflicts. Deviations or disruptions of the frame, either in terms of time or in the nature of the therapist's remarks and interactions with the client, are seen as potentially highly damaging to the therapeutic endeavour. In many publications, Robert Langs has provided examples illustrating how frame deviations, such as a therapist's personal disclosure or acts of helpfulness beyond the psychoanalytic interpretation, may be experienced consciously by the patient as gratifying and perhaps helpful, whilst unconsciously they are perceived as harmful and an expression of the therapist's incapacity to tolerate painful truth. These unconscious perceptions are communicated via disguised and displaced commentaries upon the therapeutic interaction, and are not difficult to recognise and decode once the mode of expression is understood. Langs has argued for the therapeutic importance of a secure frame, wherein, despite its potential for evoking intense death anxiety, the patient can feel supported in facing terrifying psychic truth. Regent's College, where many of the contributors to this book have trained or currently work, has been an important centre for the exploration of Langs' ideas in the UK. However, all the authors recognise that the concept of the therapeutic frame and the issues involved in its maintenance are profoundly complex.

Sometimes psychotherapeutic interventions have to take place in settings where the normal boundaries are inherently compromised – for example, hospital wards and GP surgeries. Is the provision of psychotherapeutic help impossible when a conventional boundaried setting is not available? Clearly not. The provision of empathy and understanding, and a receptivity to the communication of emotional pain, can be provided even in circumstances that are far from the normal psychoanalytic consulting room. Even within the conventional setting there are factors of reality that inevitably intrude on the transference space of the therapy – such as the therapist's illness or other disruptions stemming from personal circumstances. Moreover, it must be recognised that a rigid or dogmatic adherence to a strict psychoanalytic frame, in such a way that ordinary humanity and courtesy are compromised, can definitely be damaging – and can model not sanity but a brittle and anxious clinging to rules and procedure. How are we to reconcile the apparent contradiction between, on the one hand, the human mind's frame-sensitivity that Langs has emphasised and illustrated persuasively with innumerable clinical examples of patient's unconscious commentaries and, on the other hand, the reality that the optimal psychotherapeutic frame that he advocates is often not possible to achieve? Perhaps the point is that if a therapist is responding to a patient thoughtfully and receptively, rather than defensively, then psychotherapeutic work is viable, even if the overt structures of the 'frame' deviate from the optimum.

This excellent collection deeply explores these and many other issues and nuances of the therapeutic frame. It will surely be of interest to all psychotherapists.

Phil Mollon, PhD., Psychoanalyst

References

Langs, R. (1997) *Death Anxiety and Clinical Practice*, London: Karnac.
Milner, M. (1952) 'Aspects of symbolism and comprehension of the not-self', *International Journal of Psychoanalysis* 33: 181–95.

Acknowledgements

Words of encouragement and inspiration always come in abundance from my sons Andros and Ricky. They are the pillars of love and vitality, the source of influence and inspiration. I thank them for being there in more ways than words could ever capture.

I wish to thank friends and colleagues for their emotional support during the writing of my own chapter and the sequencing of the work in its final phase: Ann Henry-Stuart, Malcolm Stuart, Athena Christodoulou and Pavlina Georgiades. A special thank you to Nick Zinovieff for his comments on my chapter and to Debbie Killeen for her technical advice and assistance. I especially wish to thank my brother Michael Luca for his love and kindness.

Thanks also are due to Claire Lipscomb, Helen Pritt and Joanne Forshaw at Brunner-Routledge for their assistance in producing this book.

I am grateful to my patients, supervisees, students and colleagues alike, who inspired me in producing a book on the therapeutic frame. My thanks go to all of them.

Chapter 11 was first published in 1989 and is reproduced with permission of *The International Journal of Psychoanalysis*. All rights reserved.

Reflections on the therapeutic frame

Maria Luca

> One can only give one's audience the chance of drawing their
> own conclusions as they observe the limitations, the prejudices, the
> idiosyncrasies of the speaker... Lies will flow from my lips, but there
> may perhaps be some truth mixed up with them; it is for you to seek
> out this truth and to decide whether any part of it is worth keeping.
>
> Virginia Woolf, *A Room of One's Own*

This book is a journey. In a recent conversation with friends who know
little about psychotherapy apart from being on the receiving end, I was
asked what the book is about. I paused and thought to myself: what can
I say about the technical aspects of my work that can be understood in
language that is ordinary? It is about the rules of therapy, I said. About
time-keeping, about breaks, about money, about boundaries, about . . .
I felt dissatisfied with my answer. Somehow I could not encapsulate
the essence of the book in accessible language. Perhaps this is what the
book is about, I thought. An attempt to demystify the parameters of a
therapeutic relationship. How our therapeutic aspirations have limitations.
The conversation was livened up by one of the women, a friend of a friend,
who was going through a divorce. She began to share her experience of
therapy, and described a recent incident during therapy in which she felt
most embarrassed. As her session ended she went to the cloakroom and
on her way out accidentally smashed a very beautiful vase belonging to
her therapist. 'I did not wish to disturb my therapist, because she went
back to her consulting room, probably waiting for her next patient,
so I didn't tell her there and then', she said, looking rather coy. 'But
I couldn't wait until my next session to speak to her and apologize
either. It was such a beautiful piece', she added. 'So I phoned her.' I
refrained from the temptation to interpret the breaking of a vase. I needed
a break!

This book is not about fomenting ideological extremism on the frame. Neither is it about preaching on the puerile nuances and trepidation of framework conditions. As Jean Hantman puts it: 'If Freud had been around to see the fetishization of the frame by the neo-classical analysts who mistook the letter for the spirit, he would have seen how the frame, instead of facilitating analysis, had in some hands come to block it' (2000: II). The frame, like a marriage, follows universal lines, but the participants party to the contract interpret it, relate to it and are guided by it according to their own personalities and idiosyncrasies. Once the frame conditions are owned by therapist and patient the aim must remain focused on facilitating therapeutic work. The frame then can be climatized by the therapeutic interaction.

The idea of writing a book on this subject emerged through many years of teaching and practising psychotherapy. In my own journey of discovery I have come across many people who have influenced me in important ways. I have been influenced by my patients, whose wisdom has been a source of inspiration, in ways too numerous to mention here. My friends and colleagues, whose loving challenge has stretched my imagination, coloured my ideas and given shape to my thought. My students, whose enthusiasm for knowledge has provided the conditions for fruitful discussions. It occurred to me that whether it was an academic seminar or clinical supervision, trainee therapists often wanted to know what kind of frame conditions they should apply in their work with patients. It seemed that the nature of the question had ideological undertones whilst it branched out to the clinical domain. But no amount of numerous reflections and debates on frame conditions, over years of discussions in clinical seminars, led to a magic solution. The statement most repeated that became the *sine qua non* of our discussions was 'It depends on . . .' The views seemed related to the setting, the context and, most importantly, the trainee's own ideological position, personal style, as well as psychological make-up. Returning to the question of 'it depends on', the general opinion on this matter was tinged with moral and ethical undertones, especially on the importance in being guided by the principle that the frame must be in the best interests of the patient. But what if there is disagreement between what the patient thinks her/his best interests are and what the therapist thinks? Again we stumbled. One thing we agreed upon was that frames are the result of trial and error as well as modifications that often go undetected. But just as the construction of a building needs solid foundations, we thought that we need clear contracts negotiated and agreed by the dyad. We also felt that because therapy is a process of constructing and reconstructing understanding on the nature of Being, it was inevitable that the therapeutic process might call for frame modifications that enhanced the relationship rather than hindered it. We all have an idea about healthy professional relationships that are non-exploitative and are designed to be helpful to our patients. We also know and are trained to detect whether a patient can tolerate a boundary crossing or deviation or whether she/he feels traumatized by it. Patients come to us as experts and as professionals who are trained to know and apply what is helpful. A therapist who loses sight of this power dynamic is likely to be myopic to the patient's reactions to boundary crossings and deviations. The literature is replete with examples of patient acting out, but when it comes to therapist acting out we hear about it on the grapevine. 'Acting out' refers to breaking the rules, going against authority – and this applies to both participants in the dyad.

The intention of this book is to situate theory in clinical activity. It sets out to examine some of the issues intrinsic in the frame and to illustrate how certain frame conditions, whether contextually driven, ideologically established or clinically influenced, inform our work. The aim is to stimulate further reflections on clinical practice within contemporary contexts. The contributors represent different schools of thought: Psychoanalytic, Jungian, Existential/Phenomenological, Humanistic and Integrative. The chapters are born out of the heart of practice. They reveal, amongst other things, each contributor's style of work and nature of therapeutic relationships. In their own individual ways the contributors are guided by the sense of what is helpful to the patient and to what extent theoretical principles on the frame can be applied. In the process of trying to be helpful to our patients, aiming to hear their narrative, to understand and be guided by them, we also try to tune in to the inter-subjective world that each therapeutic encounter produces. It is within this domain that each encounter is unique and peculiar to the two participants. It is within this sacred space, within the 'fifty-minute hours' that our minds meet, that our understanding is refined. We can have frames to show us the way, but each frame is pushed and pulled elastically by the participants, by the threads that bind them together. In the labyrinth of an uncertain journey, with faith as our companion, we immerse ourselves in the process – but without losing sight of ourselves. The frame is nothing but a gentle envelope. A garment protecting us from exposure. What emerges in our thinking about the frame are all the predictions from our theories and all the surprises about our theories. It is here that clinical experience teaches us to be flexible in our thought and to continue re-evaluating and modifying our practices, until they hold true to our aims. Letting go of theory that no longer holds true, and letting go of our convictions, demands solid psychological foundations. But what can be more creative than fluid theory?

In the diversity of clinical and theoretical perspectives in the chapters there is a common language revealed through the wealth of clinical illustrations. The material drawn upon by the authors has been carefully chosen to illustrate aspects of the therapeutic frame. It has been heavily disguised so that the anonymity of patients is protected. They do not portray any singular therapeutic encounter, but strands of practice woven together to highlight practice issues. I trust that the reader will hold in mind that clinical illustrations represent real possibilities – as opposed to real experiences in clinical practice – and still benefit from the exploration.

As in all books, what is often the essence of experience cannot be communicated. In my mind the inevitable limitations of language mean that every time we speak we are being selective. The words are structured together to formulate an understanding. But we can never, not quite, reach absolute expression. However, through my selection of themes and range of theoretical and clinical perspectives, I have attempted to portray the key issues by way of enlarging and widening ideas on the frame. The ideas in the chapters are the product of diversity and difference. They do not present a unified theoretical framework. This was intentional on my part. It was an attempt to create a platform where difference could unfold and ways of understanding could be voiced without supremacy. What binds the chapters together is the shared struggle to grapple with, to reflect upon and to understand the central threads around the therapeutic frame.

I have considered organizing the text into different sections. But each time I tried to find a way of selecting the parts I came away feeling ambivalent. So I decided to allow each chapter to be in-itself and to speak for itself. However, I have decided to sequence the chapters to create an organic whole.

Chapter 1 is an exploration of the figurative meaning in the patient's relationship to the frame. Through the use of fictional or heavily disguised clinical material, I focus on teasing out boundary issues, and examine these in relation to technique and therapeutic approach. The discussion highlights the limitations of a rigid, literal adherence to the therapeutic frame and implies the need for a re-evaluation of clinical practice and for a more 'elastic', 'attuned' and authentic encounter.

In Chapter 2 Nick Zinovieff introduces the therapeutic frame as it applies to work in general practice. The idea of a universal therapeutic frame is challenged here. What might be regarded as 'deviant' by tradi-tional thought is the reality in general practice. The chapter looks at issues in communication between the counsellor, the GP and other medical staff and provides a useful guidance on how to deal with basic frame conditions that facilitate the work.

In Chapter 3 Deborah Killeen presents a personal account as a patient in therapy, highlighting how different therapists managed the therapeutic frame at crucial points in the process. She discusses examples of therapeutic successes where the therapist's management of frame issues ended positively and felt beneficial, and therapeutic failures where she experienced careless or inappropriate management of the frame, which felt damaging and unhelpful.

In Chapter 4 Stefano Ferraiolo presents the experience of a male psychotherapist within a hospital maternity ward. He delves into Greek mythology and metaphor to examine the dynamics of gender and frame conditions that promote a holding therapeutic relationship, a relationship that nurtures the creative forces in womanhood and contains destructive ones.

In Chapter 5 Anne Brockbank provides a moving, personal account in her journey through a life-threatening illness, presenting her struggle to manage her own reactions and impact on her work as a therapist. The potential effects on clients of sudden and premature endings are discussed, as well as the impact on her therapeutic practice. She illustrates the difficulties surrounding the management of the frame in the face of uncertainty. Anne provides reflections on practice guidelines to cover the sudden illness or death eventuality of a therapist.

In Chapter 6 James Pollard explores the difficulties of unplanned contact with patients, 'to help clinicians think about the issues raised by unplanned contact with the patient and to manage these situations more effectively'. Pollard draws on the history of psychotherapy to show the paradox of theory and practice and the conflicts and contradictions in the application of the frame. With clinical illustrations, he examines the 'significance of unplanned meetings and how these might be understood'.

In Chapter 7 Paola F. Valerio enters into a polemic about notions that therapist 'acting out' is of necessity harmful. She suggests that 'boundaries get broken all the time', even though few therapists are prepared to admit it. Valerio presents the idea that therapists are not immune from transgressions in the frame and that minor transgressions, as distinguished from violations, are therapeutic: 'they tell us a great deal about the unconscious marriage between therapist and patient'.

Chapter 8 by Paul Smith-Pickard is a bridge to Chapter 10, from direct practice in an acute hospital ward to supervision of a team of therapists practising in this setting. He explores the paradox of a frame that is tailored to meet the need of the patient in a particular moment in time. The work takes place on the wards, with acute illness and by the patient's bedside. This is 'the greatest challenge to the therapeutic frame'. Smith-Pickard discusses how a team of therapists, in the absence of certain frame conditions, such as regular time and place and outside the confines of a consulting/private room, tends to work effectively. The chapter introduces two new ideas: *embedded supervision* and an *extemporaneous frame*. The ideas are existentially driven and are based on the experience of supervising therapists who work in the acute ward.

In Chapter 9 John Beveridge looks at the dilemma in trying to find scientific credibility in psychotherapy, a practice that engages with the intangible manifestations of the internal world, of dreams, fantasies, the exploration of emotions, the lifting of repression and the clinical application of intuition and insight. This difficulty, he argues, 'is compounded by the intra-psychic and almost telepathic phenomena that occur in psychotherapy, including parallel process, countertransference and projective identification. The long and evolving relationship between the therapist, the patient and the therapeutic frame parallels the conflict between the inner and outer worlds.' As the title suggests, 'The exclusion zone' is a metaphor reflecting the limits of the encounter.

In Chapter 10 Greg Madison describes some dilemmas of frame therapy highlighted by psychotherapeutic practice in an acute general hospital setting. He examines the frame by looking at the needs of clients (and their relatives) and the obstacles of adopting a frame-based approach in a hospital setting. He argues that despite these obstacles deep thera-peutic work can be achieved, which leads him to question the necessity of frames. Rooted in the existential/phenomenological tradition, Madison's philosophical account describes the assumptions and dilemmas of frame therapy in an acute general hospital.

In Chapter 11 Andrea Sabbadini examines the dimensions of 'time' in psychoanalysis. What happens inside and outside the fifty-minute space is seen as central to analytic understanding. As the author states: 'To know a country, you must become acquainted with its boundaries.' He situates the psychoanalytic situation in its specific temporal structure, consisting of a complex inter-connection of different temporalities that guide the analytic participants along the continuum. He suggests that to keep the unconscious process free of impingement we must not impose an artificial date for termination of the analysis.

In all the chapters included in this book we see an emphasis of new ideas and the place they give to the frame in modern practices. The viewpoints represented reflect different styles and theoretical modalities. They all have something useful to say. The book was designed with trainee psychotherapists in mind, but clinicians may find it useful as a platform for fruitful reflection on their work.

References

Hantman, J. (2000) 'On the frame', viewed 25 April 2003, http://therapyathome. org

Woolf, V. (1977) *A Room of One's Own* (first published 1929, The Hogarth Press), London: Panther Books.

Chapter 1

Boundary issues in psychotherapy

From the literal to the figurative frame

Maria Luca

> And yet all the qualities of a good friendship – a welcome, an acceptance, a letting be, a hospitality, an attunement, an attentiveness, a suspension of self-interest, a questioning, a criticism, a distance that does not pretend to objectivity, an engagement, a faith in the other, a commitment to truthfulness, and above all perhaps a responsibility to the other – these surely are the qualities also of an ethical therapy.
>
> Paul Gordon, *Face to Face – Therapy as Ethics*

The increasing professional demands on psychotherapists to adapt to the changing culture surrounding the field, with the need for more evidence on therapeutic outcomes and tighter regulation governing the profession, have led to a climate of anxiety. As psychotherapists we are surrounded by a multiplicity of theories on what it is to be human, coupled with a plethora of ideas explaining away the human condition. Jargonizing existing ideas tends to provide temporary relief for our desire to come up with something new, something which will mark our own territory. Words become epidemics that sweep away even the most acute minds. Within a few months of the publication of Gerrard's paper 'A Sense of Entitlement: Vicissitudes of Working with "Special" Patients' (2002), I have heard the term 'entitlement' being applied by psychotherapists a number of times. The paper encapsulates what many therapists already know from experience, and having a term to describe this provides a kind of known territory, a relief. This kind of infection is, I believe, driven by our doubts on the legitimacy of our theories, mobilizing our need to give intellectual authority to a profession surrounded by uncertainty and constant media scrutiny. The popularity of ideas against therapy, such as claims that people are better off talking to an intelligent friend (Persaud, 2003), still prevails. For psychotherapy to exist as a valued form of help in the twenty-first century we need to transgress from our conventions, let go of our theoretical orthodoxy and reach out towards a world of open debate on therapeutic forms, their value and limitations. The best teacher is clinical practice. My focus in this chapter will be on selected issues relating to therapeutic boundaries. I will attempt to tease out, from clinical experience and disguised vignettes, issues of technique as they relate to the therapeutic framework. The clinical material comes from different sources, including colleagues and therapists in supervision.

The therapeutic frame and the management of boundaries are increasingly under scrutiny. Some authors (Gutheil and Gabbard, 1993; Langs, 1976, 1992; Lazarus, 1998; Young, 1998), have attempted to define and to clarify the 'rights' from the 'wrongs' in clinical practice. The literature is replete with concepts on ideal frames, ideal conditions, ideal outcomes. Little is written on therapeutic technique that is outside the remit of these idealizations or on therapeutic failures, therapeutic mistakes and transgressions that prove valuable. Yet learning, as Patrick Casement (2002) has demonstrated, comes from our mistakes; and therapeutic failures are the result of being married to our theories, as Valentine (1996) rightly argues. These authors remind us of the value of common sense and of moments when we realize that despite our fears, a frame modification, or crossing, had been, to our amazement, fruitful.

In our zeal to be the good disciples of leading figures we employ therapeutic approaches that are more in line with tradition (for the sake of tradition) than with common sense (for the sake of fruitful, innovative knowledge). Psychotherapy would benefit from a dialogical relationship between tradition and modernity. Traditionally spontaneity (Berry, 1987) and elasticity in therapeutic technique have been frowned upon. We only need to remind ourselves of the plight of those who challenged the orthodoxy of psychoanalytic technique, such as Ferenczi (1928), to know that flexibility comes with a price. In our attempts to validate the paternalism and maternalism of our forefathers and foremothers, we perpetuate the dogmas at the expense of creativity. But therapeutic inventiveness does not have to be harmful. As Winnicott (1971) showed, therapeutic play is essential to healthy living. It is synonymous with the humane aspects of therapeutic interaction, which, in hindsight, enhances an otherwise mechanistic encounter. 'Our confidence in our theories should be only conditional, for in every case we may be presented with a resounding exception to the rule' (Ferenczi, 1928: 262).

It would be a mistake to assume that modifications in the agreed ground rules and flexible boundaries of the therapy do not have wide-ranging implications for practice. This would be just as naïve as to believe that a rigid framework would protect us from behaving detrimentally towards our patients. The emphasis on how a therapist should speak, how a therapist should listen and what kind of clothing a therapist should wear is a pressurizing factor on the person of the therapist. I remember as a trainee psychotherapist my bewilderment at the comment from a fellow trainee that my long hair and long ear-rings were 'seductive devices' and must be avoided at all costs. On reflection, it is our fears of seducing or being seduced, as well as the demand on us to work with the complexities of erotic transference and countertransference, that create the desire to control the external environment. I still wear my hair long and the long ear-rings are still a constant in my personal presentation. Being who I am evokes all sorts of reactions in my patients (see Luca-Stolkin, 1999), these becoming essential material for the work. I firmly believe that no matter how neutral we try to be, patients will have a reaction to the subjectivity of the therapist. Working with and understanding what we evoke in our patients by who we are is part of a therapeutic, inter-subjective interaction. I give the following example to highlight this point:

A therapist I supervised presented the case of a patient who persistently arrived at least fifteen minutes late for her sessions. The therapist felt increasingly irritated by this, as she felt the patient was wasting valuable therapy time. Without much exploration about the meaning of this lateness the therapist made a statement reminding her of the agreed contract and how she hoped the patient would adhere to this, as she had indeed agreed to during the initial session. She also added that they had limited time together and lateness reduced their ability to create fruitful work. The therapist felt that she tried her best not to ignore this frame challenge and was surprised that her patient missed the following session. We discussed the impact of her intervention on the patient, including the possibility that she might have felt punished and not understood by the therapist. The therapist's focus and preoccupation with the concrete aspect of the lateness had led to a concrete management of the frame. Her need to reclaim control of the frame led to her neglecting the qualitative aspects in the patient's expression of lateness. This meant that the understanding of the lateness had been partial, externally focused and interpreted, ignoring the underlying, perhaps unconscious communication the patient was expressing by being late. The supervisory exploration prompted the therapist to look at the deeper meaning in the patient's use of time, including missing the session. The therapist understood her attempt to take control of the external frame as a blind countertransferential attempt to control erotization of the therapy. She related this to her increasing fear about the patient's declarations of love and desire for her, sometimes communicated through sending her gifts. She felt that her own fears and anxieties in not managing her 'territory' blocked her ability to tune into her patient's meanings.

It is underestimated how much of our character is revealed, despite all our efforts to hide. Our patients know a great deal more about us than we allow ourselves to believe. Patients' antennae perception of their therapist often comes as a surprise to us. To this end, presenting a false self would be just as compromising to an authentic relationship as would behaving in ways that disregard the patient and totally serve our own narcissism. The highly charged energy in the interaction and the kind of intimacy that develops through the way we work can be emotionally stifling for both participants. It is important, therefore, to step outside our therapeutic frame and give ourselves respite from the confines of introspection and inward searching. The focus on what goes on inside the frame as a demarcation for the treatment leaves little room for reflection on the outside world. As clinicians we are all too familiar with the incestuous quality characterizing our profession and of the threat of litigation hanging over our shoulders each time we transgress professional boundaries. But isn't it time we took a fresh look at this, open our consulting room windows a little and free ourselves of the frantic search for certainty? 'Certainty can imprison the analyst just as much as it may threaten the patient' (Casement, 2002: 16). Holding the treatment task in mind whilst situating it within the external world is likely to be more therapeutic and growth inducing than compliance to theory.

The essence of the frame

Without rules there would be anarchy and chaos, and exceptions to the rule are often a direct result of knowledge drawn from experience. Rules are created by humans to serve the human condition. When they cease to have this function it is important that they are reconsidered, or abolished. The frame, the setting – otherwise referred to as the therapeutic space – is a structure with rules. Just as Freud advocated the importance of ground rules, especially the fundamental rule of 'free association', Milner (1952) coined the term 'frame' to distinguish 'the different kind of reality that is within it from that which is outside it' (see Warburton, 1999: 80). For Milner, the area inside the frame has a symbolic function, and outside a literal function. This inside and outside of the frame has a crucial boundary function. Even though 'Freud and Klein took a distinctly laissez-faire line concerning the frame' (Smith, 1991: 168), the orthodoxy of some psychoanalytic practitioners is reflected in their strict, sometimes dogmatic adherence to the ground rules – an adherence that ignores the individual needs of patients for modifications to the frame that serves their therapy. Some psychoanalytic practitioners (Gutheil and Gabbard, 1993) tend to view frame elasticity as belonging to the more supportive therapies. The authors apply the language of 'deviation', 'boundary violations' and 'boundary crossings' to psychoanalytic practitioners who do not strictly adhere to the classical view of the frame.

Modifications, however, if indiscriminately made and without a clear rationale, can have an impact on the holding of the therapy and can lead to premature termination by the patient. If changes to the frame are made, whether deliberate or unplanned, it is important that we consider the implications to our work rather than fear that changes would damage the patient or ourselves. 'To be healthy, every intimate rela- tionship needs space and personal boundaries, and a corresponding respect by each person for the "otherness" of the other. Frequently, however, this space is either lacking or contaminated by intruding influences' (Casement, 1990: 160). I imagine all psychotherapists recognize the value of establishing a secure frame; but let us be clear that this does not imply an agreement written in stone.

Some authors (Langs, 1992; Smith, 1991) emphasize the importance of the rule-abiding, abstinent therapist, whilst others (Gray, 1994; Lomas, 1987) present a more flexible notion of the frame. Lomas (1987) spoke against the analytic emphasis on discipline, reticence, toughness and control – qualities he described as masculine – and believed that creative play must prevail. There is a real risk to our creativity, that in our fears of acting out on impulse we tend to ignore the value of spontaneity as a channel of communication, that is more likely to inject the encounter with an affective connection than will measured thought.

A number of analysts (Casement, 2002; Ferenczi, 1928; Klauber, 1987, Kohut, 1978, Lomas, 1987; Resnik, 1995) have all, in their own individual ways, challenged the rigidity of psychoanalytic technique, advocating for more flexibility, spontaneity and naturalness on the part of the analyst. In reference to the therapeutic contract, Resnik argues that:

> A good contract, just as in fair play, means that you can make the rules clear during implementation: it is creative, meaning that technique and schools of thought are less important than style and personal ethics. Living in a contractual society, we need to reach

agreement about rules, but we have to leave some opening for inventing those most appropriate to each case.

(Resnik, 1995: 24)

Similarly, Laplanche (1989) recognizes the importance of a flexible setting, saying that it is not a ritual or a technical appliance or an arbitrary law. He argues that '[p]ure formalism is as meaningless as the unthinking rejection of form . . . It is essential to adjust techniques to the needs of analysands and to introduce variations, but we have to justify them' (p. 155).

We therefore need to consider the usefulness of tentativeness in our approach and for this purpose I use the term 'elasticity in the frame'. This is not to be confused with a poor frame that confuses the patient. In the same way that Picasso, along with other modernist painters, could do a pretty good life drawing of classical proportions and beauty before he ventured into Cubism, the therapist needs to understand the rules of the frame before employing the 'elastic attitude'. Unless we are clear about the constituent parts, it would be difficult to be creative with the frame in its entirety.

One question that inevitably arises is 'Who is the Frame for then, the analyst or the patient? The patient whose transference will not unfold properly without it, or the analyst who might be driven crazy with less structure in place'? (Hantman, 2000). It is hard for us to accommodate changes in structure when we know that the majority of our patients are likely to react in ways that demand more of our energy. When I moved my consulting room to another area one of my patients decided to terminate; another became curious about my personal life, wondering whether the change was as a result of a breakdown in my relationship. Some patients hated the new room, and for another patient the car parked in the driveway symbolized my financial means. It was interesting to work with the intensity of the individual responses to this structural change. Patients, each in their unique ways, expressed mixed feelings ranging from anger, outrage, empathy, envy, triumph, curiosity, loss, sadness and fear. I found it very demanding to process such intense feelings in the patients whilst trying to understand my own responses to the patients. For the first few months I suddenly found myself the object of scrutiny. Whereas before I could sink in the comfort of familiarity, continuity and therapeutic distance, I now had to deal with intensified transference and counter-transference simultaneously; not an easy task for any practitioner. What was before inaccessible was now lived out. It was precisely this accident of life that widened the therapeutic space and vitalized the relationships.

The therapeutic frame is a structure that sets the rules of therapy and holds and contains the participants' behaviour. Most importantly, if appropriately utilized, it can create security. If play is guided by the sentiments of trust, ethical responsibility and professional care, so too creativity, imaginative exploration and mutual respect can be developed. Spontaneity is not a cardinal sin, and it does not infiltrate and damage the therapy. The principle of psychoanalytic abstinence in its extreme can sever spontaneity and block the patient from feeling free to desire and free to want. Of course therapy does not make promises to satisfy the patient's desires and wants. Rather, it tries to create a space for these feelings to be voiced and understood. Without spontaneity, frameworks become rigid and the patient's mind closed off. The teasing out of affects buried under the weight of defences requires an affective relationship between client and therapist. As I mentioned earlier, a structural change whether planned or accidental can mobilize affects buried under the weight of 'normality'. As Nicole Berry (1987) puts it: 'the analyst learns how to make the patient accept rules and limitations, but at the same time he learns how to act naturally' (p. 107).

Ms B completed her therapy two years before I met her on the tube one morning. 'Hello', she said, with a big smile. 'The weather is not so good today, is it?' she continued. 'Yes, it has changed this week', I replied with a smile of acknowledgement. She then buried herself in her newspaper. As it was time for me to get off at the next station, I said, 'Goodbye, Ms B, have a nice day.' Her face lit up and she replied in a similar manner. As I walked up the escalator I thought about our exchange. Our sense of being in those moments was in attunement with each other. Although we both felt uncomfortable, as the context meant that for the first time we were thrown into a new frame, we sensed the unease in each other. I tried to behave naturally and to acknowledge her existence, but without intruding into her social envelope either. Having used her name to say goodbye, she felt remembered and acknowledged by me. Intuitively I knew that in its ordinariness, the encounter was extraordinarily healing. As simple as this may sound, by referring to her by her name she felt remembered and not 'just a patient'. I saw no harm in serving the patient's need to be special and human in my eyes.

Technical tools, ethical ideas and knowledge of what the common therapeutic factors are, are some of the elements that inform practices and influence the nature of the frame. There is no question in my mind about the importance of having a clear frame at the start of the therapy that specifies the conditions within which therapist and patient begin to work with each other. A secure frame aids a secure relationship. To the therapist this means holding an informed therapeutic stance with the patient's interests in mind. To this end the frame is much more than the rules which define it. It is

> a 'non-process' . . . a state of mind – a mental space . . . a facilitating environment and a container . . . It needs to be a safe enough place for psychotherapeutic work to occur, a place where the patient can allow herself or himself to speak about things which are too painful or taboo or embarrassing to speak about elsewhere.
>
> (Young, 1998: 1)

An elastic frame is like the mind's eye reflecting on itself and acquiring a self-consciousness about the clinical realm. The frame from this point of view promotes an understanding of what goes on in the minds of the therapist and patient. This includes an acknowledgement by the therapist of his or her own thoughts and unspoken desires to turn the thought into reality. In essence, moment by moment mental knowledge of the subjective experience is necessary in order to capture the modulating of the affects in the patient's process. For example, how we manage confidentiality, the fee, missed sessions, telephone calls between sessions, holidays, the setting itself with the inevitable intrusions, as well as role boundaries, must be informed by our understanding of the inter-subjective process.

Frame challenge and modification

As the relationship progresses and the working alliance is established the structure of the frame may be challenged by internal or external factors. There are many examples of frame challenges:

> Miss X challenged the boundaries several times. She sometimes demanded longer sessions, other times she arrived when not expected. On one occasion I answered the doorbell in my shorts to find her on the doorstep. I felt utterly embarrassed and confused, and for a moment I thought I had forgotten about her appointment. She came at the right time, but wrong day. Miss X often expressed the frustration at having her sessions at prescribed times and not when she desired. One persistent boundary challenge was her arriving early

for her sessions and waiting on the doorstep, watching the previous patient leave. I often felt watched and protective of the other patients, as well as irritated. During one such experience I felt a flash of anger and immediately focused my attention on the patient's frustration in having to share me. My language was more assertive and truthful than usual. This spontaneous moment led to an intense unfolding of aggression and themes previously not accessible. The most pertinent of these was that the patient was acting out feelings of anger related to her knowing that a man she was acquainted with was also in therapy with me. She could not take the risk of confronting the painful issue of being on the periphery in her father's life. Nor could she share this knowledge with me and risk losing the comfortable position she had gained through pleasing me. Sharing the parent contained a core conflict for this patient. Her habitual ways of dealing with her pain was to avoid and to be compliant. The frame became the only means by which she could let me understand and subsequently help her deal with her avoidance. My observation of the patient's use of the frame enabled me to tune into her inability to deal with anger and to link it to the transference. My previous attempts to interpret frame challenges failed; my sense of the failure was that I could not reach the patient in some important way. As the frame challenges became more persistent the encounter became full with feeling; the patient and I finally met each other at the deepest recesses of her psyche. Here we found the darkest secrets. The understanding was mutative and the frame was our guide.

How we manage framework challenge must reflect the therapeutic climate. Interpreting a patient's forgetting to pay the fee as withholding behaviour when I know that the therapeutic alliance is not yet established and the patient is too fragile to entertain painful feelings, would be anti-therapeutic and untimely. Persistent challenge to the frame often indicates a persistent need to communicate something to the therapist, who may be oblivious to the patient's core conflict:

Mr C loathed paying his therapist. On the sessions when he was due to pay, he often presented in a foul mood, being aggressive and critical of his therapist. He would use this as an opportunity to vent his aggression as well as evidence that the money was the only reward for the therapist. This patient had been abandoned by his mother at four months and spent his early years in a residential establishment. He surrounded himself by 'needy' people, as he often referred to them. It seemed safer for Mr C to place the neediness in others and not in himself. We discussed his anger at the professional nature of our relationship and he saw this as proof that his needs will never be met. 'See? What's the point of trying to voice my needs. When I leave from here I'm on my own again. On Sunday I was feeling desperate for someone to talk to. I cried on my own and I must admit I thought of ringing you, but I knew it was wrong.' He was right. Neither I nor his partner, nor anyone, could replace his infant needs to be physically held by his mother. Had I deceived myself that I, as his therapist, could fill this void I would have denied him the opportunity to be sad and to cry in rage against those who had pained him. His protests about the fee were cries of sadness for what he had missed out on. I knew that my love for him had to be expressed through helping him to grieve and let go. This, in my mind, would make it possible for him to accept the reality of his childhood. As he was saying goodbye to me at the end of our work, he turned and looked at the little bird sitting on the garden fence, just outside the consulting room window. 'It loves sitting on the edge of your fence', he said. 'It's not scared of the squirrels. You know, I never told you this, but as a kid I used to search for bird nests and throw stones at the baby sparrows.' A secret tear rolled down his face. Thinking about his remark it struck me as a cry of freedom.

It is inevitable to expect variations in practices pertaining to the framework, partly due to ideas employed by therapists and the emphasis they place on certain aspects of technique and partly due to therapists' personal views and ideological allegiances regarding the frame. For example, some therapists may be strict on maintaining the same fee throughout a patient's analysis, whilst others may decide to increase the fee in line with inflation. Similarly, some therapists believe in being firm about keeping the day, time and place of sessions consistent, whilst others pay lip service to these rules. Another example is of self-disclosure versus neutrality and abstinence. The same applies to open-ended therapy versus time-limited therapy with a fixed date for ending. Therapeutic technique, especially in the psychoanalytic modality, has undergone extensive modification in the last decade. With regard to frame modifications, what really matters is that the therapist homes in on the unique ways patients use and relate to the frame as a central vehicle of the unconscious.

In some contexts, such as therapy with terminally ill patients in hospitals, the therapy is inevitably frameless. In these situations the standard rules (such as, for example, same room and regular times for sessions) cannot be established because the patient may not be fit to participate in a session, or that other medical treatment is seen as more of a priority. However, I was concerned to hear of a therapist who, without warning or discussion about termination, would pass on patients she did not like to a colleague, telling them that she was sending them to a specialist. In my view this would be confusing to patients and would perpetuate the feelings of isolation a lot of these patients experience. It is crucial that a clear contract is made where the non-negotiable aspects of the frame are explained to the patient from the start. In this way the boundaries are drawn and any challenge or acting out by either of the participants can be identified and addressed.

Involving patients in frame modifications makes it less of an imposition and demonstrates respect for the patient's own life and other commitments outside the therapy. Some practices are informed more by the omnipotent belief that the analysis is central and other aspects of the patient's life are peripheral. As a result even the most minute manoeuvre is interpreted as resistance, acting out or transference. In these, the fundamental reality outside the frame can be missed:

> Mrs J was referred for therapy a few months following a stillbirth. At the first session she accused her therapist of not caring and of being insensitive. She left the session in a fit of rage without clarifying what she actually meant. If the therapist did not take into consideration the fact that the consulting room was adjacent to the baby delivery room within the hospital, she might have interpreted the patient's rage as resistance, or negative transference. This patient is one of several others who felt shocked and angry at the location of the therapy room. Patient behaviour is not expressed in a vacuum. The context and the setting are external factors influencing the treatment and must be given a place in our understanding of the process.

The objectification of patients by some therapists not only compromises the work but also risks alienating people who are considering therapy. As psychotherapists we know from our training that we swallow ideas; often we question them and digest them so they take shape within the reality of our practices, but sometimes they become fixed and inert, weighing heavily on our minds, or turn into ghosts that haunt us. If the latter is the case, it is to the detriment of the therapy. Indeed, fitting our patients into our fancy theories may offer us temporary relief from our anxieties of not knowing – but how does this serve our patients?

Theoretical religiosity may serve to enhance our patients' perceptions of us as experts, but how alienating this must feel for the individual on the receiving end.

Boundary issues

Although my allegiance to the theory of relativity has never been strong, when I think of the frame conditions they are in my mind relative to other conditions outside the therapy, which create impingement, call for crossings or influence deviations. If there was ever a place in our mind, where the common-sense principle could prevail, it is in the need for 'non-dogmatic evaluations of boundary questions. Individual differences should be emphasized rather than subjugated to rigid standards' (Lazarus, 1998: 24). 'Crossing certain boundaries may at times be salutary, at times neutral, and at times harmful' (Gutheil and Gabbard, 1993, p. 189). As clinicians we are responsible for boundary maintenance, and if boundaries are crossed we must be aware of any implications and discuss the effects with the patient. Although reparative work is not always possible where boundaries have been crossed or violated, awareness of the impact on the process helps contain further leakage.

As a therapist I have had patients expressing desires to cross boundaries in all kinds of ways. Some examples include an offer by a patient to decorate my house and a patient who hit financial hardship in the process of therapy who offered to clean my house. Another patient persistently expressed the wish to take me out to dinner; yet another offered me the use of her flat abroad – she seemed to be expressing curiosity about my choice of destination during my holidays. I have had several experiences of patients expressing curiosity and the need to challenge the professional work by asking personal questions such as where I purchased certain garments of clothing and items in my consulting room. Moreover, my experiences of frame challenge branch out to patients complimenting me on my appearance, or in not being paid on time. I had a patient who disappeared without paying the fee, as well as a cheque going missing through the post. Another patient was in the habit of making telephone calls half way through the sessions from which he was absent, both to check out whether he had me pinned to my chair waiting for him or to replace the face-to-face contact with a telephone session. A trainee psychotherapist told me of how she had been followed by a patient in the car park of the institution where she had been practising.

Anticipating how we will respond to a boundary challenge is an impossible task. Our response is unique to the individual patient, even if the frame challenge appears to be the same. Managing a frame challenge without the risk of a therapeutic drift requires awareness and clarity over the therapist's own subjectivity in relation to the patient. A therapist I supervised mentioned how she once met her patient in the car park by coincidence, and having found her in distress, because a motorist had smashed into the rear of her car just before she was due in for her session, had helped her call the car rescue. She then spent time chatting to her patient, whilst waiting for rescue. Subsequent to this incident the patient was complaining of her therapist not being sufficiently attentive. The informal interaction during the incident changed the nature of the relationship, and fed the patient's fantasies of a close, non-professional relationship. The work could not continue along the same lines as before the frame crossing. The therapist needed to abandon the established process and turn her attention to the task of dealing with the theme that emerged from the boundary crossing, which seemed to be the primary focus for the patient. Often the kind of relationship a patient desires, or recreates with their therapist at any given time in the process, mirrors relationships outside. It is the task of the therapist to identify what aspect in the patient's inner world is represented in the transference and be ready to suspend attention from one primary concern to another in the effort to deal with affects in the here and now. A crisis in the patient's current situation may be a catalyst of feelings that become primary. The frame is often a medium and a catalyst of these feelings, requiring a newly formulated therapeutic device.

As Gutheil and Gabbard (1993) state: 'clinicians tend to feel that they understand the concept of boundaries instinctively, but using it in practice or explaining it to others is often challenging' (p. 188). I relate to this difficulty and think that handling boundary issues can at times be tricky and complex. I will present more clinical examples to illustrate some of the technical problems relating to the frame.

Intrusions

The competition for room space within certain public settings creates tension between different professionals. Therapists working within a hospital sometimes find themselves having to explain the importance of having the same room for the treatment, to the puzzlement of medical doctors, nurses and other staff. Thus managing intrusions or changes to the consulting room becomes part of the job:

> A woman patient in her late thirties asked her GP to refer her for therapy to deal with a persistent problem. Her presenting problem

was the inability to form intimate relationships and repeatedly entering into brief sexual encounters, feeling used and ashamed. She was successful in her career as a nurse, but felt empty and thought it was time to have children, which mobilized her to seek therapy. During one of her sessions she tried to convey to her therapist that her family had harshly treated the man who had sexually abused her between the ages of nine to fourteen. The family reacted angrily once she disclosed 'the sexual involvement', as she had described the abuse. This man, who was a relative on her father's side of the family, was a medical doctor and much respected by the family and the community. 'He was tender and kind', she said, and provided the attention she felt she needed as a neglected child in a very large family. The issue was sensitive and the therapist was trying to help the patient explore her need to protect the abuser. While this was taking place a medical doctor opened the door of the consulting room. He apologized once he realized that he had intruded. The therapist felt annoyed, as clinic staff often ignored signs, and remarked to the doctor that there was a 'do not disturb sign on the door'. The patient responded by saying: 'Don't be too harsh on the poor doctor.' In that moment the patient's early conflict was being re-enacted, which produced the same behaviour in the transference. The intrusion to the privacy of the consulting room symbolized the patient's early trauma, and the therapist's remark was protective. The patient's transference to the therapist was as the harsh parents. The situation provided the opportunity for the patient to face the memories and mourn the loss of the idealized good object, qualities she had invested in the man who sexually abused her. Mourning the loss of this fantasy could potentially free her and open up the possibility of a real relationship.

Patients need to please the therapist and their desire to be liked by her or him can mask their real feelings and reactions to boundary crossings. We must therefore recognize this and look beyond a patient's reassuring words, as these sometimes camouflage conflictual feelings, as in the following case:

When I moved my private practice to a new building there were building works taking place at the premises. On one occasion I made a request to the builders to work at a different part of the building for an hour, away from my consulting room door. They reluctantly agreed. Whilst they complied to my polite request and stopped the drilling and the noise, they ignored my request for them to keep away from the consulting room. At one point I saw one of them walking on the scaffolding outside the consulting room window, whilst I could hear the mobile phone of another ringing. The latter stood not far from the room, chatting away on his mobile phone; it was obvious that the conversation could be heard from inside. I started to feel increasingly irritated. I apologized to the patient for the situation in the corridor, remarking that he must feel angry that I had not protected the privacy of the session. He smiled and said it did not bother him at all and continued to talk about an issue with his mother. I thought that at this point he was not ready to acknowledge his angry feelings towards me and dropped the subject. Two weeks later, the patient talked of his anger at the people next door to his flat who were having renovations, describing them as noisy and inconsiderate. This, he said, made him feel unprotected and intruded upon. Intrusion was a big issue in the patient's early life, and much of the therapy was spent working with his rage at not being protected. I realized that some of these remarks were directed at me for not being able to protect him from the intrusive builders and remarked at his need to reassure me, ignoring perhaps his own feelings of rage at the intrusion. His response was immediate and fused with satisfaction that I understood the dynamics of his compliance and his need to protect me, when in fact he wished to be protected himself. He was able to identify that this was in fact a pattern in all his relationships, and his protectiveness towards others was expressing the wish to be protected himself.

Therapists are not always successful in their efforts to preserve the space as free of interruptions, noise and other related intrusions. Having a consulting room in one's private dwelling is not always an ideal place, especially if the room is not separate from one's habitat. If the therapist shares their home with a family, or they have guests, it creates difficulties for all involved. Family members may feel curious, or excluded from the intimacy between the therapist and patient. Consciously or unconsciously family members may act out. A colleague mentioned her dismay when her eight-year-old son knocked on the consulting room door calling out for his mummy. Her patient, who was not ready to deal with sibling rivalry, stormed out and never came back. The following scenario illustrates the pitfalls in working from home. It is from the practice of a male colleague working with a male patient. The therapist had guests staying with him at the time, who incidentally ignored his request to avoid coming down the squeaky staircase during the session:

A few years ago during a session with the patient, some footsteps could be heard from outside the room. The patient furiously accused the therapist of not caring about his feelings, knowing very well, as he put it, that the patient did not want to know of his partner. 'You are trying to spite me, aren't you? To provoke a reaction in me. Do you have any idea what it is like to know that he gets to sleep with you, eat with you, take holidays with you, when all I get is fifty minutes of your day?' he said to the therapist. Apparently the patient once saw a man leaving the house and assumed this was his therapist's partner. He kept quiet about it at the time, but now it became an issue. This opened up the erotic desires in the patient and it became possible to address fantasies otherwise kept at bay.

Intrusions can sometimes be felt within the consulting room itself. Changing the interior of the setting, including furnishings, can feel unsettling for some patients, whilst others completely ignore it. For patients who are acutely sensitive to the internal space, small changes are immediately noticed and reacted to. A patient who spent most of her childhood in the country always remarked about the flowers in my consulting room. If they were pink roses she felt cared for; if they were white carnations she experienced me as distant and cold. The flowers became the focus of her internal space, an opportunity to tell me how she experienced me. I learned not to take for granted the meaning patients give to items inside the frame.

It took only one glance at the couch for one of my patients to notice a human hair. 'Ooh', she remarked, 'I'm not lying on that! There's a hair, it's somebody's hair . . . and I don't know whose it is.' And after a pregnant pause she asserted: 'Not sure if it's yours!' With an assertive air in her tone she made it clear that she was not willing to share her territory. She much preferred the comfort to rest in the thought that the consulting room is her own space, her own territory free of intruders. The same patient found a banana skin in the bin when throwing a used tissue into it. This sign of unknown, undefined life was so disconcerting to her that she clearly felt cross. Finding a hair is bad enough let alone a banana skin. 'Who has been eating bananas here', she remarked. 'Yuck!! Ooh, I don't like the thought of someone eating in here.' She then paused, laughed, and said: 'It's most probably you!' Aha. She found the culprit. This finding of hair and a banana skin were so significant

– they led to the most fruitful exchange and understanding on intrusion and exclusivity. We came to realize that recently she has been exploring her need for exclusivity in her relationships and the narcissistic wound in discovering that she is not special in ways she thought she was. The thought of sharing me with other patients was also painful. So banana skins may not appear in my bin again; but who can prevent human hair from settling on my couch? One thing is for sure, when traces of the outside world reveal themselves on the inside of the therapeutic space, and if they are noticeable and significant to the patient, they simply cannot be ignored. Regardless of the apparent insignificance of the 'intruders', the psychological meaning underlying the client's response was immensely significant.

A chance meeting between therapist and patient can also be felt by either as intrusive. Patients tell their therapists aspects of their private lives that they want to talk about. A chance meeting can reveal details that may create inroads to further fruitful work, or be catastrophic. The following scenario belongs to the former:

The therapist goes to an expensive restaurant out of town with a group of friends to celebrate his birthday. As he was eating his meal he became aware of one of his patients. This gave him the opportunity to be composed, and when it was time to leave the restaurant he asked his friends if they could leave first. He then greeted his patient by saying hello, as he was making his way out. The patient was so deeply shocked to see her therapist that she made a loud scream. During the session following this event, the patient was furious at the therapist for intruding into her world and expressed how unforgiving it was that she didn't get a chance to see who her therapist was with. This unplanned contact opened the floodgate for material, which took months of work. The most important theme that emerged was about intrusiveness, which tracked back to maternal post-natal depression that neither the patient nor the therapist trod into before the incident. It became evident that this material was core to the patient, and it was this that took the work into depth. Whilst prior to this meeting the patient spent her sessions talking small talk, she was now able to access affects not accessible before.

Money

The fee is charged with tension because it is a demarcation between a friendship and professional work. It is experienced as a business transaction. Paying to be understood and helped reinforces people's feeling that love is conditional. For some patients the money symbolizes paying for 'personal services', as one of my patients put it. In a conversation with a colleague I felt uneasy to hear him describe our being paid to heal people as a kind of prostitution. Yet money is so tied up with symbolic meanings, such as power, control, nurturing, withholding, to mention but a few, that it is not uncommon for patients who are afraid of intimacy to associate paying their therapist with paying a prostitute.

The fee comes more into question in private settings than within other settings where the patient receives 'free' therapy. I have found that private patients think twice before missing a session if they have to pay. Patients who receive their treatment through the NHS, or charitable organizations, are more likely to do so. The fee transaction is nonetheless a dynamic pertaining to any setting and it needs to be acknowledged and worked with. Jeremy Holmes (2001) exemplifies the importance of the fee in his statement that '[a] therapist who sees her patients for love will be far less predictable and professional than one for whom there is a sound financial contract' (p. 122). He adds that 'financial exchange forms part of the framework of safe therapy, akin to the need for regularity of time and place, and consistency of approach' (ibid.: 123).

I remember a patient who was in receipt of therapy under the NHS due to depression and anxiety following the death of his mother. At the end of our work, whilst saying goodbye to me, he said: 'Let me know if you ever need anything done around your house. You know, painting, wallpapering. I'm quite good at those sorts of jobs.' Was this his attempt to continue having contact with me and avoid another painful loss? I didn't think so. It felt that it was more his need to let me know that he can cope, that he is resourceful and that he had the desire to nurture me back. Not paying the NHS therapist directly leaves some patients with the need to give something else back: to nurture the therapist. The nurturing can take the form of gifts, offering services, or persistent expressions of gratitude.

Each time the patient pays the therapist he or she is reminded of the professional nature of their relationship. Some patients forget to pay, others delay payment, whilst some relate to the fee as the safeguard against intimacy. The fee becomes a vehicle for expressing all kinds of feelings:

> Mr A decided to end his therapy, at a time when he felt extremely vulnerable and unable to tolerate being seen as 'needy'. It was at a point when negative transference had set in and we were looking at his dependency needs, his frustration with his tendency to be passive and compliant, and the central issue of his aggression – affects he had so far sexualized. He announced during one of his sessions that he was not coming back anymore and warned his therapist against attempting to persuade him to do otherwise. It was a familiar pattern in his life to break off his connections suddenly and violently with anyone who got too close or who was non-compliant to his demands. The patient went on the attack; he raved like a wounded man who wanted to destroy anything he believed stood in his way of exit. I felt 'grilled' in this session. Feelings of fullness, nausea and aggression ran through me like wine through my veins. It felt like being in a state of drunkenness. Have I reached my limits? I thought disconcertingly. I wondered how best to respond and doubted whether he could hear or receive anything I had to say. I felt sad and concerned whether I could contain my countertransference, avoid acting it out and help him work with the intensity of his feelings. The pressure of this being the last session sabotaged any desire on my part to do some fruitful work. As I was uttering my interpretation of the patient's feelings, I was shocked with the tone and quality of my voice. It was loaded with angry undertones. 'You are bloody good doc!' he exclaimed triumphantly. His excitement lasted for a few minutes and he once again sank in his chair. I noticed how relieved and empty of his aggression he looked. He managed to locate these feelings in me. We had finally met each other, just as we were saying goodbye. In my heart I knew the crucial work had only just begun. The ending felt premature and abrupt. But I also knew that the groundwork had been done, and had the patient decided to return in the future I would consider resuming the work.
>
> As he was leaving his session he handed over a cheque, which I discovered later carried an exorbitant amount of money: it was three times the amount he had been invoiced for. This gesture of 'paying extra' seemed linked to this patient's want to make reparation and compensate for his aggression and hostility, feelings he was fearful of as he believed they would damage me. I returned the cheque to

him asking for the correct amount. Had I colluded with the patient's need to appease it would have strengthened his propensity to avoid dealing with his aggressive feelings.

I have learned many lessons in handling patient communications and reactions to the fee. My very first experience was in my own analysis. I cite this example to demonstrate how the mishandling of an aspect of the frame led to my desire to terminate my analysis:

After leaving my session in which my analyst handed me the bill for the month I discovered that I had been given a bill with the names of two women, neither of which was my own name. I became curious, wondering whether my analyst also practised couple therapy. How is it possible to confuse me with these two other individuals? By this time I was well versed with analytic language, so my freely associative energy took only a few minutes to be mobilized. Does this mean that he sees me as too much? After all, this is the invoice of two people. Does he not remember who I am? Am I indistinguishable, just one of many? The blow to my narcissism was indeed severe. The worst of this was that I felt ridden with guilt; Suddenly I was party to a truth that I felt uncomfortable with. My conscience troubled me. The voice that says 'you shouldn't look' was now taking enormous proportions in my free associations. I hurriedly folded together the paper and forgot the names of the patients written on it. But I could not forget the amount, which stuck in my mind like glue to paper. I was furious that these other individuals, whose names I had forgotten – and dared not remind myself by taking another look at the invoice as I felt I would be committing the sin twice – had been charged a sizeable amount less than me. I had the urge to obliterate these other patients by tearing the bill apart. But, like a good patient, I took it to my analyst the following session and rather sheepishly mentioned the blunder. He briefly apologized and said he would prepare another bill. For months since this incident I had the urge to terminate my analysis, but, again like a good patient, refrained from the urge. Instead, I often lapsed into painful silences fearing that if I opened my mouth something harmful would escape. On one occasion when I was late (I was normally never late for analysis) I explained that it was due to the traffic, and my analyst accepted this without question. I felt increasingly discontent and had thoughts that my analyst was useless and had no understanding of me. Of course at the time I made no direct link to the boundary blunder. Having had to cope silently with the overwhelming feeling of anger for months I finally made the decision to tell my analyst how upset I felt every time he yawned. He apologized profusely and suggested we change the sessions from an evening to a morning, as he accepted that he was tired and less available in the evenings. This could have been a turning point in my analysis, had my analyst been tuned into my affects. But it had taken another year before my negative transference could be acknowledged. It was years later that I realized how much my analyst's lack of awareness of my anger was reinforcing a position I had in my relationships to keep my anger at bay. My desire to terminate my analysis was linked to my analyst's failure to tolerate my anger. An acknowledgement by the therapist that he or she has made a mistake can be helpful to the client; but if this is devoid of understanding of the implications on the patient, as had happened on this occasion, it can feel rejecting and lead to early termination of the work. Luckily, my positive feelings towards my analyst held the fracture in the alliance and served the continuation of the work.

As a general principle I avoid taking a patient's request to change the frame at face value. I believe it is essential to first explore the external factors demanding frame modifications and also the underlying unconscious wishes expressed through aspects of the frame. The following example is of a situation involving renegotiating the frame, to respond to an external demand in the patient's life, which made it difficult to continue therapy:

Ms G lost her job at a crucial phase in her therapy and had no other financial means to continue. We had reached a crossroads: I thought it would be detrimental therapeutically to offer this client free therapy as she was likely to experience this as a devaluation of myself, which might reinforce her own sense of low self-worth. To stop the work and resume later, once her employment status changed, would be a fracture to the process and an undermining of the work so far. I decided that continuing with the work was a more desired option than ending it prematurely. So I offered the patient a period of six months during which she could continue with our work and pay the fee by the end of this period. She felt so mobilized emotionally by this gesture that she actively sought and found employment within a month. Being flexible on this occasion helped reinforce the therapeutic alliance and enabled the patient to delve deeper into herself, something she previously felt fearful of. She was clearly moved and tearful that I had made this allowance for her, explaining that she thought therapists had no feelings, that they are simply doing a job.

A year later the patient announced that she could no longer afford therapy during the winter months, even though she had just purchased an expensive car, and that she would like to meet once a fortnight until her situation improved. I wondered what message this was conveying, whilst thinking that if I agreed to this break in the frame it would be a disaster for the treatment. Although my earlier, flexible stance to renegotiate the fee was rooted in the treatment aims I misjudged the implicit message that I was giving to the patient as being special. The second time she challenged the frame was in the context of her recent feelings of being rejected by me. This happened in the context of changing the time of her sessions to accommodate changes in her working arrangements. Instead of arriving for her session in the morning, as we had agreed since we decided to change the time, she arrived late at night. I turned her away, and when she came back for the following session she was furious. She accused me of being inhuman, cold, and of not appreciating how difficult the journey was for her to make it to her sessions. The least she would expect, she said, was for me to be friendly. Her request to attend less frequently and pay half the fee during the winter months seemed to me to be a direct expression of her anger towards me and her punishing me for being rejecting. It was also an attempt to re-establish her special position in my mind again, which she felt she lost. This example highlights the importance in identifying acting out behaviour and making it explicit. Breaks in the frame are complex events for the therapy. Although a break may serve the patient in some respect, at the same time it sets up new rules and new expectations, with inevitable implications. Had I taken the patient's second challenge to the frame at face value, I think it could have potentially compromised the safety of our work.

At face value elasticity in the frame may threaten the security in the relationship, but in some circumstances, such as the immediately preceding example, it can be fruitful and rewarding. The interpersonal component found in negotiation mobilizes the agency in the patient and lies at the heart of a more sensitive therapeutic interaction. But, as the previous example also indicates, although on the surface the patient's requests to renegotiate the frame the second time round were similar, each carried an implicit and unique meaning. Put in Ferenczi's words:

The analyst, like an elastic band, must yield to the patient's pull, but without ceasing to pull his own direction, so long as one position or the other has not been conclusively demonstrated to be untenable.

(Ferenczi, 1928: 262)

Unplanned contact

Unplanned meetings are often feared by therapists as they present a new challenge to the work and may sometimes sabotage the therapeutic process. To preserve their anonymity many therapists tend to take all kinds of measures to avoid meeting the client outside the domain of the consulting room. Conversations with colleagues suggest that we tend to be cautious and watchful in public places in case we are seen 'misbehaving' by patients. Understandably so, as this would impinge on our spontaneity and the freedom to express ourselves in ways afforded by other professions. We often hear of the difficulties unplanned meetings pose for the therapy and rarely of examples where they presented opportunities for useful work. During the course of our working lives we are bound to meet a patient unexpectedly:

> A colleague mentioned to me that during a visit to the theatre that he realized that the woman in the row in front of him cuddling up to a gentleman was his therapist. He was so astonished, shocked and furious, that he had palpitations and felt restless throughout the play. When at the interval he saw the therapist buying her companion an ice cream, he felt that that was the icing on the cake. To vent his murderousness he stormed out. He felt that this incident took the therapy into deeper territories and helped him confront his feelings of rejection and inadequacy. What he never forgave his therapist for was that he missed half of the play. He made up for this by going to a second viewing three weeks later. What helped him deal with the feelings evoked from this unplanned meeting was his therapist's willingness to stay with the material evoked by the incident, albeit to her obvious embarrassment.

The following example is given as an illustration of how therapeutic work is compromised if the timing of unplanned contact fuels existing psychic tensions:

> Three years into therapy the therapist met one of her patients at a dinner and dance party. It was towards the end of the evening, so she assumed she had either been spotted earlier and avoided contact,

or that the timing of the meeting was by chance. The patient immediately praised the therapist's dancing! The therapist felt numb and exposed, but managed a composed smile. The patient then began to appraise the party and asked what the therapist's connections were. She politely declined a direct response to her question and said that she felt it would be best if they did not engage in further conversation. When the patient arrived for her session after the unplanned contact she made no mention of the dinner party, although she was visibly irritated. She described her frustration with a friend who avoided having arguments at all costs. The patient felt that arguments are healthy, and she felt distant from this friend who was frightened of any display of anger. She continued talking about this half way through the session. The therapist wondered how much of this was related to the patient's frustration in not being able to talk about the unplanned meeting at the party. She took this up with the patient as her referring to her own frustration of feeling unable to voice her reaction to the unplanned contact. She replied: 'What do you think? It's like having your parents watching you flirting at a dance. It spoiled my evening. Not because you were there, but because you were not serious. I saw the ordinary side of you, the sensuous side of you, and I felt anxious and confused. But then what really did it for me was that you spent more time with X (referring to a friend she saw the therapist talking to) and ignored me. I was hoping you would talk to me for a bit longer.'

To be ignored or rejected by the therapist is one of the worst nightmares of many patients. In this case the patient felt excluded, and was not quite ready to delve into this in her therapy. She also felt unsafe, as she was confronted with a reality she had to face, no doubt prematurely, that her therapist has a life outside the framework. No amount of reparative work could remedy the fracture in the frame discussed in the previous example. The timing of the unplanned contact had militated against the therapeutic alliance. The patient was not ready to give up her fantasy of a serious, composed, safely maternal figure and replace it with the reality figure who can be shared and who is as human as everyone else. She terminated the work prematurely.

Milner's (1952) metaphor of the inside and outside reality of the frame is useful in understanding how a patient can obliterate the presence of his therapist if he meets her outside. Obliteration can be a way of coping with the unexpected, shocking and uncontained reality away from the therapeutic space. The scenario that follows raises the dilemma of a therapist who was unsure whether to present reality to a patient, following unplanned contact:

> The patient was nine months into treatment and into his second break. He was in denial about the significance of the break, even though attachment and separation were major issues. His first therapist emigrated to another country, and from starting work with his second therapist he persistently referred to her as Lesley, his first therapist's name. During the break the therapist saw the patient across the room at a Christmas office party (the patient was there in his own right), caught his eye and acknowledged him. He turned away and appeared very cool about it. So the therapist thought it was her own anxiety, and that seeing her at the party did not seem to bother him. Two weeks later the patient returned for his session and talked about events of the break, mainly family events. Then he presented a dream he had over the break that was haunting him. (This patient hardly had dreams.) In his dream he walked into a party and met his ex-girlfriend. But because he remembered so little of this dream he could not understand why he was so haunted by it. So, he had no associations to the dream and in no way found it to be meaningful in any particular way. The therapist waited before making any inroads into the meaning of the dream material and agonized whether to say anything at this stage. Following some thoughtful deliberation, she decided it would be mad to say nothing and without further hesitation said: 'Well, we had been in the same room at the Christmas party two weeks ago.' The patient, enraged, accused his therapist of making it all up, that she was manipulative, mad and provocative, as he was convinced he had not met her at a party. This provoked doubt in the therapist, who wondered whether she might have been mistaken and that the person she saw and acknowledged at the party could indeed have been somebody else. The atmosphere in the room during this exchange was tense, and both therapist and patient felt frightened. At the end of the session the patient left absolutely furious and livid, and the therapist wondered whether he would come back. Two days later he returned and rather sheepishly talked of his preoccupation with the previous session's material. He thought that he understood what had happened. He enquired whether the therapist was wearing black trousers with a cream blouse, in order to check his perception, to which the therapist nodded in agreement. Then he said that he often bumps into a woman in the corridors who looks just like the therapist, and he thought it had been her at the party.

The work now focused on the conflict between conscious knowing and unconscious knowing. Until this incident the patient did not believe in the unconscious, and he was a man who rarely showed any affects during therapy before. He was highly intellectualized and dismissive of feelings. The dream obviously signalled something very important to him, and a big shift occurred which enabled him to acknowledge his unconscious. This also opened up a memory he had completely forgotten about: that twice as a child he had been looked after by relatives, following his mother's psychotic breakdowns. His fear was linked to the dissonance between the dream, the reality and his identification with a psychotic mother. These memories could now be accessed and explored in depth.

The clinical issue for the therapist was whether it would be technically therapeutic to introduce the reality before the patient introduced it. Her decision to go ahead with this would have been to no avail if the patient had not been ready to use it in the way that he did. There is no doubt that therapists do not always make timely interventions, as it is difficult to know how far the patient is ready to entertain them. Often we rely on intuition and faith to see us through relatively unclear understanding. We can only hope that what we say or do with good intentions will lead to therapeutic efficacy.

Conclusion

Masud Khan (1974) drew attention to these technical problems, arguing that

> It is an accepted fact in recent psycho-analytic discussions that an integrated theory of psycho-analytic technique, as yet, does not exist. Of course, there are rules and procedures of conduct in the analytic situation . . . In Freud's own writings, as well, there is very little discussion on what one might call the metapsychology of the therapeutic frame.
>
> (Khan, 1974, pp. 129–30)

Referring to Winnicott's failings in his analysis of Khan, which might have led to Khan making this assertion, Goldman (2003) warns against insufficient concern with the formal structure and boundaries of analysis, whilst emphasizing that failures can be the result of overlapping areas of mutual vulnerability (p. 496). I would tentatively like to add that a relaxed frame and insufficient concern with the boundaries may be the symptoms of holding on to the therapy well after what could be achieved between the therapeutic couple had been completed. Instead of moving towards termination, the work becomes stale, lifeless and reaches an impasse that persists over a long time.

To be concerned with the way a patient relates to the frame is in my mind crucial to the therapy as a whole. The frame provides the container for a therapy of trust and a therapy of intimacy. Yet its properties to date remain somewhat oblique. I have used the metaphor of 'elasticity' to refer to the importance of a flexible therapeutic attitude with empathic, attuned, responsive and spontaneous qualities. The value of elasticity cannot be sufficiently stressed. I quite like to think of the frame as a 'secure base', the term employed by Bowlby (1969) to define the caregiving environment. Such a base demands continuity, consistency, security and safety. These variables act in the service of a structured, safe environment that has the strength to hold and contain the emotionally turbulent processes of therapy.

References

Berry, N. (1987) 'The end of the analysis', in *John Klauber. Illusion and Spontaneity in Psychoanalysis*, London: Free Association.

Bowlby, J. (1969) *Attachment and Loss*. Vol. 1: *Attachment*, London: Pimlico, 1997.

Casement, P. (1999) *On Learning from the Patient*, London: Routledge.

Casement, P. (2002) *Learning from our Mistakes: Beyond Dogma in Psychoanalysis and Psychotherapy*, London: Routledge.

Ferenczi, S. (1928) 'The elasticity of psychoanalytic technique', in J. Borossa (ed.) *Selected Writings*, London: Penguin, 1999.

Gerrard, J. (2002) 'A sense of entitlement: vicissitudes of working with "special" patients', *British Journal of Psychotherapy* 19(2): 173–88.

Goldman, D. (2003) 'The outrageous prince: Winnicott's uncure of Masud Khan', *British Journal of Psychotherapy* 19(4): 483–501.

Gordon, P. (1999) *Face to Face – Therapy as Ethics*, London: Constable.

Gray, A. (1994) *An Introduction to the Therapeutic Frame*, London: Routledge.

Gutheil, T.G. and Gabbard, G.O. (1993) 'The concept of boundaries in clinical practice: theoretical and risk-management dimensions', *American Journal of Psychiatry* 150: 188–96.

Hantman, J. (2000) 'On the frame', viewed 25 April 2003, http://therapy athome.org

Holmes, J. (2001) *The Search for the Secure Base – Attachment Theory and Psychotherapy*, Hove: Brunner-Routledge.

Khan, M. (1974) *The Privacy of the Self*, London: Karnac.

Klauber, J. (1987) *Illusion and Spontaneity in Psychoanalysis*, London: Free Association.

Kohut, H. (1978) *The Search for the Self – Selected Writings of Heinz Kohut: 1950–1978*, vol. 2 edited by Paul H. Ornstein, Madison, Wis.: International Universities Press, Inc.

Langs, R.J. (1976) *The Therapeutic Interaction*, vols I and II, New York: Jason Aronson.

Langs, R.J. (1992) *A Clinical Workbook for Psychotherapists*, London: Karnac.

Laplanche, J. (1989) *New Foundations for Psychoanalysis*, London: Blackwell.

Lazarus, A.A. (1998) 'How do you like these boundaries?', *The Clinical Psychologist* 51(1): 22–5.

Lomas, P. (1987) *The Limits of Interpretation*, New York: Jason Aronson.

Luca-Stolkin, M. (1999) 'Pandora's Box: the shadow of femininity in the treatment of psycho-somatic distress', *Psychodynamic Counselling* 5(2), London: Routledge.

Milner, M. (1952) 'Aspects of symbolism and comprehension of the not-self', *International Journal of Psychoanalysis* 33: 181–95.

Persaud, R. (2003) 'Looking for a counsellor? You need your head examined', *Daily Telegraph*, 12 March.

Resnik, S. (1995) *Mental Space*, London: Karnac.

Smith, D.L. (1991) *Hidden Conversations – An Introduction to Communicative Psychoanalysis*, London: Routledge.

Valentine, M. (1996) 'The abuse of power within the analytic setting', *British Journal of Psychotherapy* 13(2): 174–82.

Warburton, K. (1999) 'Establishing a therapeutic frame', in J. Lees (ed.) *Clinical Counselling in Context – An Introduction*, London: Routledge, 80–93.

Winnicott, D.W. (1971) *Playing and Reality*, London: Tavistock Publications.

Young, R.M. (1998) 'The analytic frame, abstinence and acting out', in *The Human Nature Review*, Available online: htpp://humannature.com/rmyoung/papers/pap110h.html (6 August 2002).

Chapter 2

Therapy in general practice – frames within frames

Nick Zinovieff

In the 1950s Dr Michael Balint of the Tavistock Clinic emphasized to general practitioners the value of listening to their patients and being attuned to their feelings. It became more apparent that some of the patients' complaints were linked to underlying emotional distress. At first, the implications seemed to be that general practitioners would, at least for some of their patients, need to become psychotherapists, as longer appointments were seen to be needed. Later, however, with the publication of *Six Minutes for the Patient* (Balint and Norell, 1973), came the realization that GPs did not have the time or the training to do in-depth therapy sessions.

It is assessed that approximately one-third of all patients who consult their GP are likely to be seeking help for the emotional distress associated with a physical illness, or for what can be termed a 'life problem' (Corney and Jenkins, 1993). Patients with emotional problems have been shown to attend their GP more frequently and show an increased demand for other medical services. In response to this, the 1970s saw the arrival of social workers being attached to general practices and the publication of papers associated to this (Graham and Sher, 1976). Papers also appeared in New Zealand on the counsellor in general practice and in Britain on psychotherapy and psychiatry being more closely involved in general practice (Strathdee, 1988). In 1980, in the *Journal of the Royal College of General Practitioners*, an article appeared outlining the effectiveness of counselling in general practice (Waydenfeld and Waydenfeld, 1980). Most of the therapists involved at that time were marriage guidance counsellors (Heisler, 1979; Corney, 1987). During the 1980s and after, the emergence of counselling and psychotherapy in general practice burgeoned such that by the end of the 1980s, when I myself first worked as a therapist in general practice, 30 per cent of practices were said to have an 'in-house counsellor'. Remuneration for counsellors at that time was shared by the Family Health Services Authority and the GPs themselves. During the 1990s, with the arrival of Fundholding in General Practice, when each practice controlled their own budget, some 50 per cent of general practices employed an in-house counsellor. Now, with the advent of the millennium, and the establishment of the Primary Care Trusts, every general practice patient has access to a counsellor.

In this chapter I wish to review the meaning of and relevance to counselling and psychotherapy practice (used here interchangeably) of the concept of the 'therapeutic frame', with particular reference to its applicability to psychotherapy and counselling in medical general practice. I will be looking, therefore, at two strands of thought: first, the origin and theory of the concept of the 'therapeutic frame' itself and its place in psychotherapeutic practice, and, second, its relevance when working as a therapist in general practice. Is there, indeed, a need when working in general practice for (or not?) a universal 'therapeutic frame', as portrayed by the psychoanalytically oriented writers Milner (1952) and Langs (1976). Is therapy in general practice, in fact, an example of what Langs might term as working with a non-ideal and 'deviant frame' (Hoag, 1992: 419)? The theory I shall be drawing on is predominantly psychoanalytic, as other orientations (as far as I am aware) have not fully addressed the theoretical position of the 'therapeutic frame'. Certainly in my own orientation, Cohn (1998: 112) is the only existential/phenomenological theorist to question and look at the concept of the 'therapeutic frame' comprehensively, and he himself comments that: 'the consideration of the "frame" has been neglected by existential therapists'.

Since it was first proposed by Marion Milner (1952), 'the therapeutic frame has been widely adopted and transmitted in a relatively unquestioned manner despite major modifications in clinical theory and practice', write Cherry and Gold (1989: 162), referring to the recent shift in psychoanalytic theory from the psychobiological viewpoint to one more concerned with the influence of the environment on the development of the individual (i.e. from the intrapsychic to the interpersonal). They also consider that while the 'therapeutic frame' originated in the psychoanalytic tradition, it has been widely adopted by other schools of therapy. In the course of clinically supervising trainees on an integrative psychotherapy training I have reason to share Cherry and Gold's view that 'the significance of the frame and its components has often been obscured when applied out of [the psychoanalytic] context' (1989: 162). Anxiety is expressed, for example, by these trainees when any change in the 'therapeutic frame' is considered. But why? For how far and in what way has the theory of the 'therapeutic frame' been adopted into the particular integrative theory and practice being considered? In a sense there is 'a divorce of a "rule" from its original meaning' (Cohn, 1998: 112). There seems to be an assumption that the 'therapeutic frame' exists and should be unchanging, if not inviolable. A wider consideration of the frame has certainly, then, been neglected.

The issue of the existence and meaning of the ideal 'therapeutic frame' (Langs, 1976) and the question of how 'secure' can the 'therapeutic frame' be in general practice (Langs, 1988), in fact, is worth exploring and I would like to look at and reflect on the experience of setting up and maintaining a psychotherapy and counselling service over the last fourteen years in three different general practices in different areas of London. The various questions I would like to address are:

1   What is the 'therapeutic frame'? What is its function? Is there an ideal and universal frame which is right for all kinds of therapy? Can therapy be effective without an ideal and 'secure frame'? Does the therapy have to be adapted to the frame? What boundaries, indeed, are essential, desirable and necessary?

2   So is maintaining an ideal and secure 'therapeutic frame' in general practice necessary, possible, or even desirable? Is there, then, the existence of a 'deviant frame' (Langs, 1988)? How influential on the therapy is the philosophy and culture of the medical setting? In a sense, is counselling in general practice the setting up of a frame within a frame? Is there, then, a need for a non-rigid and more flexible approach to boundaries and the 'therapeutic frame' when working in general practice?

The therapeutic frame

Though widely adopted by other schools of therapy, the idea of the 'therapeutic frame' originated in the psychoanalytic tradition with Freud's papers on technique and recommendations to physicians practising psychoanalysis (1911–1913) clearly setting out what he saw as the basic prerequisites for attempting to establish the analytic relationship: free association, evenly suspended attention of the analyst, neutrality, anonymity, abstinence, confidentiality, set time and length of sessions and set fee. Freud refrained from drawing up hard and fast rules but stressed that modification of these ground rules makes the patient less able to overcome deeper resistance, together with the bringing about of further consequences in the analysis. The actual term 'frame', however, was originally introduced as a metaphor by Marion Milner in a paper in the *International Journal of Psychoanalysis* when she referred to these basic ground rules and boundaries as an essential component of the analytic relationship:

> I had already, when trying to study some of the psychological factors which facilitate or impede the painting of pictures, become interested in the part played by the frame. The frame marks off the different kind of reality that is within it from that which is outside it; but a temporal spatial frame also marks off the special kind of reality of the psychoanalytic session. And in psychoanalysis it is the existence of this frame that makes possible the full development of that creative illusion that analysts call the transference.
>
> (Milner, 1952: 183)

What Milner introduces here is the notion of how adherence to the basic ground rules, and creation of the frame, 'sets the analytic relationship apart from other segments of the patient's life, creating the opportunity for the development of the transference' (Hoag, 1992: 418). In a sense, then, both Freud and Milner are laying down the ground rules of how the psychoanalyst should be with, and approach, the client within the therapeutic interaction itself. The psychoanalyst's insistence on anonymity, and therefore maintenance of the blank screen, for example, is undertaken to facilitate the client's projection of significant figures from the past onto the analyst. The origins of the concept of the 'therapeutic frame', then, very much pointed to the context, philosophy, and process of the therapy being practised, with the 'therapeutic frame' being very much part of the psychoanalytical process.

Since then, it is the communicative psychoanalyst Robert Langs (1976) who has offered the most conservative and extensive clinical exploration of the importance of the ideal and of what he calls the 'secure frame', particularly in terms of the manner in which it serves the therapeutic interaction. Frame and therapeutic process are, for Langs, closely connected if not fused. Smith (1991) has eloquently presented Langs' thinking on the 'therapeutic frame' and emphasizes the importance f management of the frame in communicative psychoanalysis as being much more than just a setting:

> The structuring of the frame, the management of the ground rules, is the real business of psychoanalysis. It is a basic communicative tenet that the management of the frame has a more powerful impact

on the patient, for good or for ill, than any other feature of the psychoanalytic interaction (including the content of the analyst's interventions).

(Smith, 1991: 164)

The ideal and secure frame includes a private setting, not office or clinic (with soundproofed room); a set fee not altered throughout the course of treatment; a set time and length of sessions, with the therapist being responsible for maintaining confidentiality, anonymity, neutrality, abstinence, the use of the couch, free association, absence of physical contact, the consistency of the setting; and the client being responsible for the termination of the therapy. This ideal and secure frame is part of the therapeutic process to such an extent that change or modification in any of the basic ground rules damages the value, even destroys the therapy and the clients' efforts to resolve their problems (Smith, 1991). It is the security of the setting that allows the therapist to most effectively contain the client's psychopathology, fostering a sense of trust and an environment conducive to a secure therapeutic relationship.

It is interesting to note, however, that there is no overall consensus regarding how much the 'therapeutic frame' is part of the therapeutic process or what constitutes an appropriate reason for modification of the frame. Which particular components to be included under the term also lack any consensus. Psychoanalytic practitioners form a spectrum with regard to their attitudes toward the 'therapeutic frame': from strict adherence to the basic ground rules (Langs, 1976), to a more *laissez-faire* attitude (Lomas, 1987). However, regarding its function, psychoanalytic thinking from Freud on has consistently referenced the frame as needing to be safe and secure (Winnicott, 1965), thus allowing the patient, for example, to regress, become dependent, and reveal hidden and disturbed parts of the self (Bleger, 1967). The need for the frame is overtly linked to childhood experience and the early mother–child relationship in terms of the maternal holding function (Winnicott, 1986) and needs for an atmosphere of safety (Schafer, 1983).

It is interesting that, subsequent to these major writers, apart from Langs, articles on the 'therapeutic frame' are rather scanty and hard to find, and it is only more latterly that a book on the 'therapeutic frame' has been published. Anne Gray (1994), in *An Introduction to the Therapeutic Frame*, describes her practice as embracing both psychodynamic and person-centred concepts, and has proposed five elements which make up the 'therapeutic frame': a private setting for therapist and client, fixed times and duration of sessions, vacation breaks stated by therapist, a set fee for sessions that have been reserved, and confidentiality on the part of the therapist. Most therapists – certainly all those that I am aware of – would agree that all these elements are essential and need to be clearly outlined at the beginning of the therapy. However, once agreed upon, the question is whether these elements should never be changed? And what flexibility might be needed?

Very much influenced by earlier psychoanalytic thinkers, Gray has thence articulated, in a comprehensive fashion, the emotional and more practical purposes of these boundaries, which she links with the infant's experience of early maternal care. Her emphasis, then, tends toward the holding and containing function of the boundaries of the 'therapeutic frame' and the provision of a safe place in which the client can begin to explore their experience, much as a child needs safe boundaries to explore its environment and learn from this experience. She therefore calls for 'a firm set of rules which have been built up through experience and are applied to all clients', but at the same time, importantly, suggests a flexibility in the way these rules are applied to individual clients: 'The frame serves the interests of both parties, client and therapist, but it is not written in stone' (Gray, 1994: 18–19).

This call for flexibility, interestingly, echoes with the existential/ phenomenological approach of Cohn (1998: 113) who advocates 'a meaningful connection between frame and aim, as well as enough flexibility to do justice to developments within therapy . . . The frame-work, in my view, is defined by the aim of the interaction but needs to be flexible enough to reflect changes within the inter-action.'

The frame of general practice

Most of the literature on the nature and function of boundaries in the counselling and psychotherapeutic relationship has focused on private practice where the client goes to the therapist's consulting room and pays a fee for the therapist's services. One of the most obvious differences between private practice and public employment in general practice is that in private practice it is the client and not the employer (be it the practice itself or the Primary Care Trust) who pays the therapist. A second significant difference is reference to the length of the therapy, which in private practice is chosen by the client, whereas in general practice only time-limited, shorter-term therapy tends to be offered. This is, in essence, imposed from without by the employer on the client and therapist because of the realities of supply and demand, and is an immediate indication of counselling and psychotherapy in general practice being the existence of a frame within the frame – and certainly not meeting the criteria for a secure frame as outlined by Langs (Milton, 1993).

The setting of a general practice surgery is an explicitly medical and public one, and is predominantly focused on a model of diagnosis and treatment with no fees paid. People who identify themselves as being ill come to the surgery to consult with the doctor, find out what is wrong, and hope to be made better as quickly as possible, usually through medication. A hectic and busy atmosphere often overtakes the surgery, particularly on crowded Monday mornings, after the build up of untreated weekend ailments. The waiting room can be shared by neighbours, friends, strangers and sometimes relatives, with the aura at times like the throng of a community centre. The receptionists, who know most of the patients and some of these very well, try to keep track and retain control of the often bulging appointment system, with phones continually ringing and needy ill patients demanding to be seen quickly.

It is within such a hectic and frenetic atmosphere that I have set up counselling and psychotherapy services in three separate general practices in three different areas of London – two in Outer London and one in Inner London. At one point during the mid-1990s I worked concurrently in all three. The two Outer London practices had previously not provided a counselling service, whereas the Inner London practice had had a psychodynamically oriented therapist, in-house, for quite a number of years. This therapist, I was told by a receptionist when welcoming me to the practice, had always seen clients in any of the available doctors' consulting rooms and did I, like her (the previous therapist), want sight of the medical notes of all the clients I would be seeing that afternoon? There was an assumption in her question that I would work similarly. I thanked the receptionist but warmly told her that I didn't need to have sight of the notes. As it was (and still is), in terms of my practice as an existential/phenomenological therapist, I much prefer to first see clients without any third-party information which might influence my experience of the client's experience.

One of my first concerns from the outset, experienced in each practice, was with regard to which room would I be given to practise in. Coming from long experience of working as a social worker in a psychiatric hospital, where room space was often at a premium, I was already very aware of the possible difficulty and importance of establishing a room designated for therapy. I knew from this experience in psychiatry that the context of the therapy room has significance and, I believe, an influence on both therapist and client, and thence their interaction (Cohn, 1998). I also particularly wanted and sought out a consistent therapy room that would not be also used by any of the medical staff (cf. Linda Hoag's experience in Hoag, 1992: 423). What concerned me, then, was the creation of some clear boundaries between the counselling setting and the medical surgery in order to assuage my own insecurities, which were perhaps around hierarchy (Jones, 1986), and also to establish the status of the psychotherapy and counselling service in the practice. In effect, to secure the context for the therapy to co-exist alongside the more established medical and nursing practice – the creation of a comfortable and safe space where clients could feel free to be open and explore the difficulties that brought them to therapy. In essence a frame, in which reflecting was possible, in a frame where reflecting was not the norm; the setting up of a frame within a frame as-it-were, but with possible cultural dissonance resonating between the two.

Molnos (1995), in her study of brief dynamic psychotherapy, has emphasized the importance of handling therapeutic boundaries correctly, especially in medical settings where 'there is no general understanding of what psychotherapeutic boundaries mean and why they are necessary at all' (p. 26). Two of the general practices were situated in health centres, each of which had available space for the asking and each gave me easy access to non-medical rooms in which to see clients; the other practice, where I, in fact, still work, allowed and continues to allow me to use the staff room with its more comfortable easy chairs, a small library, with cooking facilities and a washing-up sink. An added advantage concerning this room is that it is little used by staff in the afternoon, and, being situated in the basement, has its own outside door, so it is possible for clients to see me and leave the surgery without having to go into the waiting room at all and thus preserve privacy and safety (see also Gray, 1994). Indeed, given the opportunity to choose, clients have always preferred to come directly to this therapy room for their session rather than waiting for me to come up to the waiting room. I have to assume that this preference is related to clients' needs for confidentiality and also the fears of stigma, given the public arena of the waiting room.

In each of the general practices I set up a similar referral system, where the doctors, to refer clients, simply gave the potential client an already typed out information sheet (provided by myself) advising them to ring me at the practice during any one of four ten-minute slots on either of the two days I was at the practice (the time when I was not, of course, seeing clients) to arrange their first session. I made it clear to each of the referring doctors that I was prepared to see any client referred and assess with the client whether they wished to see me for shorter-term therapy. Nothing was required in writing from the referrer as I was more interested in hearing the client's experience directly rather than reading a probably rather hastily written if not scribbled referral. I was also well aware already that the pressure and demand on a GP's time had considerably increased and was increasing, it seemed, all the time.

I also wanted the clients, after speaking with the referring doctor, to have to make the choice and take the responsibility for ringing me personally to arrange their first session rather than have the doctor and the reception system take away that choice and responsibility. It was also a way of making immediate personal contact with clients and of lessening, I believe, the amount of unmotivated clients who wouldn't attend first sessions. Looking in retrospect, the whole process could be seen as a way of securing more of the 'therapeutic frame' in what has been called by Langs a 'deviant frame' therapy (Langs, 1988).

Through this referral process I also retained complete control of my appointment book (which was separate from the medical appointments book), except for one session a week that was set aside for urgent cases where doctors only could make the appointment. (This session had been created after a doctor on the GP rotation training scheme had anxiously rung me at home to find out when I could see one of the very distressed patients she was seeing.) The reception staff, in the main, honoured these arrangements and consistently advised clients, who, for example, rang to try to change or make first appointments when I was not on site, that they had to ring me during the ten-minute slot times when I was in the practice. This referral system was met with differing responses from the medical staff. From welcome and interest to scepticism and surprise that it could work! My own belief was that such a system would lessen first session non-attenders, which was indeed borne out by the higher non-attendance rate for first sessions by clients who were referred through the urgent appointments made only by the doctors.

It becomes clear, therefore, that the frame of the therapeutic relationship becomes much more complex and more difficult to sustain once a therapist enters the organizational context of primary care. Warburton (1999: 83) has suggested that 'not only have frame issues generally been neglected by writers concerned with therapeutic work in institutions, there is also an influential body of opinion which sees counselling in specific contexts as different in kind from counselling in other contexts'. Is the therapist's primary responsibility, therefore, to the institution or the client? Is there an assumption that the interests of the institution and the client are basically the same? The culture of general practice, in my experience, is one in which confidential information is shared amongst the members of the team, and that therefore the boundary of confidentiality tends to be seen as one that surrounds the surgery as a whole. Symbolic of this I have experienced interruptions to sessions by practice staff believing the room to be empty and entering the room; or even on one occasion, a GP knocking on the door of the therapy room, walking straight in, and openly asking whether we could talk about one of the other patients taking an antidepressant. What was interesting was that the client I was actually seeing didn't seem to be thrown in any way by the experience.

Very much in line with my own experience, Smith (1999) has thus aptly commented:

> The counsellor arriving in such a setting immediately faces a problem: how far do they accommodate to the culture of the setting in which they work, and share information with other professionals as a collaborative member of the team, and how far should they stand firm, defending the secure base of the counselling relationship, of the client's right to have a confidential and private space, alone with the counsellor, in which their anxieties can safely unfold?
>
> (Smith, 1999: 44)

It is interesting to reflect now, after nearly fourteen years' experience, on any changes in my own practice specifically with regard to my relationship with the doctors and members of the primary health care team, particularly with reference to the area and boundaries of client confidentiality. How private and secure was the 'therapeutic frame'? And what frame and boundaries were needed? When I think back to when I first arrived at the practice, where I have worked for the last fourteen years, what strikes immediately is the gradual shift from my initially more active, even evangelistic, participation in the workings of the practice, where rather like Lees (1997) my evolving style was becoming driven by the setting adopting 'the "Casualty" style of "super-hero counsellor" who was fighting the battle against illness and disease', but also feeling somewhat overwhelmed by the 'bottomless pit of suffering' (ibid.: 37). Allied perhaps to this was an insecurity in identity, driven, like Hoag (1992: 422), 'by a desire to please the G.P.s and staff and by my need to be seen to be doing a good job'.

This position has now moved on to a more secure but, it seems, also less active and slightly more removed, if not boundaried, position. For example, initially I would always try to attend the monthly primary health care team meeting, be pleased to be part of that, and, on occasion, discuss more openly the emotional state of particularly the more difficult clients I'd been seeing in therapy. How much was I perhaps ventilating and not containing my own anxiety? This approach, however, has gradually changed over time, facilitated, for example, by the experience of doctors revealing to me that they had asked my clients how they were 'getting on with Nick in the counselling'. (I suspect that this question is asked not infrequently of clients, particularly with clients who are well known to or provoking anxiety in the GP. The motives for asking will be various, and, of course, would be interesting to investigate.) In another instance, when I was concerned about a client and spoke in these terms to the GP, it transpired later on, through my client, that the GP had revealed part of the conversation with myself to that client. The client revealed in the following session a degree of discomfort about this experience, and, though we discussed and explored her feelings, it was very clear that for this particular client trust had been broken irrevocably; she ended her therapy shortly afterwards.

The therapist in general practice, therefore, must carefully consider the implications of discussing client material with the GP and the effects that such collaboration might have on the therapy. This is an area where individual clients will feel very differently. I have now decided not to attend the primary health care team meetings and have more recently spoken revealingly about clients to doctors only after client request or with client permission to do so. This might be, for example, with reference to GP letters to Housing Departments supporting applications for housing or housing transfer – i.e. using emotional and clinical insights to back up practical support (cf. Gray, 1994). I also think it is important to speak to the GP of my concerns if a client is suicidally depressed and perhaps needs to be considered for psychiatric assessment and possible hospital admission. On occasion a client will ask if what they are revealing is confidential. I will then explain that the sessions are confidential, with the overriding exception that if it emerges that a person is a serious danger to themselves or others, I might need to discuss this with their doctor to establish what further help might be needed. In Langs' sense, then, in some instances I have gradually further secured the boundaries around confidentiality and thence further secured the 'therapeutic frame'.

However, contrary to the idea of the therapist having no third-party communications outside the therapeutic relationship, and with the 'thera-peutic frame' remaining secure (Gray, 1994), interestingly, there are other therapists such as Jones (1986) who, though working with a commitment to the psychodynamic approach, found that an important part of a multidisciplinary attachment to general practice was to develop regular practice meetings where individual patients being seen for therapy could be discussed with the GPs. And also Jones *et al.* (1994: 544–5) who believe that clients experience powerful transferences to both doctor and counsellor, who are thence experienced as a parental couple. To understand any particular patient's transference, there is a need, therefore, for regular meetings between therapist and GP 'so that interaction between therapist and patient, therapist and GP and interaction with third-party GPs can be examined . . . it is the Oedipal triangle of therapist, GP and patient which is vital to have in mind and under scrutiny'. Indeed, I myself have experienced certain clients who might have known their GP for many years, have a very good relationship with and trust that GP, and who have encouraged me to communicate with him or her. Clearly, in such an instance the GP knows the client very well and the triangular relationship meets client needs to feel looked after by the 'parents' and to also feel contained by the whole practice itself. It would seem, in this example, contrary to the example above where my communicating with the GP broke trust, there are clients who trusted me to communicate with the GP with the result that trust might even have grown in a syner-gistic way? In a sense, the client had felt more held and safe through my communicating with the GP.

This same theme of what boundaries, and what therapeutic framework, are needed when working in general practice has been highlighted by Lees (1997) and Smith (1999) who both challenge psychoanalytic, if not psychodynamic, orthodoxy when they call for a need for a flexibility and adaptability of the boundaries. Smith calls for a

> degree of elasticity with regard to the boundaries whilst at the same time having a sound and firm structure, one that can hold the client, and yet move with them. I would suggest the analogy of a dance, applied to the boundaries of the counselling relationship . . . provides a framework and metaphor for articulating the nature of the boundaries in the primary care setting.
>
> (Smith, 1999: 47)

What is particularly interesting and what I like about the idea of the analogy of the dance is that there is an implication that the 'framework' is ultimately about the therapist's presence holding the client i.e. to 'hold the client, and yet move with them'? I am reminded of my own experience when, on the few occasions when the administration of the practice have needed the therapy (staff) room for a meeting etc., I have had to move the session to one of the doctor's consulting rooms. I have noticed that after my apologizing for the move to another room it is me rather than the client who is seemingly more anxious about the move to a new context. At this point, however, it becomes a matter of belief and debate whether what clients say they want or need on a manifestly conscious level is the opposite of what they want or need on an unconscious level. As an existential/ phenomenological therapist, however, I am working with the client's experience as it appears rather than assuming there is necessarily an unconscious phenomenon behind what is said. The position taken on this, therefore, will depend on the therapist's theoretical orientation.

Time-limited and shorter-term therapy are part and parcel of therapeutic work in general practice, and perhaps this is why therapy in general practice is referred to as counselling rather than psychotherapy. Within the psychotherapy profession itself, over the last forty years, there has been much debate and argument around the pros and cons of shorter-term time-limited psychotherapy, but generally a resistance has operated in the mainstream psychoanalytic orientation against shortening psychotherapy, seeing it as the poor and superficial relation of the 'gold standard' of a full and lengthy analysis. Theoretically, shorter-term therapy goes against many of the classical psychoanalytic ground rules in terms of the activity of the therapist and the needs for time and how to build up the transference relationship in the 'therapeutic frame'. The whole question of working with (or not) the transference in shorter-term work becomes the salient question and a debatable area (Handley, 1995), rather than being assumed to be necessarily the right and only way. It is not, however, within the time and remit of this chapter to explore this debate at any length. Suffice it to say that, probably because of matters of supply and demand, shorter-term therapy, is generally a requirement by the employers of therapists in general practice, be it the practice itself or the Primary Care Trust. Institutional provision of counselling tends to be shorter-term and time-limited, which will find therapists becoming more interactive and focused in their work. There is clearly a need, then, in shorter-term therapy for a more flexible approach to the classical 'therapeutic frame', which will also translate to looking at different ways of being with clients, and thus thinking of different theoretical approaches to therapy when working in general practice.

Conclusion

There are two particular areas this chapter set out to look at and explore. First, what is the 'therapeutic frame', and is there an ideal and universal frame right for all kinds of therapy? Second, drawing from my own experience of working as a therapist in general practice, is maintaining an ideal and secure frame in general practice necessary, possible or even desirable? Can the frame be modified? And how confluent are theory and practice?

Freud and Milner are very clear regarding the purpose of the ground rules and the 'therapeutic frame': to facilitate the development of the transference (within an atmosphere of safety). The 'therapeutic frame', then, is very much part of the therapeutic process and as such is even more extensively discussed by Langs. It is Langs' exposition of the secure frame that sets up the benchmark of the ideal and 'secure therapeutic frame'. This is further loaded by his description of what he calls the 'deviant frame' (of, for example, therapy in general practice or the psychiatric outpatient clinic), a definition of which, according to *The Concise Oxford Dictionary* (Sykes, 1982), is 'that which deviates from normal behaviour'. In a sense, then, there is an implication of what is deemed to be 'normal' therapy and what is 'deviant'. If, however, the therapist is not working with, for example, the theory of the deep unconscious and interpreting the transference, then the therapeutic situation and work take on a completely different hue. The frame or context of the therapy will have a completely different purpose and constituency. There will not necessarily be a need for the therapeutic process to be divorced from what Milner calls the 'reality outside'. I am sure, though, that for most psychotherapists and counsellors the atmosphere of the therapeutic setting needs to feel safe enough for a client to explore and be open to looking at sensitive areas, but the question still remains as to what degree of 'security' is needed? Perhaps this is really a question relating to individual client needs? It must be noted that I, as an existential/phenomenological, oriented therapist, will not necessarily be looking for a client to regress etc. and/or to project past experience of significant figures on to myself, as the therapist, in the present. And, rather than keeping the frame fixed, I will be looking for a flexibility to change or modify the frame according to the picture being painted via changes in the therapeutic interaction.

Regarding the area of modification of the frame which is the main source of uncertainty and controversy, there seems to be some agreement between Gray and Cohn that, first, there is a need for a frame, or framework, and also that there is need for a flexibility in approach to these boundaries. Cohn agrees with Gray that there are five elements necessary for the therapeutic situation, but suggests that this framework needs to be flexible enough to reflect changes in the therapeutic interaction (i.e. the frame is adapted to the therapy and not vice versa); and Gray, a psychodynamic/humanistic theorist, in a sense concurs with this when she calls for a firm set of rules built up through experience with a flexibility in the way these rules are applied to individual clients. What is interesting, therefore, is that there is a call for flexibility towards the boundaries and 'therapeutic frame' by two theorists from very differing orientations. It is this call for flexibility and elasticity in approach to the boundaries and frame in therapy that is clearly needed in general practice (Lees 1997; Smith1999) and links with my own experience of therapy in general practice as described above. It is very clear that with respect to psychotherapy and counselling in general practice, the institutional providers of the therapy, and therefore the therapists themselves, are certainly not providing secure frame conditions in any classical psycho-analytic or Langsian sense. The setting of general practice is a public institution and can never attain the privacy, security and length of working in private practice.

I would like to conclude with a refreshing quote by Richard House in his article 'The culture of general practice and the therapeutic frame':

> In sum, perhaps the GP counsellor's task is to be as fully aware as possible of the particular (and sometimes peculiar!) characteristics of the GP counselling frame in which they work, and to be as open as possible to monitoring from moment to moment, and then respond-ing appropriately and creatively to the complex interplay between the setting, the counsellor's and the client's personality dynamics. In this way GP counselling becomes an alive, creative, emerging experience entered into by two co-creating subjects, rather than a programmatic, mechanistic process which self-fulfillingly fits clients into a preconceived theoretical framework which may say far more about the counsellor's 'neurotic' need for security than it does about the unconscious security needs of the client.
>
> (House, 1999: 37)

References

Balint, M. and Norell, J. (eds) (1973) *Six Minutes for the Patient*, London: Tavistock Publications.

Bleger, J. (1967) 'Psycho-analysis of the psycho-analytic frame', *International Journal of Psychoanalysis* 48: 511–19.

Cherry, E.F. and Gold, S.N. (1989) 'The therapeutic frame revisited: a contemporary perspective', *Psychotherapy* 26(2): 162–8.

Cohn, H.W. (1998) 'Frames for therapies or therapies for frames? An exploration of the relation between setting and aim of psychotherapy', *Journal of the Society of Existential Analysis* 9(2): 108–14.

Corney, R. (1987) 'Marriage guidance counselling in general practice in London', *British Journal of Guidance and Counselling* 15: 50–8.

Corney, R. and Jenkins, R. (eds) (1993) *Counselling in General Practice*, London: Routledge.

Freud, S. (1911–13) 'Recommendations to physicians practising psychoanalysis', in J. Strachey (ed.) *The Standard Edition of the Complete Psychological Works of Sigmund Freud*, London: The Hogarth Press, 1975.

Graham, H. and Sher, M. (1976) 'Social work and general practice', *Journal of the Royal College of General Practitioners* 26: 95–105.

Gray, A. (1994) *An Introduction to the Therapeutic Frame*, London: Routledge.

Handley, N. (1995) 'The concept of transference: a critique', *British Journal of Psychotherapy* 12(1): 49–59.

Heisler, J. (1979) 'Marriage counsellors in medical settings', *Marriage Guidance Journal* 18: 153–62.

Hoag, L. (1992) 'Psychotherapy in the general practice surgery: considerations of the frame', *British Journal of Psychotherapy* 8: 417–29.

House, R. (1999) 'The culture of general practice and the therapeutic frame', in J. Lees (ed.) *Clinical Counselling in Context: Clinical Counselling in Primary Care*, London: Routledge, pp. 19–42.

Jones, D. (1986) 'General practitioner attachments and the multidisciplinary team', *British Journal of Psychotherapy* 2: 196–200.

Jones, H., Murphy, A., Neaman, G., Tollemaache, R. and Vasserman, D. (1994) 'Psychotherapy and counselling in a GP practice: making use of the setting', *British Journal of Psychotherapy* 10(4): 543–51.

Langs, R.J. (1976) *The Therapeutic Interaction*, vols I and II, New York: Jason Aronson.

Langs, R.J. (1988) *A Primer of Psychotherapy*, New York: Jason Aronson.

Lees, J. (1997) 'An approach to counselling in GP surgeries', *Psychodynamic Counselling* 3(1): 33–48.

Lomas, P. (1987) *The Limits of Interpretation*, Harmondsworth: Penguin.

Milner, M. (1952) 'Aspects of symbolism and comprehension of the not-self', *International Journal of Psychoanalysis* 33: 181–5.

Milton, M. (1993) 'Counselling in institutional settings – secure frame possibility? – or not?', *Counselling* 4: 284–6.

Molnos, A. (1995) *A Question of Time – Essentials of Brief Dynamic Psychotherapy*, London: Karnac Books.

Schafer, R. (1983) *The Analytic Attitude*, London: Hogarth Press.

Smith, D.L. (1991) *Hidden Conversations: An Introduction to Communicative Psychoanalysis*, London: Routledge.

Smith, J. (1999) 'Holding the dance: a flexible approach to boundaries in general practice', in J. Lees (ed.) *Counselling in Context: Clinical Counselling in Primary Care*, London: Routledge, pp. 43–60.

Strathdee, G. (1988) 'Psychiatrists in primary care: the general practitioner viewpoint', *Family Practice* 5: 111–15.

Sykes, J.B. (ed.) (1982) *The Concise Oxford Dictionary of Current English*, Oxford: Clarendon Press.

Warburton, K. (1999) 'Establishing a therapeutic frame', in J. Lees (ed.) *Clinical Counselling in Context: An Introduction*, London: Routledge.

Waydenfeld, D. and Waydenfeld, S. (1980) 'Counselling in general practice', *Journal of the Royal College of General Practitioners* 30: 671–7.

Winnicott, D.W. (1965) *The Maturational Processes and the Facilitating Environment*, New York: International Universities Press.

Winnicott, D.W. (1986) *Holding and Interpretation: Fragment of an Analysis*, London: Hogarth Press.

Chapter 3

Experiencing the frame

Psychotherapy from a client's perspective

Deborah Killeen

Although all qualified psychotherapists have had their own psychotherapy, very little is written about their experiences. In this chapter I will use examples from my personal therapy, prior to and during my psychotherapy training, in order to highlight how the therapeutic frame was managed by different psychotherapists. I have chosen examples of what I see as therapeutic successes, where the therapist's management of frame issues ended positively and felt beneficial, and therapeutic failures, where I experienced careless or inappropriate management of the frame which felt damaging and unhelpful. It is a challenge to write about personal therapy. Disclosing details of such an intimate process brings with it anxieties about what and how much to reveal; too much and I make myself vulnerable, too little and this becomes rather mechanical and empty. Writing this chapter has been a carefully thought out and cathartic process, as pulling together significant pieces of my psychotherapeutic 'journey' over the last fifteen years has made me realize quite how transformational it has been.

For a good psychotherapeutic relationship to develop, the boundaries of that relationship need to be clear. It is generally considered good practice for the therapist to set out the 'rules' of the therapy in the first session. These include explaining practical issues such as the fee, setting and duration of sessions and payments for missed sessions. The less concrete elements of the therapeutic relationship are more easily understood by being modelled rather than explained by the therapist. These are about *how* the therapy will be carried out and differ according to the therapist's orientation. When agreed to by the client, these 'rules' can be seen as a verbally binding contract, ensuring that both client and therapist understand how their work together will be conducted. Milner's (1952) description of an artist's frame still serves as a good metaphor in understanding the limitations and containing nature of the therapeutic relationship. Gray (1994) describes how the therapeutic frame contains all the interactions between the therapist and the client and provides a boundary between the client's inner and outer worlds. The frame, which is established and maintained by the therapist, is not only the holding device of the therapeutic work but a fundamental part of it too, as without the frame there is arguably no therapy. There are occasions when elements of the frame are broken, either consciously or unconsciously, by either the client or the therapist, and it is only if the frame has been clearly defined and firmly held that attempts to change it take on some meaning. Working with such material was often the most difficult part of my own psychotherapy but usually led to the greatest leaps in self-awareness. This affected my personal development and in turn has informed my own way of working as a psychotherapist.

I have had four psychotherapists, varying in orientation from psycho-analytic to humanistic. How the frame was created and managed by them varied enormously. I originally went to see a therapist in my early twenties because I became extremely anxious and developed an overwhelming death anxiety, which was totally debilitating. I had daily panic attacks, became agoraphobic and experienced numbness in my left leg for months. I had no conscious understanding why I had started to behave in this way and felt very frightened. In the same week that I had graduated from university with no future prospects, my grandmother, to whom I had been very close, died unexpectedly. This sent me reeling with shock.

Before this time I had experienced periods of depression in my teens. I grew up in a working-class northern town and had always felt attracted to women, which terrified me and made me very secretive. By the time I was eighteen I had decided that I was probably a lesbian and moved to London shortly afterwards. I had grown up with a great fear of 'going mad' as there was much mental illness in my family. To add to this, my relationship with my mother was complicated. She had been depressed and anxious for most of my life. She told me that I had screamed constantly as a baby and of her strong desire to get rid of me. She was beautiful and regularly reminded me that I wasn't, which with hindsight must have caused considerable narcissistic damage to my development and identification with her. My mother was extremely strict and often angry, and I learned how to be a 'good little girl'. I developed an 'insecure attachment' (Bowlby, 1988) towards her and my lack of stability established a particular pattern of behaviour in me.

It is with some trepidation that I write this section, but from an early age, about four or five, I began to eroticize certain relationships with maternal figures. I would 'fall in love' in the most desperate, obsessive and unrequited way, getting extremely attached to, but also terrified of my desired objects. I lived mostly in my fantasy world, which was exciting but at the same time full of shame. The knowledge that I could never be as special to any of these women as they were to me made me feel unlovable and caused long periods of sadness and depression. For many years my connections between sexuality, eroticizing and mental illness were bound together and confused. My erotic fantasy life became my 'illness' and I carried it alone and protectively.

Therapist A

When my panic attacks began some of these feelings became impossible to contain, and I felt emotionally overwhelmed and out of control. I was desperately trying alternative therapies and visiting my GP regularly when a work colleague suggested psychotherapy. I would have tried anything and so, suddenly, I found myself being a client with no clue what to expect. My first therapist, whom I shall call therapist A, worked psychodynamically. I had no concept of a frame and in the first session practicalities such as fees, payments for missed sessions and holiday arrangements were explained. My own internal boundaries were so harsh that these 'rules' were not a problem. I was very obedient and had learnt to be unquestioning. My own projections and transferences, however, were a problem. The therapist quickly became a severe and monstrous mother, and her class, apparent wealth, education and status intimidated me. I was insistent that I had not come to talk about my sexuality, and absolutely not my fantasy life, but to prevent the onset of madness or some unidentifiable illness.

Therapist A's management of the frame was firm, although from the start I did not have a regular appointment as I worked shifts. Arranging the next meeting at the end of a session was something I looked forward to, as it seemed a more 'friendly' time with her. After being late once for a session, and not been given my 'full' fifty minutes, I began to understand the boundaries of the frame and from then on I was always on time.

After a few months I was beginning to get very attached to therapist A when the first major break in the frame came. It was winter and London was unusually covered in snow, which made the journey to my session a real struggle. I rang the doorbell and after several minutes a handsome young man, about my age, came to the door looking puzzled. I explained why I was there and he said that therapist A was 'snowed in' in her other house in the country and would not be coming for my session. He then went on to tell me that he was her daughter's boyfriend and was staying for a while. I was turned away into the freezing cold and cried tears of rage for most of my journey home. I was furious; she'd forgotten about me. Ringing in my ears were his words about who he was. I began to have lots of fantasies about therapist A: was she married, divorced, heterosexual; did she have other children; where was her other house?

Feelings of anger, jealousy and abandonment stayed with me until the next session when I sat in a silent rage refusing to speak. Therapist A was apologetic for not informing me of her absence but enraged me further by telling me she had cancelled all her other clients' sessions. I was furious and filled with envy; I wanted to be her daughter and to live in her house. I was reluctant to admit to these feelings as I felt very ashamed of their intensity. This break in the frame was clearly a mistake on the part of the therapist and for whatever reason she had overlooked her responsibility to contact me and cancel the session. On a practical level she dealt with the issue but therapeutically did not enable me to voice or understand the feelings it brought up for me.

Feeling 'forgotten' had a direct impact in evoking anger, which was either missed or ignored by therapist A. I acted out my rage by sitting in silence as I thought that if I let her see how angry I was the therapy would be terminated by her. Feeling like the compliant child, I had been led into an intensification in the anger. Negative transference feelings emerged, which were not worked with. For a time this caused a fracture in the therapeutic alliance and as a client I was left to deal with these over-whelming feelings myself. This break in the frame could have served as a useful therapeutic tool in drawing a parallel with my feelings of abandonment and rage towards my mother, but instead I ended up losing trust in therapist A, wondering if she was going to be there for my sessions in future.

After a year or so, and to my horror, I began to 'fall in love' with therapist A. Some of my aggression and anger had become sexualized and the erotic transference intensified. I started to have some very erotic fantasies about her and was both excited and ashamed about these. It took me a long time to make them even slightly explicit. I did eventually voice these feelings, but wasn't entirely truthful as I implied my feelings were rather more loving than erotic. Therapist A did acknowledge my feelings and made them 'acceptable', but didn't explore them any further which I was relieved about at the time. She said they were a 'normal' part of the therapeutic process. With hindsight this may have been a missed opportunity and I feel it was her reluctance to explore further that halted the process. As with my anger, therapist A seemed to avoid engaging too deeply with the feelings in the room between us.

So although acknowledged, which was in part helpful, these feelings remained puzzling to me.

I became very dependent on my therapy and after a couple of years some significant events happened in my life which changed its course. My parents split up very acrimoniously after a long marriage and shortly afterwards my brother had his first psychotic breakdown. He'd been missing for a few weeks and turned up in Paris. I went straight to Heathrow and got on the first plane there. I found him and spent one of the worst nights of my life with him in a hotel room. He was paranoid, furious and aggressive and barricaded the door with all the furniture in the room. I had no experience of this type of behaviour and at times I was extremely frightened. The next morning he left and I had a very stressful few days before I found him again.

I had my therapist's telephone number and in desperation I rang her. I got her answer machine and left a message. To my astonishment she rang back about half an hour later. Through all the madness and chaos came a sane, calm voice. She was concerned and reassuring and I held onto her words to give me some strength. Although technically therapist A broke the frame, it was of great therapeutic value to me at the time. It disproved my fantasies that a maternal figure that I loved would not care enough about me in a time of crisis to support me.

Via incredible means I got my brother back home and he was sectioned in a London hospital. I was under a lot of pressure, coping with him and parents who were refusing to speak to each other. The distress of watching him refuse to see my mother, but break down and cry like a desperate baby in my arms, was immense. His best friend had died of cancer at seventeen and a couple of years after that he'd attempted to save my dying grandmother by trying to give her the 'kiss of life'. He had never grieved and his grief overwhelmed him and me. It seemed to go on for weeks. This was probably the time I was at my weakest ever, I felt broken inside. My own fear of 'madness' was powerful. If it could happen to him why not me, it was surely just a matter of time.

My therapy became the most important thing in my life as nothing felt safe or sane; everything was frightening. I became very anxious again, thinking I would die in my sleep. My fear of madness turned into a desire for it; just one small step and I could be there too, be looked after, be safe. I have no recollection of doing any analytic 'work' in therapy at this time. The consulting room, and therapy, became just a safe and containing place to be.

Time passed and as my brother became calmer and more medicated I became more able to contain myself. I decided after three and a half years that I had gone as far as I could in therapy. I no longer had panic attacks, I could sleep at night, my leg wasn't numb and my fear of madness had subsided to a manageable level. I was still eroticizing however. I look back on the process as being divided into two halves. In the first half I had begun a journey of self-discovery, which was halted by external events. The second half of the therapy was less personally challenging but necessarily more containing. I had experienced for the first time a containing and loving maternal figure who I knew on some level cared about me. It was hard to leave and ironically I 'forgot' about my last session until about an hour before.

Therapist B

Six or seven years later I became interested in training to be a psychotherapist, in part because I'd felt that therapy was the only thing that had 'helped' me to begin to understand myself. I started my training and went back to therapy very willingly. I chose to see a psychoanalytic therapist, therapist B, and was again on the couch. I was agreeable to all areas of the frame that were negotiated but explained in the first session that I worked shifts and that although I would be able to make almost all sessions there might be some I would have to miss. Therapist B said she understood this, and I accepted that I would pay for these sessions. This was going to be a temporary situation for a few months as I was planning to start working part-time; keeping to all the sessions then wouldn't be a problem.

From the start the frame was managed in a most ferocious way and I immediately began to feel persecuted. Therapist B had warned me that this was going to be 'hard work'. Her manner was brusque and she pushed me to work with painful emotional material at all times. If I deviated I was told that I was wasting my time. There seemed little opportunity to pause for breath and process emotionally intense material before we were onto the next painful subject. I also had a feeling of being trapped. Therapist B's chair was in front of the door, which made me feel uncomfortable. There was a tension in the room, not least of all because I'd had a very intense negative transference as soon as we met and I also began to experience incredibly erotic feelings towards her after a few sessions. The whole process was very confusing. I was aware that whilst on the couch I was in a state of terror, shaking and in tears almost all the time. I felt powerless and extremely vulnerable. Therapist B had an unusual habit of holding a small stone in her hand and moving it around. I couldn't see her, but I could hear the quiet movement of the stone. It made me feel that she was anxious, which in turn increased my own anxieties. In many ways she got a good measure of me very quickly; she identified areas that were troubling me, but there was a problem for me in her manner, which felt cynical and judgemental. I'm fully prepared to admit now that there were a lot of my own projections and transference emotions in my assessment of her at that time.

I very soon felt open, weak and vulnerable and was experiencing a lot of shame about my erotic feelings towards her, which I had voiced and had the feeling that I was being trampled on by a very 'bad mother'. The climax to my time with her came out of the blue after about three months. I was unexpectedly moved to a different department at work and my shifts were going to be altered. Ideally, it would have been better for me if I could have changed my therapy time and day, for if I kept the same time I would miss one in four sessions. I wanted to discuss this possibility and soon realised that there was absolutely no flexibility in the frame. Therapist B suggested that if I couldn't commit to my own therapy, how could I possibly commit to future clients of my own. I could understand entirely where she was coming from on the issue of commitment, but there was something very unnecessary about discussing my future clients in this setting and I began to get quite annoyed. After several minutes the conversation elevated into a row, with me somewhat defensively saying that of course therapy was important but without my job I couldn't pay for my training, or my therapy, so I had a difficult balancing act to do.

Therapist B began to wonder aloud what type of person chose to work shifts, implying my desire for unpredictability in my work was an indication of my inner chaos. My job in the media was demanding and required commitment, and I was expected to do irregular shift-work including nights and weekends. Rather than help me understand my reasons for these choices I felt I was being punished for them. Therapist B was right to explore my unpredictable lifestyle choice, but her manner seemed unprofessional. She then went on to criticize my choice of psychotherapy training and training institution. I felt wounded and misunderstood.

Without realizing it I was challenging the boundaries of the frame. What would have been helpful at the time was an interpretation to help me understand my behaviour. Instead therapist B retaliated and acted out her blind countertransference by becoming critical, leaving me feeling attacked and undermined. Therapist B wouldn't answer any questions except with interpretations, and my level of frustration grew to an unbearable rage. I then said that I had no choice, I would have to find another therapist who could see me on a different day. It felt like the session was totally out of control, and it was with great difficulty that I stood up and said I was going to leave. Through my tears and rage it suddenly became clear that I couldn't get through the door because she was sitting in front of it. I was feeling like a wild animal now, trapped and had to get out. I was pumped with adrenaline and absolutely livid. I stumbled towards the door and practically climbed over her chair and squeezed out of the room. She remained seated and didn't make any attempt to get out of the way. I remembered that I had written a cheque for her, which was in my pocket. I attempted to give it to her as I passed but somehow it got stuck to my hand and as I was shaking it off I literally threw it at her. I ran down the two flights of stairs and by the time I got to the door I hated her. I couldn't decide which would infuriate her most, leaving the door wide open, or slamming it as hard as I could. In an attempt to behave properly, I closed it quietly. By the time I got home I was a gibbering, shaking wretch. My partner was astounded to see the state I was in. I decided that I couldn't possibly continue my psychotherapy training as I was obviously totally unsuited to it. My therapist's judgement carried such weight.

When I'd recovered a little I started to feel quite triumphant. It was the first time I'd ever dared to walk away from a situation with which I was uncomfortable. The problem was that the feeling didn't last. In spite of my concerns about the way in which she had handled the situation I knew there was some truth in it. I knew of course that I needed to be committed to my own therapy, and that I needed to try to understand the powerful feelings I had about her. I was aware that I had acted out something in a fairly spectacular way but didn't understand what. I had powerful feelings of rage, hatred, desire and victory – a confusing cocktail.

A few days later I received a letter from therapist B, suggesting I returned to my psychotherapy and that I was expected at my next session. Just reading the letter sent a shiver down my spine. I spoke to a tutor at college who suggested that if I did want to change therapists, it might be productive to have a better ending with this one, so I went back for one final session. I was shaking with fear as I rang the doorbell and waited. I refused to lie down but sat up on the couch and explained that this was my last session and I couldn't continue. In fairness she didn't try to convince me to stay, but again repeated all her criticisms about my lack of commitment and my 'terrible' training. My fantasies were that she hated me. She thought I was a useless, stupid, horrid, little girl who was entirely unsuited to train as a psychotherapist. Of course my therapist's rejection of my training was a second wound. Like my mother wished for a different little girl to feed her narcissism, so too did my therapist. The atmosphere was too punitive for me to tolerate and safely explore these feelings at the time. With hindsight I feel therapist B touched a very psychotic part of me but wasn't able to contain it. She also appeared to have a complete lack of empathy. The way the frame was handled, together with her acting out her countertransference, encouraged me to act out rather than understand what was happening.

The experience of an extremely harsh frame was helpful in my understanding of the importance of setting up and maintaining therapeutic boundaries. Langs (1992) describes the therapist's management of a secure and unambiguous frame as the most important element of the therapeutic relationship. He warns, however, that although a 'secure' frame provides a positive unconscious image of the therapist it can, in extreme circumstances, give rise to death anxiety and mobilize paranoid-schizoid anxieties. On the other hand a 'deviant' frame gives an image of the therapist as being unable to manage his or her own inner world and be 'pathologically gratifying'. My experience of an almost non-existent or 'deviant' frame with my next therapist was valuable too.

Therapist C

After my unsettling departure from therapist B I was left feeling totally useless and wanting another therapist. I returned to the UKCP list and after several phone calls went to see a humanistic therapist, which with hindsight was a total waste of my time. I'm sure it was a reaction to the previous therapist, but I felt like I needed someone less challenging – and I certainly found her. After a few sessions I knew that, even though she was a nice woman, she wasn't for me. But my fear of failing again, or not being 'appropriate' for therapy training, stopped me from moving on and I stayed for far too long – about a year in total. The first few months were spent trying to understand what had happened with therapist B. Therapist C seemed keen to report her to the UKCP to try to get her struck off. I didn't want to pursue this as I had a strong sense of my own part in the conflict.

What I learned with therapist C was how not to be a therapist, or at least not the sort of therapist I wanted to be. What I became aware of was, first, how important the frame was and, second, my personal preference for working with transference material; even though it was painful, it was the clearest way of recognizing my own behaviour. I asked therapist C about this way of working and she said she might work with the transference, only if there were really apparent issues between us, clearly not registering my total frustration with her. She had fixed ideas about me, which were wrong, regularly suggesting that I was an artist and should turn a room in my house into a studio and paint. Therapist C spoke as much as I did in the sessions and often interrupted me. I did bring this up, but instead of working with my frustration she appeared to feel very criticized and hurt. She broke the frame often by inappropriate self-disclosures, talking about irrelevant details of her family life. I always saw other clients on my way in and out and often felt sorry for them, feeling that I was in a position of knowing that there were other therapists available and maybe they were not. I began to get more and more bored, felt like I was wasting my time and twice I totally forgot to go to my sessions, which was probably a way of expressing my frustration and aggressive feelings towards her. This was only acknowledged as my 'forgetfulness' and not understood or interpreted as an attack on her, the frame or the therapy.

I knew I had to move on, but it was difficult negotiating an ending. In the final session I colluded with therapist C as she wanted me to list all the positive experiences I'd had with her. It was a short list, but my guilt allowed me to do it. The frame had been vague, I had turned up for sessions on time, she was there and I paid but nothing much had happened. It wasn't that I felt unsafe, I just didn't feel anything other than frustrated. I knew I had a lot of important material to work through but somehow I instinctively didn't trust her to manage it. Good management of the frame facilitates transference material, and the lack of this left me feeling dissatisfied. Because of therapist C's poor management of the frame our relationship began to disintegrate and eventually became non-existent. Without a frame there ceased to be any therapy.

At the same time that I was with therapist C I began supervision for my first psychotherapy training placement. Not unexpectedly I experienced the supervisor as a bad and terrifying 'mother'. Those old feelings of neediness, together with fear of being pushed away, started to surface and my well-practised erotic transference arose again. Although my supervisor made it explicit that she was not in a position to work with my transference, as this was a matter for my own therapy, she highlighted my behaviour by asking just a couple of very simple questions. She spoke openly about what she understood to be my erotic feelings, whilst acknowledging that supervision was not the place to analyse them. I finally began to see a pattern in my behaviour, and at first this was very alarming. I really wasn't quite ready to acknowledge my feelings and felt ashamed and embarrassed to the core at being 'seen'. I knew this had to be put on the back-burner until I found a therapist I could trust and open up to. Although the transference couldn't be worked with I felt quite contained in supervision, and in terms of the frame I felt like a baby in a big safe playpen. At first I sat in the middle in my own strait-jacket, and it took me a long time to realize that I could move around and had a reasonable amount of freedom. The frame felt firm, totally holding and very loving and I became for the first time consciously rather than unconsciously aware of the need to love and be loved back by a maternal figure.

After therapist C I needed another therapist, but felt quite cautious. I wondered if the outburst with therapist B had been more of my fault than I'd originally suspected and decided to see if I could go back. I wrote a letter and she offered me an appointment the following week. I was terribly nervous and aware that I was coming across as child-like. She seemed anxious, still playing with her stone and explained if I continued I would be on the couch and I *would* commit to regular session times. It just didn't feel right, she still felt persecuting and I was perturbed by the fact she couldn't look me in the eye. I decided not to continue with her and felt that perhaps some of my original feelings about her were right; not all of them were transferential and some were based on reality of her as a person.

Therapist D

I decided I wanted to see a male psychoanalytic psychotherapist. I made several enquiries and for various reasons none of the four or five men I contacted were able to see me. So after more phone calls I went to see another female therapist. Therapist D worked psychoanalytically. I made a promise to myself, and to her, in an early session that this time I was determined to get to the bottom of my behaviour and understand myself. I'd always been very secretive, even in therapy, and decided that no matter how painful, it was these secrets that were the key to my self-awareness. I'd never spoken about my sexuality, sexual fantasies and ways in which I eroticized. I felt like I now had a three-pronged attack: my relationship with her, my relationship with my supervisor and my own growing understanding of myself through my studies.

This time the frame felt secure. Therapist D was firm, but gentle and caring. I was plodding along being painfully honest for the first nine or ten months or so when events overtook me and I was able to get in touch with the most painful feelings I've ever experienced. A major motivating factor was whilst writing a piece of work I did a lot of research about erotic transference. One paper in particular I found very shocking; it could have been written about me, and as I read it over and over I began to break down. The penny dropped, I understood on an intellectual and emotional level at the same time how the structure I'd held in place held me together. My erotic transference defended against a deep depression, together with my fears of 'madness'.

An external event finally lit the fuse. I was lying in bed late one night and a baby was crying next door. I expected the baby to be comforted and stop crying, but it seemed to go on and on. The baby was getting more and more desperate and to my astonishment so was I. I began to sob uncontrollably and cry like I had never cried in my life. Suddenly I was in touch with the desperate crying baby in me and it was so painful. My crying continued for the whole weekend, almost continually and then pretty much for the next few weeks. I had fallen into the depths of depression without my defence mechanism and finally I was grieving for the crying baby and sad little girl that had needed motherly love. The depression felt very heavy, but unlike other times when I'd felt depressed I didn't fear madness. This was a depression I had to let myself have in order to move on. My partner felt very worried that I was having some kind of breakdown, but I became aware that I felt regressed. As well as grieving, I became extremely vulnerable and childlike. I remember saying to therapist D, 'I don't *feel* like a baby, I *am* a baby.' I had to take time off work, and made a conscious decision to stop eroticizing and to try and understand my depression. Without my elaborate fantasy life, what was left of me felt raw and unprotected.

Therapist D was able to offer a safe and containing frame. I had built up trust in her and we had established a good working alliance. I had only ever cried alone in the past and I broke down and wailed for a whole session and allowed myself to lose control totally. I had no idea where I was or how long I'd been crying for. It felt like I'd lost consciousness of time and it was almost orgasmic, deathlike. When eventually I looked at therapist D she seemed to be pinned back in her chair, she had one hand on her chest and her head turned slightly to one side; her eyes were shut. She looked like she'd been hit by some great tidal wave. She opened her eyes and looked at me, she was still there. It was only through feeling safe and contained that I was able to let therapist D see how vulnerable I felt.

Some time later there was an interesting turn of events, when what I refer to as a 'mistake' was made by therapist D. I was touching on some very painful, secretive and sexual material that I'd kept totally to myself. This felt quite dangerous and at the core of my fantasies and who I am. Therapist D gave me the impression that, like my mother, she might not be able to cope with this information and may need to refer me to someone else more 'specialized'. This sent me into a rage and I acted out by missing the following session. I was so furious with her for her threat of removing my safe space, together with fears of not being acceptable and being abandoned. Whether she was just voicing countertransference feelings or not I won't ever know, but the rage that it brought up in me was incredible. I spent several months barely being able to contain my anger and hatred towards her. The fear of being pushed away and not seen or tolerated by her fuelled my narcissistic rage. I became very aware of the same feelings towards my mother.

We had a bumpy ride together for a while but I was finally able to work with these feelings and be honest about them. Before this I had a fear of being seen, as if this would lead me to being pushed away. Therapist D, like a good mother, was not perfect and made 'mistakes', but on the whole was able to both hold me and frustrate me. She injected reality into my fantasy world of an idealized maternal object and at the same time contained me far more than the others. It was only when I felt safe that I could get in touch with the most vulnerable parts of myself. She was able to tolerate whatever I brought to the sessions, and that, together with my willingness to open up, was enormously facilitating. In my time with her I began to achieve a new confidence and openness after my shameful feelings were worked through.

Summary

How the therapist manages the frame directly influences the client's experience of the therapy. In my experience, breaks in the frame which were managed 'successfully' by the therapist led to a greater increase in self-awareness, whilst those which might be seen as therapeutic 'failures' resulted in my acting out old patterns of behaviour and not achieving any real understanding. For me, being forgotten, getting an unexpected phone call and forgetting or walking out of sessions were all in some way relevant to past experiences. The ways in which these breaks in the frame were managed taught me first about myself and second about what is important to me in a psychotherapeutic relationship.

What I discovered over many years of therapy is that in order to feel safe the frame needs to be secure and loving and the therapist's own internal boundaries need to be good. Breaks or violations in the therapeutic frame were always extremely revealing as they pulled certain behaviour patterns into sharp focus. With the right care and sensitivity I was able to look at my behaviour and explore and understand it. It took

me a long time to realize that a big part of feeling contained was acknowledging and making explicit whatever feelings were in the room between
myself and the therapist. *All of me*, particularly the 'worst' parts, needed
to be seen and tolerated by the therapist. It was usually the most un-
pleasant feelings that gave rise to most self-awareness, and, in fact,
an unwillingness on the part of the therapist, for whatever reasons, to
attend to these feelings left me feeling unheld and uncontained. I realized
that if the other was able to tolerate my feelings then I could tolerate them
myself.

Through my own personal psychotherapy I slowly unravelled a baffling
pattern of behaviour and came to understand how my eroticization hid
my depression. Eroticizing was a way of being in control of a situation,
to have a conscious idea of a desired outcome and to deny my painful
feelings. Acknowledging and understanding the erotic transference has
been personally liberating. As Mann (1997) writes, the erotic transference
signifies the client's deepest wish for growth, it binds individuals at the
most intimate level and if worked through properly offers a huge potential
for transformation.

The importance of managing the therapeutic frame well is absolute,
and I hope that through some of my experiences as a client I've gone some
way to learning how to be a decent therapist.

References

Bowlby, J. (1988) *A Secure Base. Clinical Applications of Attachment Theory*,
    London: Routledge.
Gray, A. (1994) *An Introduction to the Therapeutic Frame*, London: Routledge.
Langs, R. (1992) *A Clinical Workbook for Psychotherapists*, London: Karnac.
Mann, D. (1997) *Psychotherapy, An Erotic Relationship. Transference and
    Countertransference Passions*, London: Routledge.
Milner, M. (1952) 'Aspects of symbolism and comprehension of the not-self',
    International Journal of Psychoanalysis 33: 181–95.

Chapter 4

You have been framed

Maternity and the male psychotherapist

Stefano Ferraiolo

When a training psychotherapist joins the front line of his or her new profession, practical issues relating to the therapeutic frame become essential factors, thus promoting the trainee's evolution from theory to hands-on professional reality. My aim is to identify the characteristics that contribute to establishing and working with the therapeutic frame, taking into consideration the therapy context, which is within an NHS hospital maternity ward. I will also examine how the gender of the therapist impacts on the therapeutic frame and outcomes.

Introduction

Greek mythology provides us with a rich and colourful spectrum of human unconscious and collective archetypical patterns of the psyche, as for example in the historical recounting of creation. In the beginning there was Chaos, pure darkness, nothingness. There was no beginning or end to Chaos, no foundation and no confines: just an unknown dark void. Chaos gave birth to Gaia, the Earth. Gaia, the goddess and universal mother, had a visible configuration unlike her creator. There was a form, a refined space, where gods and eventually human beings could exist. Gaia embodied a solid plane, her peaks projected towards the light, whilst under the earth she was darkness. Gaia gave birth to Ouranus the sky and Pontus the water. They undoubtedly were their mother's off-spring yet very different to each other. As soon as he was born, Ouranus lay down in perfect symmetry on top of his mother, two planes perfectly superimposed, perpetrating a state of darkness. Ouranus was repeatedly copulating with and inseminating his lover. Gaia was constantly pregnant, but the fruits of her union could never see the light since she had become a prisoner of her own creation. Gaia tried to convince her progeny to rebel. Only Cronus, the young Titan, agreed to help his mother. When his father once again gave way to his sexual urges, Cronus got hold of his father's genitals and amputated them with a sickle forged by his mother. Ouranus screamed in pain as he was separated from Gaia and froze in shock. He was still perfectly symmetrical to Gaia in that by looking up from earth he could be seen as the sky. By castrating his father, Cronus had separated his incestuous parents and allowed evolution to follow its course. Ouranus could no longer copulate with Gaia but found another outlet for his creative needs by fertilizing her through the rain, his tears, generating new life on earth (Vernant, 1999).

The establishment of boundaries defines the history of creation. Eventually, when life is snuffed out by a blind search for gratification of primordial sexual urges, the need for a defined space arises once again. A space is shaped, where the development of creation can run its course, through the paradox of good and bad, light and dark forces chaotically enmeshed. Creating a frame requires an 'act of betrayal' (Carotenuto, 1991) which originates from the acknowledgement of limitations and the consequent challenge of a previously established equilibrium. For life to flourish on earth, boundaries set within a frame are vital. One must remember that working with the therapeutic frame requires weaving a path through the ever-changing life-cycle factors. Boundaries, which make up the therapeutic frame, cannot remain static: they have to allow for the life-cycle evolution; from the womb to being born, in love and out of it, in a relationship and out of it, from life to death. Gaia symbolizes the universal mother, the womb, the generator of life; her development is relative to renegotiable boundaries.

The aim of this chapter is to underline the structural importance of the therapeutic frame for clinical work in a maternity ward. After a brief excursus on the theory of the therapeutic frame, I focus on the impact of both the external setting and the therapist gender, providing various extracts of my experience as a male therapist in a maternity unit. When I first began to practise, the reality I was faced with at the beginning of my clinical placement was a far cry from the one I had expected. Ironically, it was I who had been framed! The location, the time, the day, the fee, had all been pre-arranged; was I not the one who was supposed to set-up the therapeutic frame? In this setting, 'being the psychotherapist' was the only variable I could count on to provide a frame encompassing the mental and spiritual element within the existing physical setting. For the first time I experienced the tri-dimension of the therapeutic frame.

Theoretical considerations on the frame

> The frame marks off the different kind of reality that is within it from that which is outside it; but a temporal spatial frame also marks off the special kind of reality of a psychoanalytical session.
>
> (Milner, 1952: 183)

Is the therapeutic frame an important feature of psychoanalysis or just another comfortable notion to be disregarded, as and when the need arises? Literature on this subject is abundant, with powerful statements on the importance of setting-up and maintaining the analytic frame, even though I have witnessed and read of numerous exceptions. Although views differ, most psychotherapy schools have found common ground when considering the therapeutic frame an essential theme to psychotherapy. Life itself provides examples of the frame; a human being is initially framed in his or her own body and subsequently in his or her mother's womb. Contrastingly, examples of a frameless reality can be defined by birth and death.

'Life itself, in existential terms, is the appropriate frame' (Madison, 2001: 89). There is an external frame, a 'given' in existential terms: life, a motherland or a maternity ward, and then there is an internal frame: the metaphor for a womb or a state of mind – the therapeutic frame. The existential view, which encompasses life as a frame in itself, disregards the therapeutic frame as being central to psychotherapy, whilst the traditional psychoanalytical view sees the frame as a basic tool and ingredient for the success of a psychotherapeutic intervention.

One of the most important contributions Freud made to psychoanalysis was the creation of a scientific model. Freud's effort in creating a science (Schwartz, 1999) was mainly rooted in applying a neurologist's well-known framework. His evidence-based observations had him conclude that some fixed constants would create the best possible environment for the healing process to take place. In doing so, he was creating a 'laboratory' where he could locate the psychoanalytic process and extrapolate the data. In psychoanalytic terms, the location, the frequency, the confidentiality, the fee, and in dynamic terms the psychotherapist, are the factors which define the frame. I previously suggested that a therapeutic frame should be set on three levels: physical, mental and spiritual, facilitating the creation of a therapist's frame of mind; a constructive attitude towards the analytic process and grant the space for a spiritual quest, engaging in what Carotenuto (1988) defines as a 'western form of meditation'.

'If I listed all the factors making up the analytic frame, I would still miss out some things and not capture its essence' (Young, 2002). I felt that searching for the ideal frame would result in taking on a Sisyphus task; theory should never impair a psychotherapist's work but support it. A frame protects and preserves an object from being damaged by external agents whilst exposing its shortcomings. The frame creates a safe environment for the client to confront the threatening outside world in manageable doses:

> If the home can stand up to all the child can do to disrupt it, he settles down to play; but business first, the tests must be made, and especially so if there is some doubt to the stability of the parental set-up and the home (by which I mean so much more than the house). At first the child needs to be conscious of a framework if he is to feel free, and if he is to be able to play, to draw his own pictures, to be an irresponsible child.
>
> (Winnicott, 1964: 227)

Winnicott's inspirational depiction of a constructive parental setting introduces the valuable notion of testing the dynamics of the therapeutic frame, whilst the latter part metaphorically defines the therapeutic frame in simple terms: a space, safe enough to play and experiment in. Winnicott's idea originates from a child's incapacity to relate openly to the dangerous external world. This stage of ego development foresees testing the external world. The parallel between a child's reality and the client's difficulty in living his or her own daily life is therefore easily identifiable. Winnicott's definition of an ever-changing space within clear boundaries introduces the temporal space of the analytic frame, basic to the development of the therapeutic encounter as a process in motion.

A therapist's priority lies in moulding the frame and providing the space in which to engage, by accepting, understanding and supporting a human being. A beautiful frame will enhance a work of art. Accepting limiting external conditions and putting them to constructive use requires skill, as for an artist working with limited resources. The psychotherapist refines a frame, moulds it accordingly and ultimately embodies his or her creation. The therapeutic frame, and therefore the psychotherapist, becomes a point of reference for clients:

> If you know the point of balance
> You can settle the details.
>> If you can settle the details
>> You can stop running around.

If you can stop running around
Your mind will become calm.
 If you will become calm
 You can think in front of a tiger.
If you can think in front of a tiger
You will surely succeed.

(Mencius, in Richards, 1996)

A hospital-based psychotherapeutic intervention and the therapeutic frame

Although psychoanalysis remains a luxury for those with the required resources and time, the development of psychotherapy has helped to dispel the snobbish aura attached to psychoanalysis and made it accessible to a larger audience. Therefore, the traditional psychoanalytic theory is challenged. It would be unreasonable to aim for the ideal theoretical model of the therapeutic frame in deprived areas:

> Langs . . . questions the viability of treatment in settings such as the one described, settings with what he calls pervasive 'framework modifications'. The ideal therapeutic frame is composed of ground rules that include: (1) total confidentiality; (2) privacy; (3) predictability and consistency, manifested in a set fee, location, time and length for all sessions; (4) therapist neutrality; and (5) therapist anonymity.
>
> (Cheifetz, 1984: 216)

I work as a psychotherapist within the Women's Services division of a NHS hospital. The service was designed to support women and families who have experienced trauma as a result of termination of pregnancy and miscarriages. The users of this service are mainly women from deprived, multi-ethnic backgrounds with abuse, refugee status, culture and gender issues. The area is a melting pot of nationalities where psychotherapy offers a common language, which helps to ease the inevitable cultural differences and minimize the social divides.

Psychotherapy, an invention of the western world, is a new form of interaction and is not always embraced by different cultures. If the language of love is universal, then so is the language of distress; in the consulting room, it promotes understanding and acceptance. I have witnessed all walks of life engage in the healing process which psychotherapy facilitates. In the beginning of a therapeutic relationship, a psychotherapist should provide the necessary space to explore cultural projections and look beyond preconceptions. This approach provides invaluable insight in structuring the therapeutic frame.

The hospital's consulting room is located in the maternity ward, which has often contributed to clients reliving their traumatic experiences of loss and bereavement. There are no other options. Is it healthy to provide therapy to parents who have suffered the loss of their child so close to where the drama initially unfolded? This example of an external reality demonstrates how the frame is handed out and underlines the importance of addressing the initial structure or the 'given' characteristics of a therapeutic frame.

The consulting room is reasonably quiet, apart from the ward's daily humdrum. A consultant and the ward's midwives also use the room. Unfortunately, privacy, total confidentiality and therapist anonymity in this setting are unrealistic. The voices of the hospital staff, their unannounced intrusions, a noisy fax machine receiving medical reports for the consultant's team, the incestuous exchange of the client's health reports amongst the hospital professionals, are all continuous violations of the traditional therapeutic frame. In the public setting of a low-income, multi-ethnic community, ground rules laid by Langs for an ideal therapeutic frame cannot realistically be met. As violations of the frame seem to be unavoidable, therapists are required to manage their impact on the work. In spite of all theoretical considerations, the designated room is often shared with other members of staff and scarce resources dictate the frequency of the sessions. Today, almost thirty years after Cheifetz's (1984) study, the situation seems to have remained static.

A maternity ward

> In reality, the primordial Goddess was female, Gaia, the goddess of Earth and then male warriors created a male God. At this point women were relegated to a lesser role and God was transformed into a strictly male figure, an executioner, always ready to punish, with a thirst for blood . . . Religions stripped God of His feminine side, therefore denying humanity, compassion and love of life . . . Creation is a feminine process, slow, mysterious, unrelated to male logic; a woman is the patroness of life and does not love wars which kill the fruit of her womb. The female and therefore the feminine energy is sacred, she who stops a wall being erected between sacred and profane: she is the logic of mystery, of the incomprehensible . . .
>
> (Arias, 1999: 109, 113; my translation)

The world's navel and motherhood are associated with the process of creation. The womb represents the frame for excellence, the laboratory where life is created, the metaphor for a safe environment. What could be a greater tragedy than to find that a mother's womb is in fact a poisoned space, a deadly trap? In psychoanalytical terms, the hospital symbolizes the mother; it becomes the place where women search for their lost mother and motherhood. A maternity ward represents a surrogate womb; the most primitive and perfect frame nature has to offer. However, an environment which should be the ultimate containing and safe space often proves to be a frightening experience. A client who has failed to internalize a 'good enough mother' will look for confirmation that a maternity ward is unable to provide 'good enough care'. A hospital is rarely geared to care for emotional traumas, especially when resources are limited.

The stages of a woman's development are also centred around maternity and motherhood. Maternity encompasses sexuality, creation, separation, gender and identity. For some women a maternity ward is the last resort, a place which may offer the containment they are failing to provide their baby with. Just as a foetus needs a safe environment to develop in, a client needs a 'therapeutic womb' to grow in. A problematic pregnancy often mirrors a mother's discomfort in relating to motherhood on a physical, mental or spiritual level. The amniotic bag is the physical space surrounding the foetus; the mother's frame of mind is the emotional container for the developing foetus, and the perfect symbiosis of these two human souls provides a frame with spiritual meaning. On a parallel the psychotherapist's frame of mind and spirituality of the therapeutic encounter help define the 'good enough therapeutic frame'. A client's negative attitude towards the frame is indicative of her or his discomfort in relating to psychotherapy and the sign of a damaged internal frame:

Mrs X, a middle-aged woman, often hears a voice ordering her to kill her children. Terrified that one day she might actually obey this voice, she sought therapy after falling pregnant again. Mrs X shared her wish to spare her children the painful experience of living in a foreign country or eventually returning home, where she had witnessed her parents' killing and had been subjected to abuse and torture during a civil war. Motherland had failed Mrs X; there was no safe haven for her. Mrs X was continuously challenging the frame: she was always late and she did not show up for several weeks, only to reappear without warning. She wanted to dictate how, when and where she would be in therapy. Mrs X was acting out her despair at having lost control of her life and was using the therapeutic frame to communicate her problem.

Mrs Y, a troubled young woman, was referred to the service after having suffered five consecutive miscarriages: in her own words, 'she was going mad'. Her pain and distress were unbearable when she acknowledged responsibility for the losses she had suffered. Her murderous rage would manifest itself in the form of recurrent obsessive fantasies about her own death and that of others. To be in a room with Mrs Y and her guilt was a chilling experience. It is common for women who have suffered serial miscarriages to believe that their unresolved hatred may have contributed to their damaging the developing foetus. The expression of this feeling is usually a landmark in the therapeutic process. Mrs Y seemed to have settled down in therapy and completely surrendered to the therapeutic frame. In retrospect, the traits of her obsessive personality probably helped her relate to therapy in a systematic manner, therefore finding a container for her 'madness'. How long could her new-found safe container withstand her internal world? A few months later I witnessed a major attack on the therapeutic frame, when she stated her need to attend therapy as and when she needed and outside the consulting room. She needed to establish whether the 'therapeutic womb' would survive her 'intrinsic claustrophobia' (Bell, 1998). My attempts to avoid a 'therapeutic miscarriage' were in vain, as she left therapy because, as she put it, 'she was feeling much better'.

The frame as an institution is the receiver of the psychotic part of a personality, i.e., of the undifferentiated and non-solved parts of the primitive symbiotic links (Bleger, 1967: 518). In an interesting excursus on the subject of the analytic setting, Etchegoyen (1991) quotes Bleger's idea, on how an unchallenged frame might conceal a psychosis. His contribution is important, as it calls for the therapist to monitor the unrealistic behaviour of a client in full acceptance of the therapeutic frame and how this might collude with her psychotic side. In a maternity ward, the potential failure of a mother's uterus to carry out its function amplifies the therapeutic relevance of the frame. The womb has failed motherhood and the mother's inability to bring pregnancy to full term gives way to feelings of inadequacy. This trauma is brought into the therapeutic space, often reinforced by resurfacing unresolved early childhood traumatic memories. Echoes of pain infiltrate the therapeutic womb, poisoning it and making it unsafe. The amniotic fluid tempers the sounds of life, but cannot prevent them from homing in on the foetus. Similarly, the harsh reality of the ward's sounds pierce the consulting room's thin walls. The frame cannot shield a mother from the external world, but a carer's healthy frame of mind can help soothe intrusive repercussions. A psychotherapist's primary task is to confront these echoes by facilitating a good therapeutic alliance, especially where 'basic trust' (Eriksson, 1950) is lacking. I focus on the client's return to the 'crime scene' to confront her fear of annihilation: the unbearable pain of her trauma this time around re-experienced in a safe therapeutic womb.

In her work on motherhood, Pines (1993) often linked maternity related psychosis with early failures in the mother–daughter relationship. I would like to add to her work and suggest that one also needs to acknowledge the father–daughter relationship. A mother represents the woman role model and is therefore hugely influential on shaping her daughter's identity. The father's figure hovers in the background, hostage to his daughter's primitive desire for maternity. My experience has shown me that in the absence of a safe environment for the foetus there may also be a defective father–daughter relationship, which needs to be taken into consideration. Medea (Euripides, 1994) killed her children because she had not experienced a safe mother (motherland) and could not resolve the relationship with her father, Aeetes, whom she had betrayed for a doomed love with Jason. Medea's feverish act of love ensured that her wish for her children to be spared the pain of life was made a reality and provided her with the opportunity of discharging her murderous feelings towards her man. Greek mythology offers a good illustration of a woman's developing identity without neglecting the male component. Encounters with the father have to be constructive in order to plant the seeds for development. If the daughter has not been 'emotionally inseminated', and the Electra complex takes over, her ambivalent sexual fantasy becomes obsessive, stunting her development. The tarnished father–daughter relationship assumes a repetitive obsessive compulsion pattern, and in the daughter's unconscious an absent father becomes her unique and persecutory sexual partner:

> The obsessional process seems to be a displaced form of mourning in its preoccupation with the loss of good objects. As often happens in 'normal mourning' the thoughts become a form of persecution thus preserving the object, not in an ideal form, but in a persecutory form.
>
> (Bion, 1962: 112)

A troubled mother might be identifying herself with her own mother, thus unconsciously substituting herself in the parental couple. Simultaneously, the parental intercourse metaphorically enacted by Gaia and Ouranus might become sexually obsessive, repetitive and ultimately claustrophobic; this would prevent a woman from bringing her child into this world. The masochistic acceptance of Ouranus' sexual addiction symbolizes a daughter's attempt to resolve her murderous feelings by sublimating them in a passive but pleasurable act (Glasser, 1979). Taking a closer look at the father–daughter relationship may shed more light on the reasons which prevent a woman from fully enjoying motherhood.

In my experience a woman who has experienced a healthy relationship with her father is more receptive to psychotherapy. By this, I am suggesting that most women who struggle to come to terms with motherhood might also suffer from an unresolved Electra complex. As in the case of Medea and Mrs X, murderous feelings towards one's own children are also a displacement of hatred towards an idealized father figure who is physically or emotionally unavailable. The biological reasons behind a miscarriage may aggravate an existing unresolved psychological matter.

As in Gaia's case, settling for the possibility of a distant fertilization, a woman needs to allow for a creative intercourse with her father, metaphorically being inseminated and thereafter conquering her individuality by separating from her partner.

Gender and the frame

> Fathers come into this, not only by the fact that they can be good mothers for limited periods of time, but also because they can help to protect the mother and baby from whatever tends to interfere with the bond between them, which is the essence and the very nature of child care.
>
> (Winnicott, 1964: 17)

In my experience as the only male therapist in this maternity ward I can offer a unique point of view. Once I had joined the counselling team I was taken for the introductory round and met with some members of staff, who all happened to be women. When introduced to one of the senior consultants, a well-groomed professional looking lady, she welcomed me with a quizzical look. It was the same look I am given by most female clients seeking therapy for maternity related issues. 'What is a male psychotherapist doing in a maternity ward?' they all seem to wonder. The consultant looked puzzled. She knew of only one other male therapist working with women in a hospital. 'Do you know Bob?' she asked. My project manager could not remember. 'Come on, Bob, the guy in a wheelchair!' she insisted. 'He is a good therapist and the women I have referred to him have been very happy.' I could not help taking the message very personally and had a tough time digesting it; a man with a handicap, or 'castrated' in psychoanalytical terms, would be safe to work with. The consultant's message was the clear signal of a gender issue, which I have had to address repeatedly. The therapist needs to be responsible for the frame, and, being part of it, he must acknowledge the influence that gender may have on the frame itself. A good therapist should encompass a well-balanced animus–anima in order to facilitate a client relating to the ideal parental couple, which he or she represents through a healthy frame. This profession requires a well-developed feminine side or anima, and although I spent many years refining mine I have nonetheless experienced isolation.

When approaching psychotherapy, people naturally tend to 'do gender' (Gilbert and Scher, 1999). In transference terms I have found myself taking on the role of father, partner, brother and doctor in a 'fifty-minute' hour. More often than not, I am identified with the father figure, who is called upon to mend a broken relationship with the mother and with motherhood. When I initially thought of training as a psychotherapist I imagined being surrounded mostly by male figures, father surrogates, who would provide me with the support I had missed out on in my early years. To my surprise I found myself unconsciously replicating my family environment and surrounded myself with women. I felt trapped by my own destiny and, after having perused Freud's, Jung's and Winnicott's biographies, I understood that an exposure to female upbringing or to female figures with a life-lasting impact is not uncommon in the profession.

A couple of years ago, I was invited by a well-respected senior psychoanalyst to appear in front of an audience of psychotherapists and present my clinical work. I was both worried and flattered to be given this opportunity as a clinician. I met with my supervisor an hour before the presentation and was immediately reassured by the apprehension he shared with me. I presented the case of a woman, whose passive aggressive personality, coupled with masochistic undercurrents and a capacity for 'somatization', had brought her under the surgeon's knife ten times in eight years. She had suffered the surgical removal of her entire reproductive system at various intervals. The supervisor focused on my denial of sadistic fantasies in the countertransference, and just when

I took a back seat, having surmounted this challenge, a black female psychotherapist took to the microphone and gave free rein to her anger for what she defined as a piece of offensive interaction between two male psychotherapists. She accused us both of racism and of diminishing the profile of a woman belonging to a minority group. How could a clinical case be used to fuel polemic echoes of racism and gender-related issues? I was upset, and this incident has haunted me throughout the writing of this piece. On reflection, I could understand how two male psychotherapists sharing intimate details of a therapeutic relationship and focusing on hatred, as it was experienced in the countertransference, was too much to bear for the female therapist. Equally, my countertransference was indicative of the hatred that first my client and the female therapist later on were experiencing. My supervisor and I were perceived as unskillful perpetrators, invading the female domain. We were the phallic intruders, just like the surgeons who had ravaged my client's body. The therapist who had raised her concerns about male attitudes towards women in therapy left abruptly in a rage. I found this even more disturbing as I was suddenly deprived of my interlocutor. She was unavailable to engage further and I was dismissed. Similar incidents happen when cultural and gender issues enter the consulting room and there is no capacity or desire to face what lies behind it.

'I suppose that is clear to everyone that, in normal times, it depends on what mother does about it whether father does or does not get to know his baby' (Winnicott, 1964: 113). Women do not naturally allow a man into their domain if they got to know their father through their mother's filter, or fantasized about a relationship which did not develop beyond the cultural legacy. The male therapist in a maternity ward takes on a role of great importance. In transference terms, the female client is confronted with living out a real relationship with her father. The transference offers women the opportunity of looking deeply into their relationship model, without neglecting their role as a mother. The therapist and the frame provide the necessary containment supporting the female client in experiencing her independent role as a mother. The possibility for a woman safely to explore her erotic transference may help her ultimately to retain the 'fruit' of a creative intercourse. The male therapist therefore becomes the father or the partner, who does not actually gratify the incestuous fantasy, but helps a woman to explore her fantasy, developing the creative side of an 'emotional intercourse'.

A woman's identity in a maternity ward

In a maternity ward Gaia, Electra and Medea, three women perversely enmeshed and representative of a woman's multi-faceted identity, assemble to meet the psychotherapist in order to conquer wholeness.

Mrs A had been referred to psychotherapy a few months before undergoing a hysterectomy, which she had postponed for five years and was still hoping to avoid. She could not hide her disappointment in meeting with a male counsellor. Her anger was so obvious that I acknowledged the urgency of addressing her relationship with men. My openness had an immediate effect. She smiled, relaxed instantly and told me about the pain of her father leaving the family when she was a baby. A few sessions later she asked me if I could see her privately. I explained that I would not be able to see her privately and reminded her that we still had time left over. The positive transference was instantly wiped away. Mrs A became aggressive and uncooperative. She started to come late to every session, was both seductive and impersonal, or very aggressive in questioning my competence. Unfortunately, at the time I could not properly see through her seduction scenes, which were the sublimation of her aggression in the transference. Her behaviour irritated me and I felt lost. An individual with extreme survival skills, which her deprived and painful childhood had instilled in her, meant that she became very manipulative in order to drive her point home. She made clear in our first session that men cannot support or help a woman, and although quite happy to reconsider her belief further down the line she was steadily working towards proving this belief. Her hatred paralysed me and hindered my therapeutic work. In retrospect, I had failed to acknowledge her initial and dutiful respect of the frame. In our last sessions her behaviour became erratic. These sessions consisted of her attempts to disrupt the frame. Mrs A was consistently late and would leave early. Her last session summed up what she was trying to prove. She arrived 20 minutes late and left the session 10 minutes early. She had come to say what a waste of time our meetings had been and did not know why she was bothering to show up at all. Her anger was blinding. I had failed to address the disruption, which originated from the absence of a benign father and her consequent disturbed relationships with men. With cold precision she deliberately pursued to castrate the therapist's efforts; but at what price? The impossibility of imagining a creative intercourse was translated into her womb being removed. In psychoanalytical terms, Mrs A was castrating herself and wanted me to experience how she was feeling. Her womb was useless. The therapeutic womb or the frame could not be put to good use, there was no space for a creative relationship: we would never be able to 'conceive'. If the therapeutic process is on the right track, psychosis will filter through a good enough therapeutic frame sooner or later.

Another interesting case is that of Ms B, a woman in her mid-thirties, who was initially referred for psychotherapy in the wake of a miscarriage. The baby she was unable to mother was supposed to fill the void of her father's death. Her father had died the year before and she was devastated. I remember her look of disbelief when she met me for the first time: 'How can a man relate to a miscarriage?' We worked on the gender issue, and whilst being supported by her positive transference she developed trust and confidence. A few months into the therapeutic process Ms B was pregnant again. She set out to ignore her pregnancy, a defence against her fear of yet another miscarriage. She also developed a strong erotic transference, which soon affected me to the point where I found myself confused and terrified of my special feelings for a pregnant woman, who had soon become my favourite. I avoided looking into my countertransference, kidding myself with a false sense of security provided by her pregnancy. The therapy stagnated. Putting aside my shame, I shared these feelings of attraction for Ms B in supervision, after which I finally came to terms with my erotic countertransference. I was suddenly free to address the erotic transference. She began to describe dreams, where I would appear to be her partner, who would reject her after a seduction scene. She was able to link the transference with her desire for her father, who was obsessively appearing in her dreams and had become the 'persecutory lost object'. Ms B would often share feelings of warmth and happiness when dreaming about her father, but became unusually upset at his increased appearances, which she began to perceive as an invasion. Being father's favourite child, Ms B fantasized that she could have saved him from a terminal illness had she been allowed to take her mother's place. In her fantasy, her father had seduced her only to betray her with mother and had now abandoned her forever. She acknowledged the link between her child's conception and her father's death and was able to identify the baby as a separate entity to the unresolved pain and anger she carried towards her father's premature departure. Her 'act of betrayal' consisted in developing a nurturing relationship with her psychotherapist, which led to a strong attachment to both her baby and the therapist. Her pregnancy was now desired and she entered a state of bliss, which she was loath to let go of. Soon enough, therapy focused on separation from her baby at birth and Ms B began to consider ending therapy. She gave birth to a boy and brought him into the first session after the summer break. She was able to look at the relationship she had with her mother, acknowledging it was fraught and poisoned by many unspoken secrets. We spoke about the safety net her baby had provided, and she decided to look for child-care during our sessions; this way she was stating her identity as a client, a wife, a mother and a daughter. Metaphorically, she had taken on the roles of Medea, Electra and, ultimately, of Gaia. We tackled many other issues as the therapy progressed. For the last session, Ms B arrived a few minutes late. I was emotional, but at peace. She had managed to speak with her mother and was sad, but now ready to move on with her life. The anniversary of her father's death was the following week and she could now let him go. Ms B would have closure with her father's death and with me, her therapist. She stated that she was looking forward to life with her family and putting aside her mother and extended family. We looked back on the work we had accomplished. She thanked me for supporting her during her pregnancy and for helping her to understand that she did not need to fall into bed with the first man who showed some care. Time was running out and we both simultaneously looked at the clock on the wall. I stood up as she collected her belongings. She put on her raincoat, turned around, smiled at me and said: 'I hope you do not mind.' Before I could understand what she meant she was hugging me. I froze. Instinctively I knew that I should not be in this position, but also realized there had been nothing sexual to it. This was saying goodbye to her 'father'; her arms were up over my neck, as a young girl would hug her father. I held her in my arms loosely and pressed my palms to her shoulder blades so she would know that I had not rejected her. She said: 'Thank you for all you have done for me.' I stood back and smiled as she walked through the door. I was immediately reminded of a tutor, who had shared with his class that after 20 years in his profession, nowadays, clients did not hug or try to touch him any longer. I wondered if it was my fault. Relieved by the feedback from my clinical supervisor I felt it was okay to have broken the frame in the end, as a closing statement; a gesture of separation, grounded by the in-depth work which had been accomplished.

The frame, or one could say the therapeutic womb, is the result of a successful relationship defined by stable boundaries which respect gender identity. Ouranus still fertilizes Gaia from a respectful distance when it rains, and the male psychotherapist can effectively establish a creative relationship from a respectful distance by exploring the fantasies which lie behind unresolved relationships.

Conclusion

Reminding myself of the 'saviour complex', the delirium of omnipotence common to all psychotherapists wishing to heal another human being, I realized that there is often little I can do to set up the frame as textbook theory had taught me. The cases I illustrate contain a common denominator, a peculiar psychoanalytical reality where some characteristics of the therapeutic frame are a 'given', the result of limiting external conditions. They provide important clues on how a client relates to the therapeutic frame and, in this case, to the male therapist. When the structuring of a therapeutic frame is impaired by external reality, confronting it becomes an urgent matter. A psychotherapist needs to accelerate the natural pace of a psychotherapeutic relationship, even though the client may initially find it threatening. Defining the frame becomes the first therapeutic task.

Ms B's case is the best constructive example of how the therapeutic frame acted as a therapeutic womb, enabling the client to bring her pregnancy to term. The container had survived the threats of life and Ms B could now constructively internalize the therapist. Violations of the therapeutic frame often indicate a potential negative transference, which needs to be addressed. Ignoring it may result in what I referred to as the 'therapeutic miscarriage', the premature expulsion of a client from the therapeutic space. Violations of the frame become signals of the mirroring of a distorted interaction with the external world. A client who violates the frame demonstrates his or her attempt to regain control of a situation in which he or she feels threatened and where irreparable damage is forecast. Having witnessed an array of attempts to disrupt the therapeutic womb, I can list a few: bringing the infant or a family member into the consulting room, challenging the frame by being absent or constantly late, continuously trying to reschedule sessions or trying to relocate therapy elsewhere. It is important not to disregard a client's need to disrupt the therapeutic frame. The therapeutic frame must be solid, but flexible enough to allow for experimenting: 'the more the therapist is able to tolerate anxiety of the unknown, the less need is there for the therapist to embrace orthodoxy' (Yalom, 1989: 36).

When my work with Ms B ended I realized that the client's gesture of breaking the therapeutic frame was through a goodbye, a final act of separation. Ms B had reclaimed her power through her strengthened ego. She bade farewell to her therapist, her father and to all the men who had 'imprisoned' her body and soul. A long-term therapeutic relationship had cleared out all ambiguities from within the consulting room. I would advise against any breach of boundaries during the therapeutic process as a general rule, but I realize that at times it happens. It is important to move on from this breach by simultaneously investigating its significance, which at the time is often unknown to a client and his or her therapist. In certain circumstances it is proved that the process of renegotiating the frame can be viewed as a prerequisite for the success of therapy (Luca, 2003), therefore I cannot preach orthodoxy.

In psychoanalytical terms a psychotherapist is providing a supplementary ego by structuring a therapeutic womb. A therapeutic frame confirms the psychotherapist's commitment to the process, sending a message of reassurance to the client. The therapeutic frame also encompasses the therapist's own anxiety and concern for being part of this psychotherapeutic encounter. In this chapter, I have taken for granted the psychotherapist's professional growth developing in parallel with the therapeutic work in progress. A psychotherapist's professional evolution is underlined by the skilful utilization of the countertransference to gain insight in the client's pathology. If the frame is a work of art, and the therapist embodies his or her creation, it goes without saying that the evolution of the therapist influences the development of the therapeutic frame. This identification offers exceptions to the rules of the traditional therapeutic frame, thus making room for the creative use of psychotherapy in particular cases (Hale and Sinason, 1994; Madison, 2001; Cortez Marques, 2002). Although I am not a great believer in the frameless structure for psychotherapy, I question if the exception of a framed approach to psychotherapy is symptomatic of the struggle that psychotherapy is engaged in order to find a secure space in today's society.

My work in a maternity ward made me aware of the importance in providing a space for a woman to confront her distress and look into the frightening darkness of an unknown reality. For many of the women in receipt of psychotherapy I become the guardian of their identity, as a father does in the mother–infant relationship.

In a fascinating account of his work in the field of psychoanalysis, focusing on fairy tales, Bettelheim (1976) recounts how fairy tales offer the possibility of breaking free from the inhibiting and anxiety-provoking perception of reality through the enchanted world of fantasy. Experiencing a way out of a perceived deadly situation for a child or a client signifies the opening of new prospects, symbolized by the unfolding of the fairy tale. Choices offering the way out from an impasse, often wrongly perceived as deadly, provide the possibility of surviving a threatening external world, often the metaphor of one's own poisoned internal reality. A fairy tale can be seen as the container to a child's psychosis; the tale needs to be heard until the psychosis has found its own words. It is not uncommon for a child to want to hear the same fairy tale over and over again, until one day, as if by pure magic, he or she loses interest. The impasse has been resolved and the container simply disappears, just as a frame dissolves with the end of a therapeutic encounter.

In a television interview following his Oscar nomination, the film director Benigni (1999) was asked to define freedom. He said: 'Freedom is discipline. I know you will be surprised to hear it. My father taught me discipline and offered me the choice of freedom. With discipline, I have the freedom to get off track if I choose to, but also the luxury of knowing how to get back on track if I choose to.'

Can psychotherapy be effective in the absence of a therapeutic frame? Benigni's interpretation of freedom is an accurate description of how I believe the therapeutic frame should be used. A client 'disciplined' by the therapeutic frame is more free to explore their distress. As for Winnicott's child, relating to life within a safe frame is the fundamental requisite for a harmonious growth. How would fellow therapists react to the idea that the therapeutic frame can be a path to freedom?

References

Arias, J. (1999) *Paulo Coelho: Las Confesiones del Peregrino*, Barcelona: Editorial Planeta.

Bell, D. (1998) 'External injury and the internal world', in C. Garland (ed.) *Understanding Trauma. A Psychoanalytical Approach*, London: Duckworth and Co. Ltd.

Benigni, R. (1999) Interview on RAI Television, Rome, April.

Bettelheim, B. (1976) *The Uses of Enchantment: The Meaning and Importance of Fairy Tales*, New York: A. Knopf.

Bion, W. (1962) 'A theory of thinking', in *Second Thoughts: Selected Papers On Psycho-Analysis*, London: Karnac, 1987.

Bleger, J. (1967) 'Psychoanalysis of the psycho-analytic frame', *International Journal of Psychoanalysis* 48: 511–19.

Carotenuto, A. (1988) *La Nostalgia della memoria. Il paziente e l'Analista*, Milano: Bompiani.

Carotenuto, A. (1991) *Amare Tradire. Quasi un' apologia del tradimento*, Milano: Bompiani.

Cortez Marques, M.A. (2002) 'The home visit. Considerations of the frame and boundaries', Unpublished thesis, City University, London.

Cheifetz, L.G. (1984) 'Framework violations in psychotherapy with clinic patients', in *Listening and Interpreting: The Challenge of the Work of Robert Langs*, New York: Aronson.

Erikson, E.H. (1951) Childhood and Society. London: Imago Publishing Company.

Etchegoyen, R.H. (1991) *The Fundamentals of Psychoanalytic Technique*, London: Karnac Books.

Euripides (1994) *Medea* London: Nick Hern Books Ltd.

Gilbert, L.A. and Scher, M. (1999) *Gender and Sex in Counseling and Psychotherapy*. Boston, Mass.: Allyn and Bacon.

Glasser, M. (1979) 'Some aspects of the role of aggression in perversions', in I. Rosen (ed.) *Sexual Deviations*, Oxford: Oxford University Press.

Gray, A. (1994) *An Introduction to the Therapeutic Frame*, London: Routledge.

Hale, R. and Sinason, V. (1994) 'Internal and external reality: establishing parameters', in V. Sinason (ed.) *Treating Survivors of Satanist Abuse*, London: Routledge.

Luca, M. (2003) Containment of the sexualized and erotized transference', in *Journal of Clinical Psychoanalysis* 11: 643–68.

Madison, G. (2001) 'Framing death: (or, What's so existential about communicative psychotherapy?)', *Journal of the Society for Existential Analysis* 12(1): 85–101.

Milner, M. (1952) 'Aspects of symbolism and comprehension of the not-self', *International Journal of Psychoanalysis* 33: 181–5.

Pines, D. (1993) *A Woman's Unconscious Use of Her Body*, London: Virago Press.

Richards, I.A. (1996) *Mencius on the Mind: Experiments in Multiple Definition*, New York: Curzon Press Ltd.

Schwartz, J. (1999) *Cassandra's Daughter*, London: Penguin Books.

Vernant, J.P (1999) *L'Univers, les Dieux, les Hommes. Recits Grecs de Origin*, Paris: Editions du Seuil.

Winnicott, D.W. (1964) *The Child, the Family, and the Outside World*, New York: Addison-Wesley Publishing Company, Inc.

Yalom. I. (1989) *Love's Executioner*, Harmondsworth: Penguin.

Young, R. (2002) *The Analytic Frame, Abstinence and Acting Out*, Available online: htpp://human-nature.com/rmyoung/papers/pap110h.html (6 August 2002).

Chapter 5

Therapist illness and its impact on the therapeutic frame

Anne Brockbank

This chapter recounts my experience as a therapist being diagnosed with a life-threatening illness, my personal response to this and how I handled my professional work with clients. The potential effects on clients of sudden and premature endings are discussed, as well as the impact on my therapeutic practice. Alternative strategies are considered and compared with actual events. Reflections include practice guidelines to cover sudden illness or death eventuality of a therapist.

I found the lump in my right breast one morning in bed, during that languorous stretching and self-stroking that is part of waking. I felt the lump and my heart sank. I had had lumps before and I knew this one felt different. Then I felt panic. How long had it been there? How had I missed this in my regular self-examinations in the shower? Had I been forgetting to check? I couldn't remember when I last checked my breasts. Had I stopped bothering about myself, not caring whether I lived or died? I remembered that after having some joint therapy sessions with my partner I had felt utterly hopeless about my future life with him and wondered if I would die of it. Now I felt fatalistic. Perhaps this is how my struggle to be happy is going to end. I could feel almost resigned to the inevitable. I began to take a deterministic stance, which I believe now was a familiar defence against the fear and terror I was experiencing: '*If this is it, so be it, but I won't go down without a fight.*' I acted immediately, getting a doctor's appointment within a week. He was reassuring. 'I'm sure it's just a cyst', he said, and this was more than likely as I had a history of lumps which turned out to be cysts full of fluid rather than tumours. My regular mammogram was due the day after and as I climbed into the van marked 'Health of the Nation', which housed the breast screening unit, I was very aware that this 'gram' could reveal cancer in my breast. The technicians took note of the lump and marked the films for special attention at the one-stop breast unit located in my local hospital

Within a week my partner B and I attended the breast unit, with some apprehension, but were reassured by the professional atmosphere. When we saw the doctors they were confident that there was nothing to worry about as the mammogram was clear. I persisted with my feeling that something was different and there was a new lump in my breast, just near my right nipple. Ultrasound established that there was a mass present and the FNA (Fine Needle Aspirant) procedure produced blood and the cells were sent for analysis there and then. So this time it was not being dismissed as 'just a cyst'. They were taking it rather seriously, so I knew there must be something wrong. I was feeling wobbly and uncertain. I had not been here before. It had always been OK or a false alarm before. This time it could be serious.

We waited anxiously in the waiting room, neither daring to speak, and each studying the *Guardian* ostentatiously. When we were recalled we were told that the FNA cells were abnormal and that a more invasive procedure was needed to look at the actual cells in the lump. The consultant radiologist appeared and carried out a core biopsy on my breast, under local anaesthetic, using a kind of gun to aim a large needle/scalpel into the lump to scoop out some tissue for analysis. We were told we would have a definite diagnosis within a week.

That week was the longest in my life, and probably my partner's, as we both avoided the subject but cried quietly with each other, just living the hours to what could be a death sentence it seemed. It felt like a nightmare – I may or may not have cancer and I'll find out in a week. I couldn't work, concentrate, or relax until I knew definitely one way or the other. If the lump was cancer I could be facing a painful death quite soon. I began feeling a deep sadness and a fear of the future as unknown and threatening. I wondered if I was beginning the long wait for death

Just before the appointment I decided it was time to tell my daughter, A, herself a doctor, about the potential diagnosis, and I called her the night before the appointment. She was concerned about my 'holding' the situation for so long without telling her; I promised to let her know the result as soon as I could.

The day came and we went into the room to hear my fate. 'I'm afraid the lump in your breast is cancer', the surgeon said. I was stunned, even though I had been preparing for this for a week. I never thought this would happen to me. Breast cancer is what other women got, not me. Linda McCartney died and she had every treatment money could buy. So did Dusty and Marti Caine. Will it be radiotherapy and chemotherapy? Is that the one where your hair falls out? I was not sure I could cope with this.

I was advised by my surgeon to have a mastectomy. When I asked about my likely survival chances, responses were cagey: 'That all depends on whether you are node-negative or node-positive'. 'Negative' means that when the lymph nodes (under-arm glands) are examined under a microscope the cells show no evidence of breast cancer. 'Positive' means they do and the chances of spread to the nodes was around 10 per cent; that is, one out of ten women with breast cancer had cancer that had spread to the nodes. When I pushed for detail I was given the assurance that, with a mastectomy, and a node-negative result, my chances were as good as those of a woman who has never had breast cancer (a statistic which I still find it hard to believe). If I turned out to be node-positive my chances of survival after ten years was 55 per cent, and in the UK one in 12 women die of breast cancer every year. Clearly it was a very good thing indeed to be node-negative, but I would need to prepare for both eventualities. Until the surgery was done and pathology reports made, I would not know which group I was in or what my chances were. I was scheduled for surgery within six weeks. I was unable to predict whether I would recover completely, partially or not at all.

The breast-care nurse arrived and took us away for a cup of tea while the news sank in. When the NHS gives you tea it must be bad news. I was aware, as if detached from it, that the breast-care nurse had been trained in counselling skills, taking time to listen attentively and answer our questions, as well as being receptive to and accepting of our feelings. As a professional, working in the unit every day, she was used to helping people to come to terms with a potential death sentence. But for me it is my life, and the prospect of losing my breast to possibly save my life was horrendous. I was holding onto the knowledge that I could make a choice here. I knew I could refuse surgery, especially if the cancer had already spread. If so I was determined to just enjoy the time I'd got left. But how would I cope with them cutting off my breast. It felt horrific. I felt sick imagining the slicing off process. Then the thought of the sewing up afterwards made me feel even worse.

I was diagnosed with breast cancer on Valentine's Day. It was my day for seeing clients and I returned from the hospital in a dream-like state, and began to feel angry. I had enjoyed excellent health all my life and had rather taken it for granted. So I felt angry first. 'How dare my body let me down like this?' The security of good health fell away and I found myself in a very frightening place. In addition to fear I was facing a huge potential loss in my life, the loss of one of my favourite body parts, my breasts. I was unsure about how I would feel about myself without one of them. I will explain how significant this loss was for me and discuss its impact on my practice below.

My breasts featured as top-of-the bill performers in my sexual life. They were intensely sensitive and responded to the slightest touch. In particular the idea of losing my right nipple was horrific as my nipples were my favourite place to be stimulated, and the right one was the lead nipple. If the idea of a lead nipple seems fanciful I can confirm now that the left one is not sure what to do without its partner. I was just about able to speak to the surgeon about this, but she shook her head sadly, saying the tumour was too near and it would have to go. I was left with that unenviable choice: did I want to continue having pleasure or die? The operation included a reconstruction of my breast, a clever use of muscular tissue from my back inserted under my existing breast skin. This presents to the world an appearance of 'normality' but does not address the feelings of loss, as the reconstruction would have very little feeling compared to its real sister. The appearance of normality has been discussed by Julie Friedeberger (1996) as a barrier to the grieving process, as the 'missing' part is not visible, and I discuss the continuing experience of loss below. I was overcome by feelings of sadness and grief as we returned from the hospital on that never-to-be-forgotten Valentine's Day.

My partner, B, and my daughter have a difficult relationship; both are very close to me but in different ways. My relationship with B, not her father, is passionate and tempestuous, and my relationship with my daughter is like that of a sister or best friend. He finds it difficult to share me with her, and she doesn't see why she should. I'm her mother after all. On receipt of the bad news outside the hospital she made a gesture of peace to my partner and he responded positively but, in his distress, was unable to function for the rest of the day. So I turned to her for help with immediate problems. I then faced the task of dealing with my clients. There wasn't much time, as my first client was due to arrive within two hours.

The idea of a therapeutic frame was instilled in me at my first counsellor training, where we were required, while working within a voluntary agency, to adhere to a series of boundaries. These included the use of a receptionist, a waiting area, a sound-proof room without personal cues of any kind, and a strict adherence to agreed session times. We were strongly advised to limit our communications with clients outside sessions, to letters inviting or confirming appointments, limited telephone conversations, and the option for counsellors of declining to work with someone they know or know of. I didn't realize then that the frame is part of the therapeutic relationship itself, just as where a couple go out to, and when, is part of their relationship.

The significance of the therapeutic relationship in all counselling contexts has been explored by researchers, and the evidence suggests that client outcomes are less influenced by the therapeutic model used than by non-specific factors (Frank 1974). The most significant of these factors is 'the creation of a supportive relationship', and in their review Grencavage and Norcross (1990) found that 'the therapeutic alliance' attracted the highest level of consensus in professional opinion regarding non-specific factors affecting client outcomes.

For me the idea of a therapeutic frame is rooted in the psychodynamic concepts of containment (Bion 1968), 'a holding environment' (Winnicott 1960), and a secure base (Bowlby 1979). The frame holds the client within the safe environment of therapy, providing a secure base for development. Within the frame I work in a person-centred way, using the six core conditions laid down by Rogers (1992) and developed by others (Egan 1976, 1977; Mearns and Thorne 1988). I believe that Rogers overlaid his initial training as a psychodynamic analyst with his person-centred conditions, so that the therapeutic frame is invisible in his writing, being treated as a 'given'.

At the very beginning of a therapeutic relationship with my client I put the therapeutic frame in place. I begin the process by restricting my initial interactions to frame issues like available sessions, timing, fees, etc. I confirm the arrangement made in a letter to the client asking for confirmation by a given date by phone, fax or email. The status of emails is still an issue for me, although many of my clients are quite happy to communicate through this semi-public channel. My clients come to my home where I see them in a comfortable room adjacent to the front door, with minimum personal cues. There is a small bench in the hall, out of sight of the doors, where a client can wait if necessary. At the first session I reiterate the frame conditions, adding details about counselling for clients new to it. I mention confidentiality and ethics, as well as the requirement for supervision. I also inform clients in this first interview about my likely availability, and when my holidays occur. Clients are invited to decide at the end of the first session what contract they would like to enter into with me. Typically clients choose six or twelve sessions with reviews on completion with the option to renew the contract. My long-term clients start off with such a contract, and as the work to be done emerges they may opt for a longer contract.

Thereafter I use psychodynamic ideas as a kind of backdrop in trying to understand my clients' difficulties, which are often, but not always, rooted in the past, and I use the person-centred method to work with those difficulties in the here and now. This approach is sometimes referred to as an integrative model. I alert my clients to when I will be taking holidays or being away from London. I prepare a list of my session dates with the holidays/time away clearly indicated, and we discuss this three or four sessions before it occurs. When the end of the counselling is approaching I alert my client so that we begin addressing issues relating to the end of the work before the last session, dealing with the familiar longings and regrets that endings may engender.

In the case of illness or death of the counsellor there would be no such preparation for the ending. It would be sudden, premature and far from ideal, as I would not meet with them to do it. The 'story', as described by Holmes (1997), would come to an abrupt finish without the client being able to take charge of their own narrative. My clients enjoyed intimacy with me in their therapeutic relationships and were working towards autonomy. This break in the frame could potentially arrest that process. For my clients this ending would be 'involuntary' and therefore 'too early' in Holmes's (1997) terms.

When separation occurs in any relationship, feelings and behaviour may echo attachment patterns from the past, and this is true for both client and therapist. The ending of therapy should realize its aim – that is, to create a secure base from which the client can move towards autonomy. How does a premature ending affect this outcome? For client X whose anxious attachment pattern tended to be avoidant, keeping me at a distance, having experienced coldness and distance in her childhood, this ending could have felt like a rerun of the past, a break in the 'holding' she needed, before she was ready to strike out on her own. For client Y whose anxious attachment pattern tended to be ambivalent, having experienced on/off caregivers in childhood, this ending denied him the possibility of expressing his anger, which had already emerged in late attendance, missed appointments and within the therapy itself. For client W, whose anxious attachment was also ambivalent, this ending could have felt like the abandonment he had experienced in early childhood. For short-term clients V and Z the ending was 'too early', and although some preparation had been done towards an ending with them the suddenness of this ending would mean they were unable to revisit the intentions they had worked through in the brief therapy (Holmes 1997).

I addressed the task of informing my clients of my illness, with the help of my daughter, who, as women together do, 'held' me while I got to grips with the news of my illness. We discussed what to do and decided to speak directly to my supervisor first. I will discuss now the significance of my supervisor.

I have been with my supervisor since I first came to London ten years ago, and I have been well supported by him in many different ways throughout. I trust him and I trust his judgement. My supervisor is a group analyst who works within a complete psychoanalytic framework. When I bring my integrative work to him, he gives me a psychodynamic 'take' on the case material, which I find refreshing and rarely cuts across the person-centred process. In this circumstance, when I contacted him, taking account of my clients' transference and potential for fantasies, he advised that they should be informed immediately of my 'serious illness' and offered alternative therapists. On the advice of my supervisor the word 'cancer' was not mentioned.

The potential for my clients to imagine that they had somehow caused the cancer was one reason why my supervisor advised me to code the information to them. The idea that clients may fear they have made their therapist ill is a real one, especially where this resonates with early experiences, and this was mentioned by Rachel Freeth (2001: 19): 'there were other disturbing feelings, such as childhood fears that maybe I had caused her to become unwell, just as my mother had been unwell throughout a lot of my childhood'.

I found myself unable at this point to be professional. I felt paralysed by fear and utterly powerless to act. I asked my daughter to make the phone calls for me as there was no way I could have spoken without bursting into tears and collapsing. This was a breach of confidentiality as I would never have discussed my clients with her under any other circumstances. She became aware of their names and their phone numbers as a consequence, which was far from ideal. I believe the information to be secure in this case, as she is used to maintaining patient confidentiality as part of her work as a General Practitioner. I don't remember confirming with her that the information was to be kept confidential or whether it was assumed between us.

I believe now that I was protecting my clients from my grief. I did not want them to know the extent of my distress. My supervisor pointed me in a direction where I was going anyway. I wanted to remain the strong parent with my clients, just as I do with my children.

My immediate decision, in collaboration with my supervisor, was to stop client work completely and recommend referrals for my clients. I hold a list of my colleagues to whom I am happy to refer clients for whatever reason. They agreed immediately to take on any of my clients who approached them. I prepared a letter for each client with more information and a list of my therapist colleagues who had agreed to take on my clients if they so desired. My preference was to give my clients the names and contact details of my colleagues, and to leave the rest up to them. I was unable to offer my colleagues any information about my clients, even if I had wanted to, as I had not cleared that with them. Client

X and Y chose to seek therapy with one or other of my colleagues and came back to tell me about it. Client W simply disappeared sadly and I heard no more from him, although he, and my brief counselling clients, may have taken up one of the referral options, and I have no way of knowing about this. I feel confident that those clients who transferred to another therapist will have been able to deal with their issues around the abrupt and sudden ending. Their feelings of anger and abandonment will have formed part of the work they did with my colleagues. For client W, my illness may have seemed like a repeat of his early childhood experience of being 'let down' by those caring for him. I hoped and trusted that this client had established another safe frame with one of my colleagues. I have resisted the temptation to ask colleagues about my clients with some difficulty as I very much want to be reassured that they are being cared for, a feeling that I recognize as guilt about letting them down, letting them go and not being there for them.

I was cancelling my life, all my clients and the course I had created at the university – and it felt awful. Everyone was very concerned, but for me this might be the end. I might never work again. My life as I had known it may be over and I felt like I didn't matter any more. I know that's not right, but it was how I felt. In the weeks following the diagnosis before the surgery I experienced a strange feeling of being outside reality, looking in at everyone else who didn't have cancer. I even described it to someone with a wonderful Freudian slip included. I said: 'It's like I'm standing outside looking in through glass, and everyone else is inside, and they're ill and I'm not.'

My daughter A took charge of the situation, managing the messages to clients and making sure that I did not receive requests from anybody in the foreseeable future. She is a darling and I love her. When my son G contacted me I became tearful and tried to keep my voice steady while I told him I had breast cancer. He was on his way to me immediately. I love him dearly too. They both show signs of appearing strong when defending against painful feelings, and I recognize that I have presented that behaviour to them as a parent just as I have done with my clients in this case.

Fear of death and denial of dying is a characteristic of Western life and we are not used to accepting that 'death is simply a fact of life' (Friedeberger 1996). My daughter's reaction on hearing the diagnosis was 'but you're too young' – suggesting that she was not ready to deal with my death yet. My son began asking for photographs of me, which I assumed was in preparation to keep in the event of my death. For my clients, as I was going to be ill for quite a while, and may possibly die, their therapeutic frame was fractured as I was not able to 'hold' them any more. In a sense they were not ready to deal with my death yet either.

It seems it was not my turn yet as the nodes turned out to be negative – that is, the cancer had not spread. There would be no radiotherapy or chemotherapy needed, and I would return for scanning every year to the breast clinic. The day I received that news was a very happy one for me and my loved ones. We had all been carrying the potential worse-case scenario, and it was a relief to hear that the surgery to all intents and purposes had saved my life. I spent a year in recovery, visiting friends abroad, taking restful holidays, making heirloom quilts, and preparing a portfolio for BACP accreditation.

Clients X and Y chose to return to me a year later for a short contract of sessions, bringing me up to date on their progress, and taking their work a little further. This I identified as our ending, delayed by my illness. They asked about my health and seemed happy to hear that I am now well. I chose not to give details, but assured them that I am OK now. Their work included accounts of how they had fared with my colleagues, and I identified this as a form of 'see what happened to me when you were not here' and their need to tell me about it. In addition there was a sense of them reassuring themselves that I was still alive, and establishing that I would be here if they want or need me again, before being able to move on.

What have I learned from the experience? The discussion which follows does not claim to have the validity that research findings would have. It has not been possible or desirable to question clients about their experience of my illness. I am writing from my own experience as a therapist, about a life-threatening illness, and my own observations about how this seemed to affect the therapeutic frame for my clients and myself.

My dilemma, which I allowed my supervisor to solve for me, was that I could not find the strength to attend to my clients with the prospect of my own death to deal with. A key factor in their therapeutic frame was threatened – that is, the regularity and predictability of my attention to them. If I could have had surgery immediately and become available within two or three weeks it may have been possible to 'freeze' the frame for my clients. However, this was not an option as I had to wait five weeks for surgery. Though I was unhappy about waiting at first, those five weeks were an important time for me: I attended to my own needs, saw friends and family, said goodbye to my breast, and came to terms with what I might have to face. In this situation I would have been asking clients to 'wait' for me for two months and possibly three. What was difficult for me was the uncertainty of not knowing how I would be if things went badly and the cancer had spread. In such a case I would have work to do preparing for death (breast cancer kills quickly if it spreads), and I have a number of unresolved issues around in my life. Perhaps a therapist shouldn't have these, but I confess I was very focused on my own needs and wasn't even sure I would ever practise as a therapist again.

Clearly this is not how all therapists feel and others have found that getting the surgery over quickly enabled them to return to work as normal. However this has its own problems, and this is recounted well by Rosie Jeffries (2000: 479) who found that: 'it was tricky to work with her fear that she made me ill . . . I thought she might have seen my cancer as her fault too . . .'

Sometimes clients guess what is wrong and within a therapeutic alliance may feel able to bluntly say, as Rosie's client did: 'you've got breast cancer haven't you?' (Jeffries 2002: 479). There seems little sense in not being honest in such a situation, as contradicting the client's sense of reality is itself a threat to the therapeutic frame. I believe that if we undertake to return to therapeutic work it is our responsibility to ensure that the therapeutic frame remains intact.

I now wish I had been more open about my illness to my clients, and perhaps allowed them to deal with it in their own way. I am aware of feeling guilty about not giving them that choice and of 'passing them on' to others rather like a feckless parent would. I wish I had held on to them throughout my recovery so that when I was well again I could reconnect as before. I know this is an unrealistic and rather selfish wish, and I am aware that the way I was feeling about my illness and potential death my clients' needs would have been unlikely to be met in this scenario.

My illness and my unavailability without warning undermined the therapeutic frame in which my clients were being contained. Would an alternative strategy have prevented that fracturing? Had I shared the details of my illness and my distress with my clients they might have had the option of 'growing up' rather suddenly. On the other hand they might have felt guilty, angry or abandoned without their therapy to process those feelings. In the event, in defending my own pain and taking my supervisor's advice, I protected them from either alternative.

I am left with a sense of dissatisfaction about it all. If I could have seen into the future and known that the cancer had not spread I might have been able to feel differently and be more available for my clients. However, I am also aware that this smacks of 'might have beens' and doesn't take into account the grief I had to deal with as a result of losing my best breast, a loss that I live with every day. I am less sexually active than before, as something seems to be missing, and I feel not quite whole. I fear that this must have impacted on my practice, perhaps making me less able to nurture and hold my clients. I long to have my breast back and suspect that I may resent anyone with two. I am aware of being acutely sensitive to clients who bring illness to therapy, particularly terminal illness. I respond differently, consciously putting aside my own reaction to focus on them, something I was not aware of doing before. My supervisor supports and reassures me and I continue to work productively.

The illness focused my mind on what should happen to my handwritten case notes and electronic records of appointments. I have inserted a sheet within my current note folders instructing my executor to destroy them. I rearranged my archived notes, labelling them carefully, and added a covering instruction about destroying them (as well as my administrative records on disk) in the event of my death. A similar note is now part of my instructions to my executors.

I do wonder about what would have occurred if the break in the therapeutic frame had been sudden death rather than illness. My clients would have turned up at the allotted time and discovered that their therapist was dead. I can leave instructions as above, but the immediacy of an accident is unlikely to allow for relatives to have my wishes to hand on the day. I have resolved to go through a procedure with my family so that they will know what to do in such an event.

As a result of my experience of having breast cancer I have confronted my own greatest fear: not just loss of life, but loss of my strength and beauty. I believe that I behaved to my clients in a familiar pattern of denial, and deprived them of choices around my unavailability, partly to protect myself from facing the loss of my personal power. I am determined to address this embedded tendency, in my personal and professional life, with the time I have left, however painful that might be.

References

Bion, W.R. (1968) *Experiences in Group*, London: Tavistock.

Bowlby, J. (1979) *The Making and Breaking of Affectional Bonds*, London: Tavistock.

Egan, G. (1976) *Interpersonal Living*, Monterey, California: Brooks/Cole.

Egan, G. (1977) *You and Me*, Monterey, California: Brooks/Cole.

Frank, J.D. (1974) 'Psychotherapy: the restoration of morale', *American Journal of Psychiatry* 131: 272–4.

Freideberger, J. (1996) *The Visible Wound*, Shaftesbury, Dorset: Element Books.

Freeth, R. (2001) 'Ending therapy . . . when one's therapist dies', *Counselling & Psychotherapy Journal*, 12(6): 18–20.

Grencavage, L.M. and Norcross, J.C. (1990) 'Where are the commonalities among the therapeutic common factors?', *Professional Psychology: Research and Practice* 21: 372–8.

Holmes, J. (1997) 'Too early-too late: endings in psychotherapy', *British Journal of Psychotherapy* 14(2): 159–71.

Jeffries, R. (2000) 'The disappearing counsellor', *Counselling* September.

Mearns, D. and Thorne, B. (1988) *Person Centred Counselling in Action*, London: Sage.

Rogers, C.R. (1992) *Client Centred Therapy*, London: Constable.

Winnicott, D. (1960) *Human Nature*, London: Free Association Books.

Chapter 6

We must stop meeting like this

Unplanned contact between psychotherapist and patient

James Pollard

The purpose of this chapter is to help clinicians think about the issues raised by unplanned contact with the patient and to manage these situations more effectively. Such contacts have been a source of difficulty throughout the history of psychotherapy. Illustrations from clinical experience, historical and fictional, are used to illustrate the consequence of extensive contacts and the significance of even slight contacts. The implications for the transference and countertransference are considered. The problems of managing unplanned contacts and the levels at which the significance of meetings might be understood are discussed.

A history of learning about unplanned contact and its consequence

Early in its history psychotherapy developed as a series of planned encounters between patient and therapist. This gave rise to what came to be known as the therapeutic frame. The place of the frame in the psychotherapeutic process was continually under pressure from the experience of the relationships. The establishment of basic disciplines was a slow and painful process.

The earliest cases illustrate that contact outside the consulting room is inevitable from time to time. They show that it is always likely that there will be patients drawn from a community of which the therapist is also a member. These experiences illustrate the dangers and difficulties created by unplanned contacts outside the consulting room. There was a widespread confusion of roles and contacts in the early psychoanalytic community. The sense of the importance of clarity, of singularity of role, took time to develop. Only gradually was the need for clear boundaries to analytic relationships accepted. Nevertheless, there was an early realization of the significance of contact outside the session.

As early as the case presented as 'Dora' in 1902, Freud was attaching significance to his patient reading about him in the newspaper. He deduced that it was this that had prompted her to make contact with him after having broken off her therapy. He suggested that the contact had brought forward an aspect of the transference. His interpretation was that on reading about his appointment to a professorship Dora had developed a facial neuralgia. This had happened in part, he believed, because the thought of him brought forward feelings of guilt in her for her attacks upon him. This one-off visit prompted by an unplanned indirect contact was part of a messy and unresolved ending to the therapy. Freud noted caustically that the visit occurred on 1 April. There was a game in play over who was going to make a fool of whom.

Problems in containing contact have been associated with psychotherapeutic failures since the inception of psychotherapy. There is a wide spectrum of events and interactions that can come under the heading 'unplanned contact'. This includes extensive relationships outside the therapeutic setting, brief and surprising encounters, and indirect contacts of the kind that led to Dora's visit to Freud. The common theme to managing all of these situations is the awareness of the transference and the countertransference.

Freud has been criticized for not giving adequate attention to what would come to be known as his countertransference reaction to Dora. In the decade prior to Freud's therapeutic failure with Dora, Joseph Breuer had found it impossible to contain his countertransference reaction to Anna O. This troubled him so much that he broke off the treatment and left Vienna. Awareness of the countertransference is the starting point for psychotherapy. Breaches of the frame provoke strong countertransference responses, as well as bringing forward the transference.

These anxieties and other countertransference reactions to patients can lead to the development of very destructive situations. Much of this chapter will be concerned with brief and indirect contacts, but it is important to recognize the potential for extensive unplanned contact and the great difficulties that this can give rise to. One of the greatest problems with unplanned contact is the difficulty of resolving where it ends.

The cases discussed here are not presented primarily for their historical interest. The century of experience since Freud first developed psychoanalysis is the heritage of all those who practice psychotherapy. If we cannot remember and learn from this experience we are much more likely to repeat it. The clinical experience discussed in this chapter is as contemporary in its relevance as when the events recorded took place.

Extended unstructured contacts with patients

Heinrich Racker, in a paper published in 1953 (originally given in Buenos Aires in 1948), describes the difficulties of the countertransference from the point of view of a 'young analyst' (Racker 1953: 319). This chapter demonstrates the potential impact of unplanned contact developing far beyond the consulting room. His clinical description, couched in the language of classical psychoanalysis, conjures up the depth of confusion and the chaotic attachments that can follow from a serious departure into extensive unplanned contact. The patient he describes is a woman of 35 suffering from a marked melancholia and manifold paranoic ramifications (attempts at suicide, erotomania, and erythrophobia) and little awareness of her condition. He writes:

> Nevertheless, he [the young analyst] did not wish to drop the case, for he knew, so he said, that, however unlikely the cure, analysis was the woman's one real hope . . . In view of the further fact that the woman was closely connected with the analytical circle, the idea of the treatment failing took on, for his unconscious, the significance of castration, or loss of the introjected objects. Against this danger and the resulting anxiety, the analyst defended himself by (inwardly) accusing the patient. He began to hate her. This hatred aroused guilt-feelings in him.
>
> (Racker 1953: 319)

At this point the woman was left by her fiancé. She fell into a state of severe depression and thought seriously of suicide. Her feelings were now strongly focused on the analyst. Racker writes:

> The analyst, persecuted by the accusations and threats of his super-ego, utterly submitted to her oral aggressiveness and 'hunger'. He offered her his free hours, and frequently at week-ends she stayed in his house for several hours, crying, accusing him, threatening him with suicide etc. . . . . Little by little the patient got better, though only superficially . . . when she found a new love object, he agreed to her abandoning analysis, a thing he had not accepted while she was depressed. What he felt at the moment she left off analysis was a truly *manic* state. He was 'set free' of the 'bad object', and 'free' of the persecuting super-ego, both of which had been alternately (sub-)transferred to the patient.
>
> (Racker 1953: 319–20)

The therapist in Racker's story believes that he must continue because he is the patient's only hope. The therapist's fantasies of indispensability and of rescuing the patient are frequently key elements in the development of contact outside the session. This may be linked to the patient's fantasy that the therapist is indispensable to her or him. There are powerful unconscious feelings of hatred in such a relationship as the demands and intrusions, both psychic and practical, become excessive. The hatred is a counterpart to the idealizations involved.

In Racker's story it had not proved possible to contain the therapist's powerful feelings of shame and guilt. From this point of view contacts outside the session were designed to relieve these feelings and to further the projection of these feelings into the patient. The patient became more ill as she introjected these feelings. She became more dependent on the therapist as the good object, but also more chaotic, more depressed and suicidal. She escaped this by finding an alternative love object. She was then not available in the same way for the therapist's projections, and he let her go.

Retrieving something from therapies that have moved outside the frame to this extent is very difficult. The psychotherapist will need to work through the experience with the great integrity. This is not easy, as it requires the therapist to move out of the countertransference dynamics that lead to the difficulties sufficiently to work with the patient constructively. The therapist may instead develop a very negative countertransference and experience the patient as a persecutory figure. Alternatively, the therapist may struggle to recover his or her position as the therapist by determinedly, and defensively, pathologizing the patient.

A refusal to acknowledge error can be very damaging. This is a difficult balance to keep because the therapist's guilt is not the patient's problem and is of little value to the patient. A patient may come to feel passionately that what she or he wants is an apology, but the apology may bring very little satisfaction or relief if it is offered. Unless it is located in the development of a contained contact with the subjectivity of the therapist the apology can have the effect of consolidating the loss of the idealized object while offering nothing in exchange.

One of the difficult aspects of the move towards greater professional and legal accountability, necessary as these are, is that they can strengthen resistance in the therapist to acknowledgement of error. It is not just in psychotherapy that the reluctance to admit to error or to apologize is greatly increased by fear of the professional and legal consequences. This fear is to some extent misplaced. The fundamental requirement of professional bodies, the law, and insurers is that the psychotherapist acts professionally. If the psychotherapist feels that he or she has not been acting professionally the important thing is to start doing so again. Supervision has a crucial role in thinking through these problems and it is essential to take the countertransference reactions openly to supervision.

As far as managing the countertransference is concerned, whether it is dominated by love or hate, Margaret Little expresses the aim very well:

> The analyst necessarily identifies with the patient, but there is for him an interval of time between himself and the experience which for the patient has the quality of immediacy – he knows it for past experience, while to the patient it is a present one. That makes it at that moment the patient's experience, not his, and if the analyst is experiencing it as a present thing he is interfering with the patient's growth and development.
>
> (Little 1951: 35)

It is, of course, perfectly possible to view the experience as a present one rather than one that belongs to the past. However, the consequence of viewing it in that way is that the therapist stops practising psychotherapy. The therapist has in this case stopped managing his or her countertransference, and the whole contact has become unplanned.

Guilt and anxiety in the countertransference

In many cases it may be better for the patient to work with a new psychotherapist with more firmly established boundaries. Heinrich Racker's story demonstrates the importance of the social and professional framework. All psychotherapy takes place in some form of social context, and this brings pressures to bear on the therapeutic relationship. The most obvious instance of this is the relationships within communities of psychotherapists.

Feelings arising in the psychotherapy relationship are often derived from or influenced by external relationships. It would be a mistake, reading the story that Racker tells, to place the emphasis on the role of the frame in protecting the therapist. However much the patient may resist or seek to subvert the frame the frame exists primarily to protect the patient.

These themes were exemplified very clearly a quarter of a century earlier. In 1922 Freud conducted a secondary analysis of Joan Riviere, who had been in analysis with Ernest Jones. Freud described having to conduct this second analysis as 'no easy or pleasant task' (Freud and Jones

1993: 483). Jones had allowed extensive contacts to develop. He had discussed his personal affairs, including his marriages, with Riviere and had lent her his summer cottage. This had led to what he described as 'the worst failure I have ever had' (Freud and Jones 1993: 453).

Jones felt that it was he who was in need of protection. He wrote to Freud: 'she devoted herself to torturing me without any intermission and with considerable success and ingenuity, being a fiendish sadist' (Freud and Jones 1993: 454). Freud's response to Jones was to tell him

> you must be prepared to my taking her side, defending her interest and even turning against you in favour of her analysis. It means simply doing my duty as an analyst . . . There was no chance of making her see the abnormality of her reactions unless she had got the acknowledgement of your errors where you had committed them.
> (Freud and Jones 1993: 483–4)

Despite this apparent clarity the unplanned contact continued. Correspondence between Freud and Jones about the case continued alongside Riviere's analysis with Freud, and became increasingly acrimonious. The whole process became enmeshed with the affairs of the psychoanalytic societies. The difficulty is that contacts of this kind can be exploitative and at best confuse the psychotherapy. Jones acknowledged in his initial letter to Freud about Riviere that he wanted to use her. He wrote to Freud: 'Seeing that she was unusually intelligent I hoped to win her for the cause' (Freud and Jones 1993: 453). Freud agreed. He wrote to Jones: 'She seems to be a powerful helpmate and we should bring her to some good use' (Freud and Jones 1993: 468).

Jones acknowledged the difficulty this caused: 'The situation was complicated by her position in the society, which gave her a certain personal contact with me' (Freud and Jones 1993: 454). However, he later became anxious about Joan Riviere's influence and the possibility that Freud would take decisions that were unwelcome to him. He then presented the confusion as Joan Riviere's fault: 'she has cleverly managed to introduce into her analysis with you the same difficulty as happened with me, namely the intermixture of analytical considerations with external actual ones; perhaps it was unavoidable on her part' (Freud and Jones 1993: 478).

Freud found himself trying to manage a conflict between Jones and Riviere that was no longer contained in a therapeutic relationship. This was a situation from which he quickly became quite anxious to extricate himself. A powerful factor in contact outside the sessions is the attraction of the illicit, the incestuous and the secret. There is often great anxiety associated with irregular contacts coming to light. Jones's anxiety about how Freud will view his conduct with Joan Riviere is palpable. Freud was very severe with Jones. He not only criticized his technical conduct but, in the end, made sweeping criticisms of his character:

> Now what made the case so hard for me was the fact that accuracy and plainness are not in the character of your dealings with people. Slight distortions and evasions, lapses of memory, twisted denials, a certain predilection for side-tracks prevail.
>
> (Freud and Jones 1993: 491)

As the triangular relationship developed Freud also became caught up in the mobilization of anxiety and guilt.

The countertransference and brief contacts

It is clear from both Racker's case and the correspondence between Freud and Jones that guilt in the countertransference is a major factor in uncontained contact between patient and psychotherapist. In a paper published in 1951 Margaret Little gave an account from the patient's perspective of a slight contact outside of the clinical setting. In this case a patient whose mother had recently died was to give a talk on the radio on a subject of interest to the analyst. The analyst knew of the talk and listened to it when it was broadcast. The day after the talk the patient arrived 'in a state of anxiety and confusion' (Little 1951: 32).

The analyst interpreted this as due to the patient's fear of the analyst's jealousy. The patient accepted the interpretation, but two years later, after he had left analysis, a new experience associated with the anniversary of his mother's death caused him to reconsider this. The patient realized that what had troubled him at the time of the talk was his sadness that his mother would not hear the talk, and his guilt at enjoying it in her absence. Little suggested that the analyst had correctly interpreted not the transference but the countertransference. What had interfered with the giving of a more appropriate interpretation was the analyst's sense of guilt at his own feelings of jealousy.

Little writes: 'I think there is an attitude towards counter-transference, i.e. towards one's own feelings and ideas, that is really paranoid or phobic' (Little 1951: 33). Feelings associated with the transference and the countertransference are at the heart of the reasoning behind strict discipline over the boundaries of the psychotherapeutic relationship. By the same token they are important to the guilt felt by both patient and therapist when the boundary is crossed by a contact. There is a continual pressure against the basic rule of psychoanalytic psychotherapy: that thoughts and feelings will be put into words as freely as possible but not acted upon. It is this pressure that has generated the core concept of discipline in relation to contact outside the sessions; but guilt and anxiety play an important part in the severity that is often evident.

For the psychotherapist even casual and brief unplanned contacts can provoke strong anxiety reactions. The therapist faces an unpredictable encounter in what may be a difficult social context. Even if the psychotherapist is confident of his or her ability to manage the encounter she or he cannot be sure how the patient will react. It is not always easy to predict how the patient will deal with the encounter or what feelings the patient will have in response to the meeting. The therapist is also likely to experience anxieties of his or her own about discovery and exposure. These anxieties may be heightened by the specific circumstances of the contact. The story of the psychotherapist who was naked in the changing room of a swimming pool when she met her patient graphically illustrates this fear of exposure.

Even psychotherapists who maintain a theoretical opposition to the concept of the blank screen in practice seek to limit and regulate what they reveal of themselves. With unplanned contacts something is revealed of the therapist that is outside this contained framework. This can be difficult and uncomfortable for the psychotherapist and also for the patient. The patient may discover more than she or he wants to know or is ready to know. For the patient in psychotherapy, especially in the early stages of a psychotherapy, the psychotherapist is an object around whom there are many fantasies. The encounter with the subjectivity of this object is fraught with difficulties, and an unplanned encounter can greatly increase these problems.

Alternatively, or simultaneously, the patient may be extremely curious about the psychotherapist. The psychotherapist may experience this curiosity as highly unwelcome, intrusive and even persecutory. There is always the possibility that apparently unplanned contact was not in fact unplanned. The psychotherapist can be left wondering whether a contact was a chance event or not. This may be a source both of realistic concern and of anxiety to the therapist. It is not so unusual for patients to seek out opportunities to encounter their therapists outside the confines of the consulting room. There are cases of patients seeking contacts in a persistent way to the point of stalking their therapists.

However, the more widespread problem is the generation of high levels of persecutory anxiety in the psychotherapist. This can lead to the psychotherapist altering his or her routines and taking evasive actions. There may be a transfer to the psychotherapist through projective identification of the experience of fear of a persecutory object. This may be precisely what, consciously or unconsciously, the patient intended to achieve.

While concerned to maintain the boundaries to protect the patient and themselves from intrusion the psychotherapist may also fear that the maintenance of boundaries will be harsh or even sadistic. The therapist may fear that even if the adherence to strict boundaries is not heartless or sadistic it will seem so and that this will be intolerable. At one extreme of this set of difficulties are contacts that are linked to fears and threats of self-harm and suicide. Even in less extreme circumstances there is a tension. On the one hand the withholding of availability and responsiveness in the face of the patient's need may feel cruel. On the other hand the relaxation of the boundaries to offer the 'humane' gesture may be a false comfort and undermine the psychotherapeutic work.

In all of these cases there is a danger that the frame itself becomes a fetishistic object in a sado-masochistic drama. In this scenario the patient clings to a frustrating bad object while the frame itself becomes the focus of masochistic satisfactions. In these cases impingements and pressures on the frame can also form part of the sado-masochistic game. In this game the psychotherapist's refusals and interpretations are punishments that relieve an unconscious sense of guilt, while the patient senses his or her power in the reproduction of the drama.

Some therapists may be tempted to see such a patient as manipulative. This may be in some ways a realistic perception of the patient's behaviour, but the term is often used in a highly pejorative fashion and important understandings are lost. The aggressiveness of the term is a response to the painful feelings of loss of control and powerless anger that can be mobilized in the therapist. In these situations projective identification of these feelings into the psychotherapist is part of the unconscious communication. Like all such communication it is effective because it mobilizes the therapist's own responses. It is essential both to understand the countertransference reaction and to see beyond the manipulation to the chaotic attachment pattern. Feelings of shame and guilt belong to the sense of being unworthy of the attachment figure's attention. These may develop further around a sense of being an excessive burden, and again from feelings of rage linked to these painful experiences and the sense of abandonment.

Levels of understanding of the meaning of contacts

In considering how to develop a less anxiety driven view of unplanned contacts there is a need to consider each patient's growth and development and to distinguish between different levels of interaction. A schema of three possible levels is useful for thinking about this issue.

There is the social level at which it is recognized that the adult patient is exactly that – an adult. This is linked to a suggestion that there should be an ordinary human interaction and that analytic disciplines can appear, or be, inhuman. They can also appear, or be, lacking in respect. However, the existence of the therapeutic relationship necessarily means that the ordinary human interaction will not be ordinary. There is no simple answer to this. The interaction has to be seen against the background of the existence of the therapeutic relationship in a general sense and also of the specific conditions and dynamics prevailing in the therapy at the time.

The most clearly recognized of these dynamics and conditions relate to the level of early attachment patterns and the Oedipal currents that derive from them. This is the second level. It is the level at which the conflicts are most intense. For the patient the words offered by the therapist are often felt as hopelessly inadequate when compared to the need that is exposed within the therapeutic setting. The therapist can often experience a need to offer more, although it is possible to develop a defensive rigidity to exclude this feeling. Limentani, writing in 1966, was concerned that 'analysts are apt to forget that interpretations are meagre satisfactions to our patients who long for actions from them' (Limentani 1966: 279). For the patient the wish to find an action that it is hoped will meet, or at least mask, the need and the vulnerability is recurrent. This often finds an outlet in the form of an action around entering or leaving the consulting room. Such actions allow feelings to be expressed, but with the suggestion that this is to be excluded from the thought that is the work of the analysis.

Contacts beyond the consulting room allow more scope for such actions and also more unpredictability. They are regularly kept separate from the therapeutic process by the patient, and often by the therapist. For example the patient, seeing the therapist in the street, may not only avoid contact at the time but also not want to acknowledge that it has occurred in the session. Alternatively, the patient may seize on the opportunity to bring forward the possibility of a social relationship and seek to continue that into the sessions.

The psychotherapist has to respond rapidly in deciding whether and how to acknowledge the patient. The helpfulness of the psychotherapist's response will depend in part on the level of her or his awareness of phantasies that both the patient and the psychotherapist may have about what the psychotherapist means to the patient. The situation may well be one that challenges phantasies about the psychotherapist that the patient may have. These phantasies may in some cases form part of the psychotherapist's ego-ideal. These could include ideas about the psychotherapist's power, about his or her freedom from need, weakness, or fault, about her or his level of interest in the patient, or about the psychotherapist's desirability, and many others.

The situation may also be one that challenges the representation of the patient in psychotherapy. For example, an overtly angry aspect of the patient may be regularly given up on entering the therapy room. This may be to do with something that the patient wants to communicate to the therapist, or something the patient wants to avoid. There is a lot of potential for embarrassment and awkwardness.

In this sense unplanned contacts can bring forward the transference in ways that can threaten the therapy or can advance its work. This is linked to the third and often neglected level – that of post-Oedipal development. Jody Messler Davies has argued for a shift in understanding Oedipal dynamics away from the development of normative sexual patterns and resolution of Oedipal conflicts. She argues for a focus on certain critical developmental achievements. In particular she calls attention to

> the developmental shift from primarily incestuous object relations to primarily nonincestuous object relations, that is, the movement from oedipal to what I have termed postoedipal forms of relatedness in the evolution and integration of a richly textured, highly nuanced capacity for romantic passion and erotic sensual vitality.
>
> (Messler Davies 2003: 7)

Early attachment patterns and their Oedipal derivatives do not disappear but are increasingly absorbed into, and contained within, a developing capacity for intimate, inter-penetrative emotional experience. An insistence on too abrupt a confrontation with the underlying conflicts or too absolute a resolution of them may reinforce the very dissociative defences that the therapeutic process aims to overcome. An excessive emphasis on the inaccessibility of the therapist can lead to an abandonment of desire, with the retention of a suppressed idealization. It may also interfere with what is a developmental stage in its own right.

Attachment figures have an important part to play in supporting the practising and development of these more nuanced relationships, with their potential for intimacy and emotionally interpenetrating experience. It is important not to have a single idealized view of how the transference should be fostered and worked through in psychotherapy. Figures outside the therapy relationship may play a vital role for the patient in working through early attachment and Oedipal issues. The therapist may have a role in supporting the patient's capacity to develop relationships in which intense early feelings can be contained. The patient's practising in this field can be supported or crushed. Unplanned contacts can come to have a significant place in this process.

Bringing forward the transference

The level of understanding of greatest importance is the level of the transference. With the transferential mobilization of desires and conflicts even slight or indirect contacts with the patient outside the analytic setting can have a powerful effect upon the psychotherapeutic process. In the case of the Rat Man, published some five years after the case of Dora, Freud again discussed the impact of indirect contact. On this occasion the indirect contact takes place in the context of ongoing psychotherapeutic treatment. The patient met a woman in Freud's house and took her to be Freud's daughter. Freud described the patient as having developed symptoms because he could not face a conflict between his wish to marry a woman that he loved and his wish to please his father by marrying a wealthy woman who had been found for him. Freud writes:

> There came an obscure and difficult period in the treatment; eventually it turned out that he had once met a young girl on the stairs in my house and had on the spot promoted her into being my daughter. She had pleased him, and he pictured to himself that the only reason I was so kind and incredibly patient with him was that I wanted to have him for a son in law. At the same time he raised the wealth and position of my family to a level which agreed with the model he had in mind. But his undying love for his lady fought against the temptation. After we had gone through a series of the severest resistances and bitterest vituperations on his part, he could no longer remain blind to the overwhelming effect of the perfect analogy between the transference phantasy and the actual state of affairs in the past.

(Freud 2001: 199–200)

It is worth noting the obscurity of the treatment while the significant contact is not understood or not disclosed. It is important to look carefully for signs of what might have occurred if there is a feeling in the relationship that is in some way inexplicable. It may be that there has been some direct or indirect external connection. As in the case of the Rat Man, it may well be very difficult to bring this into the open. There is intense difficulty for the patient in considering the significance of something that touches so directly on the relationship with the psychotherapist and the patient's phantasies about it.

The strength of feelings evoked is very great precisely because the experience is not merely remembered but relived. Such experiences can be of great importance to bringing forward aspects of relationships that are not otherwise so accessible. Freud (1955: 199)writes: 'With the help of a transference phantasy, he experienced, as though it were new and belonged to the present, the very episode from the past which he had forgotten, or which had only passed through his mind unconsciously.'

Not only might the patient's phantasies about the psychotherapist be challenged by an encounter but the patient's phantasies about himself or herself in relation to the therapist may also be challenged. It was noted earlier that psychotherapists present themselves in certain ways to their patients and that this presentation can be disrupted by an unplanned contact. This is also true for the patient. A clinical illustration, a fiction drawn from experience, will illuminate this issue.

A man represented himself as lacking in the capacity to organize his life to achieve any satisfaction from it. He said that he could not remember clearly and that he had no idea what he wanted. He was in a depressive state, and the male therapist's countertransference was to feel intense pressure to do something about it. In particular the therapist felt the need to find a way towards the recovery of the capacity for memory and desire. This position was maintained in the consulting room, but two contacts outside raised new questions about this. On one occasion a crisis in relation to his boyfriend caused the patient to cancel a session. In the telephone call making the cancellation the patient found an opportunity to show his operative side that was evidently dealing with the crisis very effectively. On another occasion the therapist saw the man shopping for clothes with friends and seemingly enjoying himself.

This is not to suggest that the problem presented in the therapy room was unreal, or alternatively that the man shopping for clothes was a false self – although the patient himself felt both of these things were so at different times. Uncertainty over his sense of self, and a wish to protect a space in which to explore it, led to him subduing those aspects of himself that showed desire and capability. The difficulties created by the competitive and homoerotic elements of the therapy relationship added to this. The competitive aspects could sometimes be acknowledged, but with the help of a phantasy of the therapist's unalloyed heterosexuality the patient avoided any thought about sexual aspects of the therapy relationship.

The exploration of these problems brought forward feelings of anxiety, guilt and shame related to exposure of his desire to a destructive parental introject. This intrapsychic dynamic was already at work in the therapy relationship and developing as an interpersonal dynamic. The unplanned contacts brought it forward. A strong attachment was essential for working this through to be possible. Equally, working it through served to strengthen the attachment. Creating the attachment and working through the conflicts are two sides of the same coin. How such episodes are explored has to be considered in the light of the creation of the attachment as well as the deepening of the transference and the creation of insight. Without the attachment the insight will often become persecutory and the intense feelings associated with the transference will be experienced as intolerably dangerous.

The timing and manner of the exploration of contacts outside the therapy setting is therefore crucial. In the above case the contacts created the possibility for aspects of the patient to enter the therapy relationship. To actually bring them in without denying the patient's experience as represented in the therapy relationship is a very delicate matter. The patient can easily find him/herself in a position of denying the significance of the events or producing a flight into health: in either case dissociating the different elements of his or her experience. Great care is needed when seeking to overcome these dissociative defences, while recognizing that this is a key aim of psychotherapy.

The countertransference and the understanding of the contact

From the point of view of the countertransference both episodes allow for the representation of the therapy relationship in a less compelling light. The contacts at least qualified two alternative phantasies: the dream of being able to reawaken the internal life on the one hand and the nightmare of failing and being useless on the other. This may be helpful, but the therapist too can welcome the chance to escape the pressures of the transference and move to respond to the interchanges on the level of casual sociability. The need to withstand this pressure and the contingent nature of the therapist's response is illuminated by another illustration.

A therapist met a patient on two occasions in the street. The two occasions were separated by about two years. The first meeting was early in the therapy and the patient was diffident. The therapist was only mildly put out. She greeted him, and in the subsequent therapy session they discussed his surprise at the meeting. She noted his reaction to being so forcibly reminded that she did go out of her therapy room and did have a life of her own beyond being his psychotherapist. In some ways this may have been a premature encounter with the subjectivity of the object. The discovery that mother has a life of her own, relived in the transference, was abruptly brought forward.

This was no doubt a factor, but only one factor, in the development of the negative transference which emerged strongly in the therapy. A broader picture of loss, frustration and anger coloured the therapy relationship. However, some progress was made in mourning the lost, idealized attachment figure of infancy. The second meeting in the street was very different. On this occasion he greeted her in a very determined and ostentatiously cheerful way. The therapist recoiled from this and ignored him. What she felt at the time was something more than being mildly put out. It was annoyance.

What she felt was a negative reaction to an unwanted attempt at intimacy that had an edge of aggression and was not contained within the therapeutic setting. Reflecting on this as she walked away from the encounter she thought that what was happening was that the determined greeting, by seeking a social contact, was also an effort to escape from the reality of the loss as it was experienced in the transference situation. She decided to focus on these issues and was reluctant to discuss the encounter.

The greeting was a compromise formation. It contained some real feeling, it contained some of the aggression, but was also a denial of the tender and erotic feelings that were present in the therapy relationship. The patient's experience of the encounter was of a rebuff and a rejection. He also experienced the therapist as determined to be in control of their transactions. This latter point is important. It may be evident to the therapist that she or he is maintaining boundaries for the benefit of the patient, but this is not necessarily evident to the patient. The patient may well experience the psychotherapist as behaving in a controlling way for his or her own reasons. Therapies can reach an impasse over conflicts of this kind. The defensive use of the blank screen can make the problems worse. The therapist has to be fully present with integrity to work these problems through.

In this case both the attachment and the understanding of the psycho-therapeutic process had developed to the point where the relationship could survive the patient's experience of rejection, and to some extent it was possible to work this through. However, the encounter reproduced an experience that losses are absolute and crushed the practising associated with the development of a post-Oedipal interpersonal world. This practising would more helpfully have been supported. This impulse to crush this development, and to reproduce in the next generation the experience of the death of desire, was also part of the counter-transference.

The question of how to bring forward the possible significance of a chance meeting, or indeed to refer to it having happened at all, is a difficult one. If it is brought forward too soon the effect of the intrusion can be increased and the space for its meaning to the patient closed off. If it is left too long it can become the starting point for further acting out or it can be overlaid with other events and developments. It is part of the skill of the psychotherapist to sense when it is right to wait and when to bring it forward. If this judgement is reasonably successful not only can problems be averted but real gains can be made.

What might be gained by learning from experience

Much of this chapter has focused on difficulties associated with unplanned contacts with the patient. Life is full of unplanned experience, and this last illustration shows how valuable unplanned experiences can sometimes be. In this story the fact that the psychotherapist refrained from any reference to the meeting for a short period created a space into which came a dream.

Passing a patient in the street, the woman had not greeted the psychotherapist but had talked animatedly, and it seemed to the therapist determinedly, to the man she was with. This man, the therapist deduced, was her partner; this was later confirmed. She had come to therapy struggling with a relationship with a separated married man who kept her waiting and let her down until she felt distraught and humiliated. She had had many brief sexual relationships and affairs and felt at best dissatisfied and at worst that she was abusing herself and allowing others to abuse her. Behind such feelings lay parental imagos of a depressed mother who she described as useless and insignificant and a father who was experienced as demanding and powerful.

At the time of the meeting she had broken off the relationship that she was in at the start of the therapy. She had planned to have a period of independence. In the event she had quite quickly formed a new relationship which she liked and felt relaxed in, but she worried that it was dull. This man was the partner that she was with in the street.

In the dream she was in a car chase; she was not sure who was chasing her. She entered a house and the room turned into a garden in which she was approaching a man standing by a lake. She was not sure but she thought this was the boyfriend she was with at the start of the therapy, although it might have been a former boss because he had silver-grey hair as that man had done. There was something erotic between her and this man but she was anxious about her new partner who was sitting on a bench watching her. Her partner on the bench was wearing a grey suit, which was not like him. The grey of the suit reminded her of the therapy room. Thinking about the theme of grey she joked: 'I have such black-and-white thinking and you are all shades of grey.'

The dream seemed to be an attempt to think about the possibilities that had been warded off at the meeting in the street by the intense conversation with her partner. Her joke caught the progress that the dream had made and shows the possibility of a link between the excitement associated with the old boyfriend and the depressive feelings associated with the new one. She was quite proud of her vivid black-and-white world and was suggesting that the therapist's shades of grey were dull by comparison, as well as welcome.

The making of these links relied on the containment in the therapy. The meeting outside the therapy setting was a demand for work that was undertaken in the dream. She was moved to locate the therapist more specifically in her internal world as a result of the encounter and see her relationships from this third position. She had seen the therapist out of the corner of her eye and was pleased that he had seen her but not interfered. Acknowledgement in this setting would have been an intrusion. In some ways she was pleased to show off the progress she had made in moving beyond her insecure attachment patterns and her Oedipal conflicts into a more nuanced interpersonal relationship.

Conclusion

This chapter has started by emphasizing the importance of the psycho-therapeutic frame and the seriousness of the difficulties that are associated with extensive unplanned contact with the patient. A key theme in considering these issues is guilt and anxiety in the countertransference. These feelings of guilt and anxiety can lead to misjudged responses to the patient, they can interfere with the psychotherapist's capacity to reflect on his or her experience, and they can produce excessively harsh judgements, which make it difficult to acknowledge where mistakes have been made.

The chapter has looked at the sensitivity of the therapeutic process to even slight and indirect unplanned contacts. These contacts can be revealing, awkward and comical, but they can have a powerful impact on the development of the therapy. There are no simple answers to the difficult questions that arise around managing unplanned contact when they occur. The essence of the position recommended in this chapter is a sensitive adherence to the importance of the frame based on a profound understanding of the transference and the countertransference dynamics of the particular psychotherapeutic relationship at its particular point of development.

References

Freud, S. (1955) *Standard Edition of the Complete Psychological Works of Sigmund Freud* vol. 10 (ed. James Strachey in collaboration with Anna Freud, assisted by Alix Strachey and Alan Tyson), London: The Hogarth Press.

Freud, S. and Jones, E. (1993) *Complete Correspondence of Sigmund Freud and Ernest Jones*, ed. R. Andrew Paskauskas, Cambridge, Mass.: The Belknap Press for Harvard University Press

Limentani, A. (1966) 'A re-evaluation of acting out in relation to working through', *International Journal of Psychoanalysis* 47: 274–82.

Little, M. (1951) 'Counter-transference and the patient's response to it', *International Journal of Psychoanalysis* 32: 32–40.

Messler Davies, J. (2003) 'Falling in love with love: oedipal and postoedipal manifestations of idealization, mourning, and erotic masochism', *Psychoanalytic Dialogues* 13(1): 1–27.

Racker, H. (1953) 'A contribution to the problem of the counter-transference', *International Journal of Psychoanalysis* 34: 313–24.

Chapter 7

Broken boundaries

Perverting the therapeutic frame

Paola F. Valerio

It is better not to touch our idols; the gilt comes off on our hands.
Gustave Flaubert, *Madame Bovary*

Alchemy however is a chaste prostitute, who has many lovers but dis-
appoints all and grants her favors to none. She transforms the haughty
into fools, the rich into paupers, the philosophers into dolts, and the
deceived into loquacious deceivers . . .
Trithemius, *Annalium Hirsaugensium*

Boundaries get broken all the time in psychotherapy. Boundaries between
analyst and patient, supervisor and trainee, and of course psychotherapist
as teacher and student. All psychotherapists know this; few of us admit
it or talk about it. If we do admit to boundary transgressions then we are
selective about whom we tell. In fact, our decision about just whom
we do tell about our lapses can be therapeutically illuminating. Yet we
hold onto this mythology in psychotherapy, and particularly among
analytically trained therapists, that somehow we are immune from such
transgressions in the therapeutic frame. Yes, we admit some therapists
act out shamelessly, but fortunately they are few. They probably have
not been properly analysed, as if somehow the requirement for four or
five times a week analysis over many years secures us of our ordinary
human feeling; of lust and greed and envy, and so forth. Or alternatively,
we reason, at least our own analysis makes us so aware of our weaknesses
and limitations that we would never be drawn in to act upon them, and
certainly not to the detriment of our patients. This of course is not just
self-deluding – one might be tempted to say that it is a form of madness.
Furthermore, it prevents us from addressing the importance of owning
at least minor violations of the frame and recognizing their therapeutic
value and potential richness. Of course, I am not speaking about major

violations of a sexual nature, or violations made consciously or indeed unconsciously for the therapist's sole benefit. However, those minor transgressions, the acting-out that we fall into which is inevitable, tell us a great deal about the unconscious marriage between therapist and patient. If we do not own our transgressions, and particularly our negative countertransference responses, then we lose an opportunity to learn from them and we may inadvertently also interfere with the therapeutic alliance. As Binder and Strupp (1997) suggest, the ability of therapists to establish and maintain a good therapeutic alliance has been greatly overestimated:

> The reason for this is the enormous difficulty that human beings have in dealing with interpersonal conflict in which they are participants. Evidence for the ways in which therapists struggle with negative therapeutic processes – hostile interchanges between patients and therapists is traced throughout the psychotherapy research literature. It appears that negative processes are a major obstacle to successful treatment, and that its pervasiveness has been underestimated.
>
> (Binder and Strupp 1997: 1)

The therapeutic frame is often described as the ground rules of therapy. A fundamental function of the therapeutic frame is held to be the protection of the therapeutic process from the intrusion of elements antithetical to the best interest of the patient and detrimental to therapeutic outcome. Some therapists, particularly newly qualified ones, might feel that technical purity in terms of rigidly enforcing boundaries will ensure the success of the therapy. Yet dogmatic interpretation of the frame promotes conformity rather than growth and constricts the therapist's ability to be appropriately responsive to the patient.

Perhaps this conformity protects the therapist rather than the patient. Not that protection of the therapist is a bad or anti-therapeutic matter. Nevertheless, if we have to conceal from colleagues our transgressions or minor acting-out, then surely conformity functions rather like a tyrannical superego, which promotes shame and secrecy in the therapist. At a peer supervision group recently I admitted to colleagues that I had forgotten that I was seeing a patient for an early morning appointment and had answered the door in my dressing gown. This particular patient had been developing erotic fantasies about me, which he had been unable to talk about, as well as a fear of being forgotten about by me and of not being important. Thus, amazingly, I had not only forgotten about him but also revealed myself semi-clad. I felt that I had no choice but to send him home. My acting out of his very worst fear promoted a lively session when we next met and a healthy exchange, which was very therapeutic for my patient, despite, or rather because of my boundary violation. However, what I discovered in my peer group when I owned up to my transgression was that several of my colleagues had done pretty much the same thing at one time or another.

In my experience, both as a therapist and as a supervisor of trainees, I have been alerted to the difficulty in maintaining boundaries or staying within the therapeutic frame with borderline and perverse patients. Many of these patients are traumatized, who as we know routinely push at the edges. By their very nature, borderline patients are boundary breakers. Mythology has it that many borderline patients are very creative individuals. One finding, which seems as well established, as any in this area, is that creative individuals tend to be more independent-minded. They conform less to social expectation and pressures, rebel against authority and are much less likely to suppress negative personality traits. They can be refreshingly honest. Is there room then, for the creative therapist who is less conforming but not necessary less boundaried? Many therapists are creative and they are indeed boundary breakers of one sort or another, but this is not always anti-therapeutic. I would suggest that more research is needed in this area to produce less shame, and promote dialogue that is more open and which might then reveal a rich, albeit anecdotal, source of material for our profession.

In the rest of this chapter I would like to focus on the difficulty in maintaining boundaries with certain patients, particularly those who present with perverse character structure, about whom several theoreticians (Glasser 1979; Khan 1979; McDougall 1985; Stoller 1974; Welldon 1988) have written at length. However, this is often written about as if the analyst retains conscious awareness and complete control within the therapeutic frame, so we tend to hear less about therapist violations. Yet as they illustrate, in order to master the traumatic experience such patients will often reverse the abusive victim/perpetrator constellation seeking triumph over the therapist in the hostile act (Stoller 1974). We, as therapists, are routinely forced into eroticized, collusive and hostile counter-alliances (Luca 2003). I will illustrate this dynamic below with reference to my work with two perverse young men, including my instances of boundary violation, and I will discuss whether this was therapeutic or synchronistic in any sense.

I was forced into recognition and a fuller experience of this mechanism by several films that I have seen recently, and which graphically illustrate this process. The film *La Pianiste* ('The Piano Teacher') by Michael Haneke is the story of a perverse young woman. Her history fits the classical one that is often attributed to perverse character development, particularly core-complex development (Glasser 1979). The scenario incorporates an intrusive mother who lives through her daughter in both the sense of expecting her to fulfil her ambitions as well as being envious and attacking of her achievements, and an absent father – or at least so we assume from the film.

The perverse individual longs for closeness, yet experiences profound anxiety about engulfment and annihilation when intimacy and closeness with the desired object (usually mother substitute) becomes a real option. As Glasser describes it:

> In the perversions then, the ego attempts to resolve the vicious circle of the core complex and the attendant conflicts and dangers by the widespread use of sexualization. Aggression is converted into sadism. The immediate consequence of this is the preservation of the mother, who is no longer threatened by total destruction, and the ensuring of the viability of the relationship to her. The intention to destroy is converted into a wish to hurt and control.
>
> (Glasser 1979: 288)

The wish to be rid of the sexualized anxiety that contains unconscious hatred of the object, or part-object, draws the individual into a perverse act, which has often been referred to as 'making hate' not love.

From a clinical standpoint, most perversions are seen as a fragility or as a defence of the self, while at the same time conjuring up images of shame and of being forbidden or secret, both in the minds of the victim and of anyone else who is privy to the secret. It is the Shadow that outrages or provokes moral responses – some might say panic – in others. We are first aware of the piano teacher's perversion when she is seen visiting sex shops. As she watches the pornographic film, we see her removing a tissue from the wastebasket, which previous male customers have been using to clean up after masturbating to these images. She views the hard-porn films while holding and smelling this disregarded and soiled tissue. The film further develops her perversion through her voyeuristic behaviour in a drive-in cinema where she is caught by two youths she has been spying on while they 'make out'. She is caught urinating outside their car in response to her excitement. We are invited into her bathroom where we see her attack on herself, her perversion turned inwards attacking her own body, as Welldon (1988) has written extensively about. She cuts her vagina, her womanhood; an identification with the mother.

When a young pupil falls in love with her, although she is clearly attracted to him, she becomes afraid of the possible intimacy he offers. She conjures up a long list of sadistic acts she asks him to perform upon her, and presents these to him. She rejects his attempts at lovemaking, but silently masturbates him while refusing him eye contact. That would be too intimate. She puts the object, 'the penis', between them and she takes control. In turn, she is dehumanized. The way in which this sexual encounter is filmed is interesting. The camera shoots this scene, which happens in the toilets, from behind. We do not see all of the action, but see the face of the young student who is being masturbated. We are forced in an intrusive way into his experience and we are prevented from seeing him as a whole person or to imagine the couple in a close relationship. We, the audience, are fetishized and simultaneously turned into voyeurs colluding in the sexual excitement of the scene. Much of this filming is done offset, so we hear voices of characters that we cannot see, or only view parts of them, which underlies this perverse or voyeuristic theme.

Two other films – *The Piano*, which is directed by Jane Campion, and more recently, *Secretary* – are illustrative of the processes of boundary violation and their consequences for relating. *The Piano* opens with Michael Nyman's haunting music, and we are told in a child's voice, the voice we later learn is that of the main protagonist, Ada (Holly Hunter): 'I have not spoken since I was six years old, Lord knows why – not even me.' We later learn or suspect that this was the result of a broken heart. In *Secretary* the female lead, who also self-mutilates, still seems to be deeply affected by the trauma of her parent's fraught relationship and her father's alcoholism. In the case of *The Piano*, Ada is drawn into a perverse relationship with Baines (Harvey Keitel), but when he falls in love with her, perhaps through the impact of her piano-playing, he cannot maintain this perverse liaison. The arrangement 'is turning you into a whore and me wretched'. In *Secretary*, when Lee (Maggie Gyllenhaal) 'glimpses' her boss, thereby recognizing his vulnerable side and hence their similarities, sadist is also masochist, the boss (James Spader) who by now has preyed on her vulnerability and wholly perverted the relationship, becomes afraid and withdraws. The point of the perversion is distance not closeness, not intimacy, but power and control. At the point when Ada realizes she shares the feelings for her lover, her husband mutilates her trying to control what he cannot have. When the boss feels 'glimpsed' by the secretary, who falls in love with him, he gets rid of her, he sacks her.

If perversion is all about avoiding relating, about fear of intimacy, about turning the other person into an object and perhaps even a fetish

(Stoller 1986), how does this fare for the therapeutic relationship where the point, as well as the means of the contract, is all about relating, which is deeply intimate and must be so if it is to be effective?

I was seeing a young man, whom I have written about elsewhere (Valerio 2002), who came to me because of feelings of inadequacy and problems with his girlfriend. He was partially sighted so I expected to feel sympathetic towards him, but something never quite fitted and, indeed, I felt hostile towards him. He feared intimacy and related very much from a core-complex structure much as I have already alluded to. However, I failed to understand my dislike or suspicion of him except in so far as I felt there must be something in him that was hidden, some Shadow material we needed to explore. One day in broad daylight at about 11 a.m. three police officers burst into my consulting room – a neighbour, having seen him arrive and thinking he looked shifty, had called the police. I was immediately, through this synchronistic event, able to raise my own feelings of suspicion with this patient, which led to a productive exchange and in later sessions brought to light much Shadow material that he needed to integrate; some of this was negative, but there were also positive qualities of which he had remained 'psychologically blind'.

Another male patient whom I saw as part of my work as an NHS psychotherapist came to mind when I started writing this chapter. He is a 25-year-old unmarried man, without children, very attractive, and a painter. When I first met him I thought of a character in a D.H. Lawrence novel, rugged but handsome, who earned a living through his craft. He was assessed in the department by a colleague, who described him as narcissistic and reluctant to talk about anyone other than himself. He described his main problem as an obsession with horses, in particular penetrating a horse. He had had this fantasy since he was an adolescent and had first seen a poster of a girl who was naked to the waist, standing next to a horse. This started a compulsive and obsessive series of fantasies in his mind, which eventually led to him going to the stable and masturbating around the horses. The youngest of five boys, he had been brought up by a narcissistic mother and an absent father. His mother had wanted a girl and had therefore brought him up as one. He experienced a great deal of teasing in school and was called gay, although he is not aware of any homosexual feelings. He was caught masturbating by his mother at around the age of 12 and he informed me that he was made to feel disgusting by her. He had sexual relationships with women, but put a distance between himself and his girlfriends by fantasizing about penetration of a horse during intercourse. Thus, he was able to avoid true intimacy and loss of control.

He soon began to fetishize the therapy. He began to fantasize about my ankles and shoes, which he would describe in graphic detail, while I in turn felt bored and hostile towards him. Stoller (1986) talks about the importance in treating the script like any other material in analysis. We came to see that his intercourse with the horse, a powerful phallic symbol, was a way of trying to usurp it of its male power in order to repair his own broken sense of masculinity.

I found it very hard to be in the room with him and would retaliate by switching off from him when he talked about his sexual fantasies. I shamefully admit to ending a few sessions a few minutes early when it became unbearable (although consciously I had just got mixed up over when he started his session), and he noticed this. He forced me into a collusive sadistic pattern and then took pleasure from it and of his control over me. My violation of the time boundary was an attempt to reassert myself. At the same time I refused to engage with him when he tried to pervert the transference by his obsession with my body, which felt like a violation. This felt technically correct because it seemed more important to look at his vulnerability underlining his need to control me. One clear sign of perverse rather than erotic transference to the therapist is the therapist's countertransference response of hostility or boredom precisely because it is the opposite of erotic relating, of *eros* where love may be involved. It is about non-relating and is always hostile. I failed him by my boundary violation, but it was not a bad therapeutic outcome because it fostered a deeper connection between us. In her paper, Welldon (1996) refers to Carol Gilligan (1982), who supports her clinical findings. Gilligan studied normal children at different stages of development. In brief, she concluded that male gender identity is threatened by intimacy since masculinity is defined through separation from the mother, whereas female gender identity is threatened by separation since femininity is defined through attachment. As Welldon continues, when seriously threatened, or even damaged in the sense of gender identity, the man needs to be reassured in his own internal world; he needs not only to separate from his mother but also to make her the object of his eroticized hatred. This he will do through symbolism, splitting or projecting and denial. Nothing in the scenario should involve any sense of intimacy. The opposite is required: the further, more alien and the less attached the part-object, the more suitable it will be as a target for his perversion. While women interject and attack their own bodies, for both sexes the attacked object remains the female body and its maternal attributes. The father plays a decisive role in offering a process of triangulation. Often this fails due to his absence or collusion in a malignant bond with the mother against the children.

Stoller (1974: 358) also supports this view: 'Developing indissoluble links with mother's femaleness and femininity in the normal mother–infant symbiosis can only augment a girl's identity', while for a boy the whole process of becoming masculine is endangered by the primary, profound, primal oneness with the mother. Shakespeare has written much about this fear of women, of the man's struggle to denigrate or distance himself from his feminine side in order to remain manly. For example, we are aware that Lear is in a collusive and perverse relationship with his daughters. When they disappoint him, his vulnerability terrifies him. Nevertheless, in the last analysis he refuses to acquiesce in his vulnerability; he refuses to weep. Now hatred comes upon him for his daughters. If Lear had wept (perhaps if he had had the benefit of a court analyst), he would have achieved the integration that he so desperately needed to transcend his disappointment and relinquish his control. The capacity to 'see feelingly' is the play's redemptive idea:

> You see me here, you Gods, a poor old man,
> As full of grief as age, wretched in both.
> If it be you that stirs these daughters' hearts
> Against their father, fool me not so much
> To bear it tamely. Touch me with noble anger,
> And let not women's weapons, water-drops
> Stain my man's cheeks! No, you unnatural hags,
> I will have such revenges on you both
> That all the world shall – I will do such things –
> What they are, yet I know not; but they shall be
> The terrors of the earth. You think I'll weep.
> No, I'll not weep; I have full cause of weeping,
> But this heart shall break into a hundred thousand flaws.
> Or ere I'll weep.
>
> (*King Lear* II. iv. 275–89)

Do we as therapists also feel such fear of our own emotions or shame about our vulnerability? While I shamefully admit to my boundary transgressions, I report them here because I am confident that I am not so unusual. As Binder and Strupp have written:

> according to the clinical/theoretical literature the therapist's role in producing and maintaining the therapeutic alliance is to offer an empathic, respectful, warm and interested attitude towards the patient. The inability of the therapist to maintain this attitude is seen

as a deficiency in either the therapist or the patient. However research over the past few years has indicated the recurrent ruptures . . . It is our belief that the ability of therapists to implement these strategies has been greatly overestimated.

(Binder and Strupp 1997: 123)

They conclude:

As therapists we have not adequately faced up to the negative reactions engendered in us by patients who bring to our offices the products of their unhappy life experiences . . . thus, major deterrents to the foundation of a good working alliance are not only the patient's characterological distortions and maladaptive defences but – at least equally important – the therapist's personal reactions. Traditionally these reactions have been considered under the heading of counter-transference. It is becoming increasingly clear however that this conception is too narrow. The plain fact is that any therapist – indeed any human being – cannot remain immune from negative reactions to the suppressed and repressed rage regularly encountered in patients with moderate to severe disturbances.

(Binder and Strupp 1997: 125)

In our study, which they inform us relates to highly experienced, professional therapists, they continue: 'we failed to encounter a single instance in which a difficult patient's hostility and negativism were successfully confronted or resolved. Therapists' negative responses to difficult patients are far more common and far more intractable than has been generally recognized' (Strupp, 1980: 95, quoted in Binder and Strupp 1997: 126).

I am not aware of the research base in the sense of which therapists were part of their sample. It is possible that they have underestimated the capacity of therapists to withstand attacks from patients without retaliation. Nevertheless, we do retaliate at least some of the time. Boundary transgressions do occur – whether in unconscious acting-out by therapists, or more simply, hostile countertransference feelings which are not adequately processed and reflected upon before they are shared with the client. Can we avoid unproductive anxieties about 'thought-crime' and use our maturity and humanity to guide our thoughts and feelings into a mutually safe place? In addition, if the therapist commits a minor transgression, whether by unconscious acting-out or by sheer accident, can she invest this back into the therapeutic alliance? By creating a culture of openness, in which we can talk about our transgressions, we enable our supervisees and students to learn in a more open environment.

The therapeutic frame is essential as an ideal model, and effective therapeutic work requires that treatment boundaries exist. But when we do transgress boundaries, which we must from time to time, and particularly as I have suggested with certain patients, especially those with a borderline or perverse character structure, we need to be able to use the experience creatively without shame.

Judith Hubback (1988), in writing about transference and countertransference, describes an interaction with a patient in which he is recounting a dramatic and painful story to her; but she had heard it often and realized that she was feeling increasingly bored. His stories anaesthetized her and her attempts to interpret his repetitions of these painful stories were to no avail. 'The next time he speculated about whether or not I was bored', she answered, 'Yes' and adds, 'that was more helpful than interpreting had been' (Hubback 1988: 34). Now I am sure this was not the end of the discussion and I am not suggesting for a minute that we simply share all our negative countertransference feelings and thoughts with patients without reflection. Perhaps, as Hubback may be trying to suggest, sometimes it is simply discourteous and antitherapeutic not too.

From a Jungian perspective we are inevitably drawn into unconscious collusion with our patients. For Jung, analysis occurred through mutual attentiveness to multiple simultaneous fields, as each person is both an individual and part of the whole. Jung saw the intrapsychic and analytic fields as personal and non-personal, unique but also collective and archetypal. Thus, Jung talked about the transference and countertransference processes in therapy as a mutual alchemical event leading to transformation of both parties. He spoke of a *telos* that moves the interaction beyond simple fusion towards a specific type of interaction, which he called the *coniunctio*. Often referred to as the marriage of opposites, it is depicted through the alchemical pictures from the *Rosarium philosophorum* showing the mating of king and queen (Jung 1955). More recently therapists have begun to talk about the way in which the *coniunctio* can in fact be experienced in a tangible 'here and now' manner, as a truly interpersonal event, and which reflects events not so much *within* but *between* the self and another. Often referred to as an intersubjective field, attempts have been made to research this encounter as an extreme form of empathy, perhaps even a kind of telepathy, which occurs between individuals also outside of the analytic setting (Reed 1996). To meet the challenge of the *coniunctio* we need to develop the imagination, which is the capacity, as Blake said, to 'see with, not thro', the eye'. In analysis, we are called upon to develop this capacity in relation to another person in a creative manner, not in a repressed or defensive one.

Hermes was the messenger of the gods, the guide of souls to the underworld and of travellers. Hermes has been considered the father of alchemy, that arcane science that focused on trying to turn base metal into gold, and serves also as the primary metaphor for the spiritual quest that the alchemist undertakes to find: the meaning of gold in experience. Hermes opens up moments of discovery and synchronistic events – those *coincidences that turn out to be meaningful, unforeseen accidental happenings*. This spirit of adventure and quest for *coniunctio*, along with its unsettling challenges to the framework, should be valued at least as much as our conformity or adherence to boundaries in the therapeutic process.

References

Binder, J.L. and Strupp, H.H. (1997) '"Negative process": a recurrently discovered and underestimated facet of therapeutic process and outcome in the individual psychotherapy of adults', *Clinical Psychology: Science and Practice* 42(2): 121–39.

Gilligan, C. (1982) *In a Different Voice*, Cambridge, Mass.: Harvard University Press.

Glasser, M. (1979) 'Some aspects of the role of aggression in the perversions', in I. Rosen (ed.) *Pathology and Treatment of Sexual Deviation* (2nd edn), London: Oxford University Press.

Hubback, J. (1988) *People who do things to each other: Essays in Analytical Psychology*, New York: Chiron Publications.

Jung, C.G. (1973) *Mysterium Coniunctionis*, in *Complete Works*, vol. 14, first edition, London: Routledge & Kegan Paul.

Khan, M.R. (1979) *Alienations in Perversions*, London: Karnac.

Luca, M. (2003) 'Containment of the sexualized and erotized transference', *Journal of Clinical Psychoanalysis* 11: 643–68.

McDougall, J. (1985) *Theatres of the Mind*, New York: Basic Books.

Reed, H. (1996) 'Close encounters in the liminal zone: experiments in imaginal communication', *Journal of Analytical Psychology* 41(1): 165–323.

Stoller, R. (1974) '"Facts and fancies": an examination of Freud's concept of bisexuality', in J. Strouse (ed.) *Women and Analysis: Dialogues on Psychoanalytic Views of Femininity*, New York: Viking Penguin.

Stoller, R. (1975) *Perversion. The Erotic Form of Hatred*, New York: Pantheon.

Stoller, R. (1986) *Sexual Excitement: Dynamics of Erotic Life*, London: Maresfield Library.

Valerio, P.F. (2002) 'Love and hate – a fusion of opposites: a window to the soul', in *Love and Hate in the Transference*, D. Mann (ed.) London: Routledge

Welldon, E. (1988) *Mother, Madonna, Whore: The Idealisation and Denigration of Motherhood*, London: Free Association Books.

Welldon, E. (1996) 'Perversions in men and women', *British Journal of Psychotherapy* 12(4): 480–86.

Chapter 8

Challenging therapy

An existential perspective on the frame

Paul Smith-Pickard

The title of this chapter is intentionally ambiguous, reflecting both a concern with therapeutic practice that is challenging and a practice that challenges some traditional images of therapy. It is based upon the experience of managing and supervising a therapeutic frame in a specific setting within acute healthcare – a setting where it is impossible to apply many of the traditionally accepted conditions for psychotherapy. It is also a personal reflection on the boundary limits of psychotherapy and even the nature of psychotherapy itself.

I have chosen to set this reflection against a traditional or stereotypical image of therapy that may be accused of being a caricature. If it is a caricature, then it is one that I have assimilated through being engaged in the world of psychotherapy, and is therefore an image worthy of interrogation. In addition to raising questions about traditional notions of a therapeutic frame I will also be introducing two new images that have emerged out of my work in the hospital. I call these images *embedded supervision* and an *extemporaneous frame*. Whilst these images are anchored in a specific setting, they carry with them various ideas that could possibly be translated into other settings, and thereby challenge our understanding of a therapeutic frame and how supervision may be viewed in relation to it.

Sedimented images of common sense

I recognize that I have an established image of supervision, and of a therapeutic frame. It is interesting for me to reflect both upon how I arrived at these images and how they influence me as a therapist and as a supervisor. An immediate reflection is that these images have a sense of being safe, consistent and conservative. They mirror each other and highlight the importance of clear communicable secure boundaries. They provide a sort of benchmark of ethical professional practice that can unquestionably call itself psychotherapy. This stereotypical image of supervision is one that is primarily information based; a remote echo of what has previously taken place in the encounter between therapist and client. Here the imparted information is then deconstructed and hypotheses are formed from a shared theoretical perspective. As images they are distinct and different, but they remind me of Russian dolls bearing the same pattern and neatly fitting one inside the other. The client is probably the smallest doll, encapsulated by the therapist doll, the session doll, the setting, the theory and the supervision dolls. The dolls represent a paradoxical image of autonomy and sameness, concerned with the preservation of identity and the familiar. I can easily recognize the psychodynamic pedigree of these images, which is in itself interesting as my own therapeutic practice is located within an existential paradigm. In my practice I have, on occasions, frequently operated a somewhat more flexible and inconsistent approach to the frame (Smith-Pickard 2001), but it has always been against the backdrop of the awareness of this traditional frame.

'To us', says W.H. Auden, in a poem about Freud, 'he is no more a person now but a whole climate of opinion'. If this is so, we might ask ourselves if this 'climate of opinion' has produced a consensual image of the frame, reflecting an unquestioned analytic hegemony of the spatial, temporal conditions for therapy and supervision. Despite his non-conformity, R.D. Laing subscribes to this image when he states that '[t]he irreducible elements of psychotherapy are a therapist, a patient, and a regular and reliable time and place' (Laing 1990: 39). Within the setting of acute healthcare, the boundaries of the therapeutic frame are being constantly challenged and reformulated by contingency. The certainty of a secure frame frequently disappears, and often only the first two of Laing's elements are irreducible. One of my supervisees describes it in the following way:

> The richest experience is the challenge to the frame and traditional boundaries . . . being on the back foot and having to take stock in the moment, reviewing what I am doing as I do it. It's not about certainty and doing things the 'right way' – it's about the uncertainty of relationship. It's stimulating. There are some boundaries worth sticking to and others to be questioned.

Of course, the question that is left unanswered here is: which boundaries are worth sticking to? This question is often a fundamental issue in both our client work and in supervision and becomes the basis for the extemporaneous frame.

Ethics and contingency

I work with a team that includes students on clinical placement, providing counselling and psychotherapy throughout a large hospital to in-patients, outpatients, and their relations. Some of the work has a traditional format, with therapy sessions in a designated counselling room on a regular weekly basis. Other work can take place on open wards at a patient's bed-side. It is this experience of working on the wards with acute illness that provides the greatest challenge to the therapeutic frame. In the absence of a regular and reliable time and place we have come to question our practice as therapists, and explore new possibilities for practising psychotherapy outside the traditional confines of a consulting room and a conventional frame. For example, I remember kneeling before a patient in a high dependency unit. She was sitting in a chair next to her bed following recent heart surgery. There was a level of commotion around us as nurses dealt with the urgent needs of another patient. She had a number of tubes going in and out of her body and was too weak to raise her head. As I knelt before her so that she could see my face I thought for a fleeting moment of the times I had discussed with counselling students the way one might sit, the angle of chairs, and the distance between them. Convention and protocol suddenly appeared absurd in the face of this patient's need. What was her need? A large part of her need was to be offered a style of encounter that would create a space for her to become a client with existential issues, rather than a patient with a medical condition. The style of encounter here is ethical rather than theoretical, in keeping with Levinas's view of the face-to-face encounter. The Other's face presents me with a moral summons to my responsibility and obligation to the welfare of the other. 'The face', he says, 'opens the primordial discourse whose first word is obligation, which no "interiority" permits avoiding' (Levinas 2002: 520).

Reflection on the variety of my own experiences, and some preliminary research into the experience of the placement counsellors, has been the basis for the two new images that I have referred to as *embedded supervision* and the *extemporaneous frame*. These images do not provide a pre-existing theoretical and concrete framework for conceptualizing and defining practice. They are founded in a phenomenological experience of practice, leading to a style of supervision and frame management that is intersubjective and interexperiential, rather than individualistic. Supervision frequently becomes a search and research into the very nature of therapeutic practice.

Embedded supervision

The term 'embedded supervision' refers to a style of supervision where both supervisor and supervisee are working with the same client group and find themselves 'embedded' within the same setting. On the face of it, embedded supervision may appear the same as managerial supervision; however, there are clear differences and they are not the same. Managerial supervision implies a dual relationship between supervisor as manager and supervisee as worker. This can produce a situation that restricts the supervisee's ability to use the supervision space transparently, and the power differential in this arrangement is heavily biased towards the supervisor and their theoretical model. A major contention with this arrangement is that it may contaminate the anonymity of the supervisory relationship and introduce the possibility of conflict and a blurring of boundaries between clinical supervision and a managerial role.

In her book *An Introduction to the Therapeutic Frame*, Gray (1999) suggests that the supervisory relationship mirrors the therapeutic relationship. She uses a psychodynamic image to elucidate her view through the metaphor of a family, where the client is the 'child' held by the therapist 'mother' or primary caregiver, and where the supervisor has the role of 'father'. For me this infantilizing image of clients and the paternalistic image of the supervisor are problematic in its power differential and its proficiency – deficiency polarity. Embedded supervision does not have that type of polarity and neither does it have the anonymous space that we might expect to find in a client–therapist encounter. It also differs from managerial supervision in various ways that serve to reduce the power differential in the workplace. For example, the embedded supervisor would be only concerned with clinical issues and the experiences related to clinical practice with clients, plus the links with the training institution. They would not be involved with line management or disciplinary issues. In our own placement, trainees have both a supervisor for clinical work and a separate tutor for line management and workplace issues. There is also an element of equality in clinical practice. Trainees, tutors and supervisors all draw clients from the same pool of referrals, working in the same counselling room and on the same wards, interacting with the same hospital staff. This leads to a shared concrete experience of negotiating and managing the contingencies of an extemporaneous frame that aims at transparency whilst maintaining the privacy and confidentiality of client work.

The extemporaneous frame

This is a concept of the therapeutic frame that I have formed from the experience of both being a therapist and supervisor where the frame cannot be clearly delineated and decided prior to the therapeutic encounter. The extemporaneous frame is constructed *ad hoc* out of the flux of the interpersonal encounter between therapist and client in response to the contingency of environmental conditions. This raises questions – such as to what extent is therapy defined and delimited by the therapeutic frame, or is the therapeutic frame defined by each therapeutic encounter? If it is the latter, how flexible can this therapeutic frame be and still contain a practice that would be considered as therapeutic? In other words, in the absence of a traditional frame how do we know if what we are doing is therapy or not? These are questions that I will return to later in a general way, but first I would like to examine the notion of the therapeutic frame as the container for therapy.

The myth of therapy as a special kind of reality

At this point it is worth asking some questions to clarify what is at stake here with the management of a therapeutic frame: if you like, what is included and what is excluded within the boundary of a frame. This leads me to ask in what ways does the frame circumscribe what is and what is not therapy, and what are the defining characteristics of the therapeutic frame itself? It also seems important to clarify the perceived relationship between therapeutic practice and supervision, and in particular whether supervision can be contained within the therapeutic frame or whether it necessarily stands outside the frame in order to contain and support it.

The traditional image of the frame that I have carried around with me for so long is, understandably perhaps, most closely linked to Marion Milner's (1952) influential use of the image of a picture frame as a metaphor for the container or limit of therapeutic practice. Certainly there is a resonance between her metaphor and my stereotype of a universally accepted image of a therapeutic frame. Milner's image of a picture frame attempts magically to remove the reality of therapy from the mundane discourse of everyday unreflected life and transcend it. She suggests that, in the same way a picture frame contains the picture, a spatial, temporal therapeutic frame delineates the 'special kind of reality' of a therapeutic session. Milner's frame contains therapy within itself and circumscribes the practice of therapy; meaning that what is outside of the frame is another reality and not therapy. An example of this might be social conversation, or a chat, rather than therapeutic dialogue. She attempts to separate everyday reality and experience from therapeutic reality. But can we in fact make such a distinction? Cohn (1998) suggests that whilst therapeutic practice needs boundaries like any other style of meeting, it is simply one of the many possibilities of two or more people meeting each other. Furthermore, he points out that picture frames are usually constructed after the picture has been painted. Extending this metaphor, we might also say that a picture frame not only signifies completion and difference but that part of the cultural value of the painting is in its status as an independent object. It is interesting to note that Jackson Pollock, the American abstract expressionist painter who pushed the boundaries of painting beyond mundane representation, asked that his paintings should never be framed. I would suggest that we cannot make a clear distinction, as such, between everyday and therapeutic reality. Rather than delineating a 'special kind of reality', the boundaries of a therapeutic meeting must emerge from the special context and the aim of creating a therapeutic space. From this point of view, the frame and its boundaries are developed from specific needs within the flux of the therapeutic encounter, and offer flexibility within a tentative structure. However, to co-construct an *ad hoc* frame with the client requires a creative attentiveness and a willingness to be fully present in the therapy, regarding it as a shared lived experience of the moment. This can be a difficult and demanding task for both the therapist and the client.

If we return to the metaphor of the picture frame and extend it to the image of the gallery, we can say that a framed picture hanging in a recognized gallery has its status of art legitimized and confirmed through context. The gallery is simply a bigger frame. If we reapply the metaphor to psychotherapy we can see how the therapeutic frame not only contains psychotherapy as a specific activity but also legitimizes the status of that activity as genuine and distinct from everyday life. It could equally be argued that, in the setting I find myself in, the hospital serves a similar function to the gallery in that it legitimizes our activities as therapists as being worthwhile. However, had I not worked as a psychotherapist in a hospital I may have found it difficult to consider some serious questions concerning the attempt to separate therapy from the ambiguous flux of everyday life.

Some examples may illuminate these apparent distinctions between therapy and everyday life. If a client comes to me in my private practice I can usually only imagine them in their world as they describe it to me. Sometimes our worlds may overlap by us both having seen the same film, or my knowing from first hand a location they may refer to. Generally speaking what I have to work with is their descriptions of ideas, memories and experience in their spoken narrative, and a more subtle sense of them through what I would call the 'embodied narrative' (Sampson 1998). Most of what clients tell me I regard as an invitation for me to see them in a particular way. I build up a set of images of their life, the significant people in their lives, along with their styles of relationship. All this is invoked through the overt and covert invitations within their narrative and their way of being present to me. Does it matter that my understanding of their lives is only in my imagination, and furthermore limited by my imagination? Let me describe two contrasting situations to further illustrate what I mean.

Whilst I was watching a television programme a client appeared on it as a 'talking head'. It was strange to see a client in this context, and being curious I continued to watch the programme. To my surprise the partner of my client also appeared and spoke on the programme. The partner and their relationship had been the main topic of therapy for some time, and I felt that I really knew this partner and had a clear image of them. The surprise was that the partner on television was completely different to the partner in my imagination, and it radically changed my perception of my client. Everyday reality had invaded my imaginal world of the therapy.

Contrast this to sitting on the edge of a man's bed with only a thin blue curtain to separate us from the other patients in the ward. Dressed only in his pyjamas, he speaks so quietly that I have to sit very close to him in order to hear him. I don't know what is wrong with him – only that he has requested to see a counsellor, looks unwell and is somehow disconnected. He tells me that less than two hours ago he was given the results of his biopsy, and that his brain tumor is inoperable. He has been told that he probably has about a year to live, and he tells me that he can't take it in. We work together for about thirty minutes, ending only when he tires. When I come to see him a few days later he has been transferred back to his local hospital and we never meet again. This man's experience was lived out in front of me in a very real and immediate sense and, although our meeting was brief, there were moments that had a profound quality to them. These moments were unusually intimate, enabling us to speak about the unspeakable in his immediate experience and an uncertain future. The point I am attempting to illustrate and argue here is that a therapeutic encounter is not contingent on providing a separate reality contained within an external therapeutic frame.

The contents of the frame

Anne Gray (1999) points out that although there is no consensus as to which elements should be included in the therapeutic frame it has both a purpose of defining the contract and also relates to the ways in which one was cared for in the past. By this she means that from a western cultural perspective of child rearing it is widely accepted that infants and children require continuity and consistency. For her the frame provides consistency for the client and suggests that it contains the following elements:

> a private setting in which therapist and client meet; fixed times and duration of the sessions; vacation breaks which are clearly stated by the therapist; a set fee for all sessions reserved; and an internal concept on the part of the therapist that what is talked about is not talked about with anyone outside the therapeutic relationship.
>
> (Gray 1999: 7)

It is clearly evident how these elements attempt to provide consistency and confidentiality for the client, as well as benefiting the therapist. However, from the perspective of an extemporaneous frame there are other elements missing – elements that I would not only like to add to the discussion of an extemporaneous frame but would suggest that they may also be relevant to more conventional images of therapy.

One is the element of *supervision* that is integrated with the client work; another is a concept on the part of the therapist of what might be therapeutic from the standpoint of a *functional paradigm*; yet another is an element of *ambiguity and heteronomy* in the encounter that opens up the possibilities of a co-constructed flexible frame. We might also question the most basic assumption that therapy needs consistency. Why not inconsistency?

Supervision

Returning once more to the domain of stereotypes, my traditional image of supervision is one where there is an anonymous distance between the supervisor and supervisee. It would also be unlikely that the supervisor would have first-hand knowledge of the supervisee's place of practice, or of the client's lived experience. In this image the supervisor has a relationship with their supervisee that is similar to the client–therapist relationship in the majority of therapeutic paradigms, a relationship that privileges spoken narrative and an imaginal rather than a concrete world.

Here, supervision helps contain and maintain the therapeutic frame from a distance and is not an integral part of the frame as such. As I have already indicated, the image of embedded supervision is very different from managerial supervision and it seems important that embedded supervision is group supervision, as it extends the individual experiences into a shared collective experience. This is not to invoke a normalization of experience – quite the opposite. Its intention is to open up the diversity and uniqueness of experience and to encourage transparency of practice in a spirit of research and reflection. As one of my supervisees commented:

> Supervision is the work as well as the work . . . it feels integrated not separate . . . Group supervision is an important part of the work, working with others, glimpsing others' experience and extending expectations. I value the exploration of my personal process – myself in relation to the client and the team within the context of the hospital – especially the opportunity of monitoring the impact of the work on myself.

In embedded supervision there is less of a distance between participants, and the work is more collaborative. Supervisees also have the unusual opportunity to witness their supervisor as a functioning professional who is experiencing the same set of circumstances as them. This also means that there is less distance and more correspondence between the client work and supervision. There is an atmosphere of research and exploration in the supervision, with an emphasis on the experiential aspects of the work, especially monitoring the impact of the work on the supervisee.

Certain contexts, such as a hospital, can have a strong dehumanizing effect on practitioners. It seems important that all of the supervision participants have the opportunity to experience themselves both as professionals and as human beings sharing a similar experience. 'Not knowing' becomes an integral aspect of both client work and supervision, rather than a sign of incompetence and inadequacy. In short, both supervisor and supervisee become co-researchers in an indefinite field of therapeutic practice and reflection. The collaborative nature of embedded supervision encourages a sense of community within the team, which supervisees recognize as a significant element in the extemporaneous frame.

A functional paradigm

When the traditional boundaries of therapy are no longer in place it seems extremely important for there to be an internal concept on the part of the therapist of what is therapeutic and what is not. This internalized functional paradigm is more than simply a theoretical model as it allows the therapist to be (in Levinas's 1985 terms) in ethical relationship with the client. It also allows for a matrix of therapeutic and social interventions to exist side by side. One might even say that this is a portable frame that the therapist takes into the encounter. It is primarily through this portable frame that therapy can take place, and it is often, along with supervision, the only container for therapeutic work. Rather than distinguish and delineate a separate therapeutic reality this allows therapy and the lived world to meet, and therapy more closely mirrors the ambiguous and unexpected nature of lived experience.

The internalized functional paradigm is informed by a theoretical or philosophical underpinning. It needs to be sufficiently developed for the therapist to unselfconsciously function within it, but at the same time it must be available to scrutiny – in much the same way that I don't have to think about writing but am aware of how the written words appear on the page and if they make sense. It is, perhaps, possible to both make a metaphor and a parallel here with language. Spoken narrative is only one aspect of communication and there always exists alongside it an embodied narrative. If we think about how we learn a mother tongue as children, we do so in an embodied relationship with our environment. We learn an embodied narration of our experience alongside the spoken narrative that resonates and reverberates within our body. It is an experiential apprehending of alterity that takes place. We rarely think about how we use our mother tongue in the everyday negotiation of our lived world, and we rarely reflect on how we use our body. Learning a foreign or dead language is different in as much as it is against the backdrop of the mother tongue. As a child growing up in a seaside town no one gave me any instructions in swimming. I simply learnt to swim as a child by being in water, much as we learn a mother tongue through being immersed in it. However, I learnt how to ride a bicycle, and also to write, through instruction. Learning to practise as a psychotherapist involves both of these elements of assimilation and instruction. But it is always against the backdrop of other lived encounters from our social world. We learn epistemological bias from training institutions concerning the pool of knowledge and the conventions from the intellectual field of psycho-therapy, but we also learn about it by being in it with others – by being immersed in the experience of encounter with clients and reflecting on that experience with other professionals.

We may learn epistemological bias, conventions, and codes of conduct from training institutions and psychotherapy literature, but we also learn about psychotherapy through being immersed in the experience of encounter with clients and reflecting on that experience with other professionals. It is rather like the distinction between formal prosaic language and speech, where in speech there is always an ambiguous and spontaneous element in the construction of meaning.

Ambiguity and heteronomy

Ambiguity and heteronomy are to be distinguished from ambivalence and autonomy, which are terms more frequently to be found in psychotherapy literature. Ambivalence refers to the dilemma of being in two minds, or being at a fork in the road where one has a choice between two options. These options reflect a dualistic way of thinking, commonly found in our western culture, where polar opposites are set against one another. We can also see this in the Cartesian split of mind and body and in the distinction between subject and object. In contradistinction, ambiguity, a familiar image in post-modernism, brings these contrasting images together. With reference to Marcel's (1949) view of the 'body that I am' rather than the 'body I have', Merleau-Ponty (1962, 1964, 1968) reveals the phenomenological ambiguity of the body. The experience I have of touching my own body is different to the experience of being touched. My body is then ambiguously both me, and an object for me, that is always experienced simultaneously from one invariable perspective – the vantage point of my own body. He presents us with an image of the self, ambiguously experiencing itself as embodied presence to the world where: 'the body sees itself, touches itself seeing and touching the things, such that, simultaneously as tangible it descends among them, as touching it dominates them all' (Merleau-Ponty 1968: 146). From this perspective of a sentient and sensible body, the objective stance of autonomy and consistency is simply a hypothesis. It is an attempt to withhold one's inevitable and inescapable involvement with the contingencies of the world: a world of intersubjectivities, where we have no choice but to be *in* a world, and *of* a world, ambiguously with others. Others on whom, as Laing points out, we depend for our very sense of self: 'All "identities" require an other: some other in and through a relationship with whom self-identity is actualised' (Laing 1990: 82). The ambiguity of relationship, wherein identity is born through alterity, brings us together in our shared humanity as it weaves 'the circular system of projections and intro-jections, illuminating the unlimited series of reflecting reflections and reflected reflections which are the reasons why I am the other person and he is myself' (Merleau-Ponty 1968: 230). This dissolution of this autonomous self, a self that attempts to separate us from the Other, brings us to the notion of heteronomy.

Heteronomy is concerned with alterity, and whereas the egocentricity of autonomy is concerned with self-interest, heteronomy is concerned with difference and recognizes the absolute otherness of the Other. These Others who, as Harry Stack Sullivan points out, will always remain a mystery for me: 'There is an essential inaccessibility about any personality other than one's own . . . There is always an ample residuum that escapes analysis and communication . . . no one can hope to fully understand another. It is very fortunate indeed if he approaches an understanding of himself' (Sullivan 1972: 5).

In response to the uncertainty of alterity we can choose to regard the Other in Sartrean terms as a threat to our free subjectivity and autonomy, responding in sado-masochistic modes of relationship (Sartre 1996). Alternatively, we can respond to the Other ethically by putting the Other first in a way that recognizes the otherness of the Other, where the Other is someone we can serve and learn from. This paradox is not one of ambivalence but one of ambiguity, described by Levinas in the dilemma of the face-to-face encounter: 'The face is exposed, menaced as if inviting us to an act of violence. At the same time, the face is what forbids us to kill' (Levinas 1985: 86). The ethical response is not that of a detached observer but of an embodied participant. In psychotherapy terms it calls for the therapist to be a catalyst in the service of the Other, rather than an objective analyst.

Therapy is not then something that is administered to a client but a mode of relationship that both parties become immersed in. Merleau-Ponty speaks of a 'magical relationship' with things – but he could equally be speaking about people – when he speaks of 'this pact between them and me according to which I lend them my body in order that they inscribe upon it and give me their resemblance' (Merleau-Ponty 1997: 146). We cannot choose to not do this, but we can perhaps choose to deny it out of self-interest in a bid for autonomy.

Conclusion

What I have attempted to describe here is an alternative perspective to traditional images of a therapeutic frame, borne out of the contingencies of a particular setting. I have called this the *extemporaneous frame* and have indicated how it may be managed through an integrated or *embedded supervision*. This style of supervision is not outside the frame but held, in a matrix of ambiguous possibilities, alongside it and within it. The frame I have described is not a concrete rigid framework, decided in advance and applied to each therapeutic encounter. It would be misleading to suggest that it is not without expectations, or, at worst, that it can be collapsed into a *laissez-faire* subjectivism. The frame is not boundaryless, it simply has different styles of boundaries which are less concerned with maintaining a spatio-temporal consistency but rather focus on inter-subjective encounter. In this sense the frame is established more through notions of interiority rather than a pre-established exteriority. It does not aim at consistency but embraces the ambiguous nature of contingency in current lived experience. Sometimes therapy takes place at moments within the encounter and at other times it does not. In this sense, perhaps it is not so different from any other style of therapy. However, it is not an external frame that determines what is therapy as much as an internalized functional paradigm on the part of the therapist and the quality of the encounter. I have come to see the extemporaneous frame in synchronic rather than diachronic terms, and this had led me to see each encounter as a discrete unit. This is due, in part, to the uncertainty of regular future meetings, but it is also founded in the phenomenology of encounter. In the same way that Heraclitus tells us that we can never step in the same river twice, I will always be a different therapist meeting a different client. There can only ever be a relative constancy in the flux of heteronomy between his 'myself' and my 'myself'. Each meeting is a new encounter that demands the frame to be established anew, or at least re-established, and one cannot assume more than a relative continuity or consistency. The timing of fortnightly supervision groups is, however, a relatively consistent element in the experience for trainees, as is the presence of a team or a community of practitioners in all its inconsistency.

In supervision the placement therapists engage with the paradox of being members of a team whilst doing individual client work. It is in the immediate shared experience of the hospital, and all the uncertainty that comes with it, that supervisor and supervisee are brought together as co-practitioners. Here they become co-researchers into the possibility and impossibility of providing therapy within an extemporaneous frame. Not only is embedded supervision a crucial element in managing the extemporaneous frame, it is also embedded in that frame.

Finally we are faced with the possibility of translating these ideas into other more traditional settings. Clearly, for this to happen would mean a challenge to the authority of an external image of a consistent frame with invariable elements. It would involve focusing on the inter-relational possibilities of a frame – a frame constructed out of the flux of encounter in the space between therapist and client. It would require the therapist to respond creatively to the ambiguous contingencies of the embodied encounter with the client, from an ethical position of difference, regarding each encounter as a discrete unit. It would dissolve the illusion of consistency and engage with the differences between these discrete units and the fluctuating differences in my sense of myself and the client. I am not suggesting that we take therapy out onto the streets but that we conceptually shift the external authority of a therapeutic frame to an intersubjective extemporaneous frame.

References

Cohn, H.W. (1998) 'Frames for therapies or therapies for frames? An exploration of the relation between setting and aim of psychotherapy', *Journal of the Society for Existential Analysis* 9(2): 108–14.

Gray, A. (1999) *An Introduction to the Therapeutic Frame*, London: Routledge.

Laing, R.D. (1990) *The Self and Others*, London: Penguin.

Levinas, E. (1985) *Ethics and Infinity. Conversations with Phillipe Nemo* (trans. R. Cohen), Pittsburgh, Pa.: Duquesne University Press.

Levinas, E. (2002) 'Ethics and the face', in D. Moran and T. Mooney (eds) *The Phenomenology Reader*, London: Routledge.

Marcel, G. (1949) *The Philosophy of Existence* (trans. M. Harai), Freeport, N.Y.: Books for Libraries.

Merleau-Ponty, M. (1962) *The Phenomenology of Perception* (trans. C. Smith) London: Routledge & Kegan Paul.

Merleau-Ponty, M. (1964) *Signs* (trans. R. McCleary), Evanston, Ill.: Northwestern University Press.

Merleau-Ponty, M. (1997) *The Visible and the Invisible* (trans. A. Lingis), Evanston, Ill.: Northwestern University Press.

Milner, M. (1952) 'Aspects of symbolism and comprehension of the not-self', *International Journal of Psychoanalysis* 33: 181–95.

Sampson, E.E. (1998) 'Life as an embodied art: the second stage – beyond constructionism', in B.M. Bayer and J. Shotter (eds) *Reconstructing the Psychological Subject*, London: Sage.

Sartre, J.-P. (1996) *Being and Nothingness* (trans. H.E. Barnes), London: Routledge.

Smith-Pickard, P. (2001) 'Unravelling a ball of string: relationships in the world of objects', *Journal of the Society for Existential Analysis* 12(2): 188–99.

Sullivan, H.S. (1972) *Personal Psychopathology*, New York: W.W. Norton.

Chapter 9

'The exclusion zone'

A psychoanalytic perspective on the frame

John Beveridge

> The pain and panic that trained professionals can feel when faced with behaviour and mental states of individuals so afflicted that they can no longer enter into conventional human relationships, can get translated into cruel and unusual forms of punishment.
>
> Joseph Schwartz, *Cassandra's Daughter*

When a therapist begins to practise they do so in a world where public opinion is critical and suspicious of therapy. The struggle of psychotherapy[1] to be taken seriously in a hostile world has been ongoing throughout its history and is still alive today. Until fairly recently, any impersonation of a psychotherapist would be carried out in a Viennese accent, as if nothing has changed since Freud. It is not surprising that many working psychotherapeutic practitioners, when asked what they do for a living, will say that they are writers or teachers because there is nothing that kills spontaneity at a dinner party more effectively than to 'come out' as a psychotherapist. Rosie Alexander makes this clear: 'Bring up the subject of psychotherapy, in anything other than general terms, and most people will wince visibly and curdle like an oyster squirted with lemon juice' (1995: 71). There are often two conflicting images of therapists in the minds of the public. One is of a compelling 'Svengali'-like figure, who controls the impressionable and dependent patient with a stony and penetrating gaze, looking for signs of the wayward unconscious and listening in silence for mistakes and slips of the tongue which mask the sexual and the aggressive, or worse, the sexually aggressive drives, that haunt and propel us through our apparently civilized lives. Or there is another representation of the analyst, ubiquitous in cartoons, and films of the fraudulent practitioner, who is taking the client's money and doing not very much. In the film *There's Something about Mary*, a psychoanalyst, with a napkin still attached to his collar and wiping the remains of his lunch from his mouth, returns to sit behind the oblivious, talking patient, just in time for the end of the session.

Woody Allen, who has had a long and very public relationship with psychoanalysis, has done much to perpetuate an image of analysis as interminable and ineffectual, prompting one of his best jokes: 'I've been in therapy fourteen years, I'll give it one more year – then I'm going to Lourdes!'

Writing about the emergence of psychotherapy, Judith Herman (1992: 12) said that when Freud studied at Saltpêtriere Asylum, with Charcot, his revolutionary approach when treating his hysterical women patients with hypnosis was that he actually listened to their stories. The term 'hysterical' had long been a convenient description for 'troublesome' women, and Herman cites Kardiner, who said:

> The victim of such a neurosis is therefore without sympathy in court, and . . . without sympathy from his physicians, who often take . . . 'hysterical' to mean that the individual is suffering from some persistent form of wickedness, perversity and weakness of will.
>
> (Herman 1992: 24)

Prior to hypnosis, the early treatment of emotionally disturbed people suffering from neuroses and psychoses in psychiatric hospitals had evoked barbaric and sadistic treatment from psychiatric practitioners, including female castration, the extraction of teeth and the packing of women's genitals with ice.

It was reasoned that if hypnosis was powerful enough to induce antic behaviour and conditions like loss of memory and sensation, motor paralyses and convulsions, then it could also be used to cure them, as they were psychological in origin (Herman 1992: 11). Drawing from the experience of his collaboration with Joseph Breuer, Freud used hypnosis to listen for the psychical prehistory of the ailment and, using the '*instrument*' of the 'therapeutic hour' and the insights of his early patient, he began moving away from hypnosis, developing the 'talking cure' of psychoanalysis (Schwartz 1999: 60).

In its early practice, the boundaries of psychoanalysis were all over the place, with analysts touching and applying pressure to their patients' heads and analysing their own and their colleagues' children. This new treatment brought the powerful defences of resistance and transference in its wake, causing problems on both sides of the couch. Herman (1992: 18) says that the first talking cure ended with Breuer leaving his final meeting with Anna O in a 'cold sweat', having been deeply shocked and frightened by the powerful feelings that were being evoked – and not only in the patient. Breuer fled to Venice with his wife for a second honeymoon. Out of this atmosphere the therapeutic frame gradually emerged with a more abstinent and anonymous therapist, which was partially based on the dread and distrust of the 'hysterical' patient and a fear of sexual 'acting out'.

It has always been difficult to try to gain scientific credibility for something as evanescent as the interpretation of dreams and fantasies, the exploration of emotions, the lifting of repression and the clinical application of intuition and insight. This difficulty is compounded by the intra-psychic and almost telepathic phenomena that occur in psychotherapy, including parallel process, countertransference and projective identification. The long and evolving relationship between the therapist, the patient and the therapeutic frame parallels the conflict between the inner and outer worlds.

In America, Freud's revolutionary method was 'medicalized', gaining scientific credibility in psychiatry, and inheriting from the medical establishment the arrogant implication that 'Doctor knows best', so that what had started as a revolutionary movement became an orthodoxy, a 'wisdom tradition', a cult with vested interests, predominantly white, male and heterosexual, working as gatekeepers to protect its esoteric knowledge and theoretical purity. Psychoanalysis, seeking safety in theoretical ideas that had been tested in the consulting room, constructed its own protective frame, becoming very selective about who was permitted to enter this exclusive world through training. Theory evolves out of clinical experience, and the perception and interpretation of that experience is highly subjective, which results in a history of psychotherapy comprising of theoretical difference of opinion and fallings out, of fights and splits, of apostolic succession, of exclusions and banishments. It is hardly surprising that this dynamic will be re-enacted within the organizations that train therapists.

Patients should be able to enter treatment in the confidence that their therapists have been properly trained, otherwise psychotherapy could become a dangerous weapon in the hands of amateurs who might not be used to a clear and sustained examination of their own emotional responses to their patients' anguish. History shows that even people in the caring professions can respond to a patient's distress with behaviour that can perpetuate their original trauma. Being chosen for training as a therapist implies that recognition of psychological well-being is being conferred upon a student, so it might be tempting for a person to think,

when embarking upon a counselling, an analytic, or psychotherapy training, that the people you will encounter will be, if not paragons of mental
health, then they might at least be reasonably, emotionally 'sorted'.

Anyone who has sat in an experiential group and observed their peers,
'red in tooth and claw', will know that the idea that therapists, or people
from the so-called 'caring professions', hold a monopoly on mental
health is an illusion. Training institutes hold the same pathologies as
any other organization and can seem like institutes of madness, having
their share of power struggles, feuds, cliques, allegiances, and *coup d'état*,
both bloody and bloodless. The only difference might be this: in the world
of 'Psy' we learn fancier names, with which we can pathologize our
enemies.

The psychotherapy student is required to undergo their own therapy,
which forms a large part of their education, so their training is often
experienced as an expensive, traumatic and prolonged process, with
rendezvous with fear and despair along the way. The trainee therapist's
life might, at times, feel fraught with the dangers of a threatening and
differently boundaried world, where sometimes a leaky framework
between students and teachers, training therapists and supervisors,
holds invisible lines of allegiance and influence. Training institutes
might require their students to surrender to a theoretical 'party line',
expecting a degree of rigour in theoretical and ethical practice, and during
the training it may feel very risky to stray from the path of 'theoretical
enlightenment'. Will alliances or feuds lead to, or away from, future
ascendancy to committees, teaching, or, most importantly, the referral of
patients? If referrals are the nourishing milk from the breast of the mother
institute, it raises more important questions: Who is being fed? And who
are the favoured children? You don't have to be a Kleinian to go through
training in the 'paranoid schizoid' position. Participants are under constant
scrutiny from, and forming transferences with, course tutors, training
therapists, supervisors and teachers, as well as their peers, from whom
there might be envious attacks, gossip and judgement around when and
how someone might begin practising with patients. Over the years of
training, the behaviour of the student will often become more boundaried,
defensive and circumspect in what they feel they can reveal of themselves
to their peers and teachers, which can inhibit their own 'spontaneous
gestures'.

After graduation it might seem like a great relief to leave this arena of
continual observation for a relatively isolated practice, exploring private
worlds in private rooms, without prying eyes looking over one's shoulder.
But the scrutiny of the therapist's behaviour has not ended!

In order that the patient could project their revived early images of close relationships, (the transference) on to the therapist, the idea has persisted that a therapist should try to remain anonymous and reveal little of their own private life. Carl Rogers stated:

> It is surprising how frequently the client uses the word 'impersonal' in describing the therapeutic relationship after the conclusion of therapy. This is obviously not intended to mean that the relationship was cold or disinterested. It appears to be the client's attempts to describe this unique experience in which the person of the counselor – the counselor as an evaluating, reacting person with needs of his own – is so clearly absent.
>
> (Rogers 1951: 208)

As it is part of the earliest human experience that we try to discern what is in the mind of another and what motivates their behaviour, so the therapist's anonymity will only draw more curiosity. The patient begins, analysing the therapist from the moment they meet, and it is wishful thinking that the therapist might reveal nothing of him or herself. If a patient comes to a practitioner's home there are clues to be picked up and there is a lot to take in. Where is their house located on the property ladder? This might be an indication of how much might he or she could be earning. What sort of mood are they in? Would it kill them to smile? What have they got to smile about when I arrive feeling miserable? What's that smell? Who's doing the cooking? Are there signs of children, other patients, or relationships, and who are they? The patients sometimes have to use bathrooms, which can brim with clues, toothbrushes and razors being small but ample evidence that the patient is not the only person in their therapist's life.

One evening, concluding our session during my training therapy, as my analyst showed me to the front door, I noticed that something was different. The living room door, which I had to pass, was not scrupulously closed as usual but was wide open. There was an excited and excitable air of chaos in the house, a barking dog was out in the hall and a child was shouting. I turned and looked at my therapist as she tried to pick up and calm the dog, intending to give her a sympathetic smile. As her harried look met my gaze I realized that I felt elated. The usual atmosphere of calm and privacy that she maintained had broken down and all hell had broken loose! I had had a glimpse into her private life and it was not the domestic bliss in which she lived in my imagination. A triumphant part of me was making an envious attack on this woman upon whom I depended. Closed doors and the therapist's privacy can be tantalizing to the patient who longs to know more about this person whom they come to see. Stephen Mitchell has described the reasons for this interest:

> The intense and highly personal curiosity toward the analyst, which each analysand eventually develops is always partially a recreation of the child's generally thwarted and repressed curiosity about and search for the inner, personal experience of the parents.
>
> (Mitchell 1988: 104)

A patient asked me if I would like to read part of the book he was writing. When I read the account of his hero's journey to see his therapist I felt uneasy: he had written a vivid description of local landmarks, shops, road names and idiosyncratic street life that made me feel that he might as well have printed a map to my house. Descriptions of clinical meetings are most often written from the therapist's viewpoint, so it was disconcerting to see the tables being turned. It felt very exposing and I was anxious that, if the book was published (not a concern until I saw the high quality of the writing), then it would be obvious to anyone who knows me that I was the therapist who was being written about. I was therefore apprehensive about how he would perceive and describe the therapeutic encounter. His description of the patient waiting on the step for Gregory, his therapist, to come and open the door, revealed a familiar preoccupation that the patient has about the private life of the therapist. 'What is he doing in there? Is he deliberately keeping me waiting? Is he on the toilet?'

His fictional appointment was even more revealing of his inner life than he sometimes was in our meetings, and I confess to being moved to tears by his description of the warmth of the relationship between this therapeutic pair. I almost envied the easy intimacy between the characters because of the vulnerability he allowed his hero when talking to the fictional therapist. His description showed me that he had taken in the processes and the interactions between us in a way that showed a deep understanding of his own struggles. It is erroneous to assume that intuition, insight and perception are only located in the therapist.

To sit in a room with a stranger and answer questions that go to the heart of what they think and feel might be a first-time experience in the life of the patient. We expect them to tell us everything about themselves, and when they ask a direct question it is often met with another question: 'I wonder why you ask me that?'

Therapists have to find ways to protect their own privacy, whilst not shaming someone for showing a lively and natural curiosity. There can be few professional disciplines where the patient is expected, as they go along, to just pick up cues, implicit rather than explicit, with little indication of how they are doing and how a therapist and patient are supposed to behave. Many people who come to therapy may not know that the first meeting with the practitioner is a two-way assessment.

The therapeutic outcome is as much a result of personal chemistry as of theoretical technique. To be told that the sex, age and sexuality of the practitioner are unimportant might be plainly and simply wrong. Anyone can declare themselves a therapist, and the authority invested in the role does not encourage people to ask for the credentials of their prospective therapist – and would a lay person understand them anyway? It may have taken years for a patient to find a voice and the courage to articulate their pain, and then perhaps they have had to wait before they could be seen. They might wonder if they have enough material to sustain a therapist's interest and it might feel as if the meeting is about being taken on, being accepted and acceptable.

I lay down ground rules at the beginning, so that a contract is being established, for both my behaviour and what I expect from them, in an attempt to minimize the unexpected. I engage the patient in a brief discussion around their commitment to the process and the responsibilities we both have in our work. Mitchell described the unique quality of this very different relationship thus:

> The context-specific intimacy of the analytic relationship con-tributes to its oddness. So much cannot happen. The present formal structure of time and place, the almost exclusive conversational focus on the experience of one participant and not the other, the prohibitions against touching – all this makes for an odd relationship indeed that does not translate easily to chance encounters on the street.
>
> (Mitchell 1997: 229)

The relationship is not a friendship, a social occasion or a chat. There will be no outside meeting with the patient and telephone contact will be kept to a minimum. During our time, there will be no interruption to the session and no one else will come into the room. For the therapeutic hour, in concentrated attachment, the therapist listens carefully to the narrative and to what might be being communicated between the lines. If the first meeting goes well, the patient's history might come out in a reassuring rush, providing a sense of relief which might feel therapeutic. When a promising start has been made, it might seem churlish, at this stage, for the new patient to bring up any niggling doubts or raise direct questions about things they are not happy with – for example, like having to pay for missed sessions. It is always difficult to know just how much detail the new patient can take in at this time; but if something is not being expressed now it will probably be acted out later.

When someone starts to talk about the ground rules of the frame they set themselves up as an authority figure and, in our culture, a set of rules will usually evoke the role of the father as 'law-giver'. How this might be responded to can occupy a large part of an initial therapy. As the therapeutic frame represents the constraints and boundaries around the patient's access to the therapist and the practical and emotional management of the alliance, it is often along the perimeter of this frame that a relational 'push and pull' will begin. It might be the first time in the patient's history that they have encountered a firm and 'boundaried' response, but that does not mean that they are going to like it! I remember a therapist asked me *not* to bring the bicycle that I was already pushing over the threshold into the communal hall of his flat. It seemed particularly unreasonable, as there were three bikes there already, that *my* bike would have to wait outside. I mean! What if it was stolen from outside his flat? It would be his fault! I was furious that he could not see the practicality of my request. To feel myself come up against the edge of this immovable object was very frustrating. He interpreted that I wanted a closer relationship with him. I did not think so! A few days later I had a dream that when he arrived home I was already in his flat playing cards with his girlfriend and feeling very smug that *she* had let me in. I then had to admit he was onto something!

It is only natural that the patient, impelled by unconscious forces when faced with anxiety, will try, in this power 'imbalance', to push and control the frame in order to create an impact upon the therapist in a way that is congruent with the patient's relational history. There can be strong but 'sideways' communications in missed appointments, coming late, forgetting to pay, or bouncing a cheque on the therapist, and in working practice the therapist's management of the frame can often feel as if it is being created 'on the hoof', arising out 'troubleshooting' unexpected stresses. As a result, the practitioner might sometimes feel that there is a 'ball in the net' and they do not know how it got there!

Often, quite rightly, the therapist might sense that the patient is making a bid for control, and these occasions have to be addressed and challenged. A patient might try, by regularly coming late or missing appointments, to limit their exposure to the painful impact of the therapy when they are feeling 'at risk' of being overwhelmed. Sometimes a sense of futility can persist in a therapy where patients are frightened to voice their concerns with the therapy, when those concerns are about the therapist.

During my first therapy as a patient, the dialogue between the therapeutic couple often had the quality of throwing a ball at a hanging blanket. Nothing bounced back! Often, the last sentence either of us said would just hang in the air, with the words echoing and floating around in my mind, connected like links in a chain, until they became meaningless and disintegrated in the silence. The metaphors that my therapist used found no resonance in me. I sometimes had the impression that he knew something and was waiting for me to stumble across it. I thought he was cleverer than me and I just wasn't getting it! Of course now I would be able to ask him: 'What's happening here between us?'

Just sitting talking to a practitioner might be an unnatural act, which breaks an unspoken family rule of secrecy. A patient from a sexually abusive family, who found it very difficult to think about what she might be feeling, was asked if what happened in her family might have been discussed between herself and her siblings. She looked at her therapist incredulously and said: 'No, we didn't talk to each other about anything. Growing up, we took our meals alone in our rooms, like people in prison.'

When there has been abandonment or abuse in early life, when someone has been seriously, emotionally injured, it is very difficult for him or her to trust authority figures, making it difficult for them to be reached, rather like a cat or dog reacting violently to rescue attempts from the RSPCA.

There are certain patients, sexually molested in childhood, for whom sitting in quiet expectation with a silent therapist might create the expectation that something abusive is about to happen. Time can move very slowly in silence, and for the patient it can feel like a competition to see who will crack first. What is going on when the patient and analyst sit without speaking? Silence can have many different meanings and qualities, from quiet reverie to hostile disengagement, covering many feelings in between. In assessing the need to deal with silences that arise, the emotional temperature of the room must be taken and therapists must question themselves as to whose anxiety is being assuaged if the silence is broken. In a public lecture Patrick Casement, when asked about the problem of 'managing' silent sessions, said that he did not like to 'stalemate' the person sitting in silence. I will ask a silent patient if they would like me to come looking for them in their quiet place. Sometimes this might be welcomed and at other times, even with the same person, it might be seen as blunderingly intrusive.

Terror calls forth defensive behaviour, which each patient will manifest in different ways, to prevent the very thing from happening that another part of them longs for. Writing about attachment, Rachel Wingfield said: 'The terror of our longing for each other is more powerful than our anger, envy or even hate' (2002: 3).

John Bowlby (1969: 204–9) described 'attachment' behaviour, which was drawn from biology and ethology, delineating the five instinctual responses of sucking, crying, smiling, clinging and following which are designed to evoke a caregiving response in a parent and foster a child's tenacious bond with them. He saw that our anxieties and defences are rooted in the fear of separation from our attachment objects, because to be abandoned in the wild would result in death. If this early connection has been endangered, then what we are dealing with in the patient's unconscious can feel life threatening; so no matter how often the therapist calls for the patient to put their trust in them it is not always a 'given' that the patient can even begin to let the work commence.

In one of my therapies as a patient we would meet in an institute where the therapists would collect their patients from the waiting room. It took me months to try and tell him, in a very elliptical way, that I did not like the fact that he was always the last therapist to come and find me, waiting alone in the room. It seemed to me that he was reluctant to commence the session with me. This was so hard to say, and as I spoke the words my face crumpled and I felt the physical sensation of having a mask ripped away. This was the first powerful experience I had in a therapy room. His hurtful behaviour may have evoked old abandonment fears from my childhood, but this was also something very real, happening in a relationship between two adult people. There are realistic fears that many people bring to therapy that they will become dependent upon the therapist; this, in the patient's mind, means that the therapist has the power to hurt and control them.

When the practitioner begins, well in advance, to signal impending holidays, a patient with some experience of therapy will probably groan that the therapist is always going on about the breaks and that it is a cliché that they are important. But the thing about cliché is that it is based on a truth so familiar,that it hardly needs to be said.

Why might it appear that the therapist longs for the patient to be dependent upon them? Is it, perhaps, to make up for narcissistic deficiencies in the therapist's life? Why does the practitioner want it to be acknowledged that the breaks might become upsetting for the patient? It is because growing feelings of dependence upon the therapist are in danger of being exposed around the holidays so that the therapist will be most at risk of losing patients at break times. It is surprising how patients who deny the importance of the break might miss the last appointment before a holiday or the first session back after it. This makes them the 'leaver' and not the 'left', and lessens the impact of painful feelings of being abandoned by the therapist during the vacation. It is my experience that after a vacation my patients seem to be all over the place, and I often feel like Little Bo Peep who has lost her sheep! An average entry in my diary at this time would be:

> It's the middle of the first working week after my summer holiday. I've had two 'no-shows', with no telephone calls of explanation, a couple of moved appointments and two calls to check that it is indeed this week that we return. Three people have returned saying that they feel they have managed the break so well that they no longer feel the need to continue the therapy.

In her last session before the break, Bernice had given me a cheque, asking me to bank it at the end of the first week of the holiday. It was returned by the bank in the second week and I re-presented it on the following Monday of the third week. It came back again in the fourth week, the day before she returned. She was convincingly unaware that this had been going on, yet she had contrived, unconsciously, to be in my mind on a weekly basis throughout the vacation. Some patients come back to therapy after the break punctually, seemingly keen to resume the work without any apparent ill effects. However, three sessions into the new term, after returning promptly from the break of three weeks, a patient got so drunk in the afternoon that he has to cancel his evening session, apparently without thought or intention. The next time we met and I questioned what it meant when he behaved in this way, he said that, instead of talking about this, there were other things that he wanted to discuss that were getting missed. I asked him how he felt at that moment. He said he felt 'ticked off'. I asked if he thought it didn't matter to me if he missed our appointment. 'Well', he said dismissively, 'You've just had three weeks off when you were away; it didn't matter then did it?' I saw that I was being tit for tatted!

Often something dramatic will happen for a patient during the holiday, like leaving a job, or finding a new romance and taking a lover. This latter is a reproach to the therapist, indicating that someone can be found to whom they can speak at any hour of the day or night (whose access is not limited to the therapeutic hour), with whom they are allowed to sleep and who, hopefully, does not charge money!

Quentin, a recovering drug addict, wrote after the summer holiday expressing suicidal feelings and saying he wanted to leave therapy, that he was not willing to come to the room to discuss working to an ending and that his decision was final. This self-destructive act of leaving abruptly meant that his aggression did not have to be expressed in a direct attack, which might have led to an exploration of the terrifying extent of his rage beneath his abandoned feelings. To leave the therapy unexpectedly is the ultimate 'going nuclear' option for a patient because the rupture of the frame has the impact upon the therapist of the symbolic suicide it is intended to represent, leaving the practitioner feeling hurt and full of impotent anger. It is a common fantasy that therapists have all their feelings 'trained' out of them, so that they do not feel the attacks that the patient makes upon them. A counselling trainee reported, with disappointment, a story of a therapist who had cried in exasperation: 'But I have feelings too!' Rather than being an uninvolved and emotionally remote white-coated 'expert', the therapist's humanity can become their greatest asset. As Theresa Benedek said:

> The patient may grope for the therapist as a real person, may sense his reactions and will almost read his mind . . . Yes the patient bores his way into the preconscious mind of the therapist, and often emerges with surprising evidences of empathy – of preconscious awareness of the therapist's personality and even of his problems.
>
> (Benedek 1953: 203)

I noticed as my practice grew that, within a recognizable *modus operandi*, I felt and behaved differently towards each person. When patients apply pressure to the therapist, they will uncannily locate in his or her psyche the tender places and 'fault-lines' from earlier wounds, which will become responsive to the stresses from that particular patient. Finding faults will vindicate the distrust of the wary patient who may painfully feel the failures of previous practitioners. The early perception of the demanding patient invading the calm interior of the practitioner has had to be reworked to allow for the part that the therapist's emotional contribution plays in these encounters. The patient is aware at some level that their demanding behaviour is having an impact upon the therapist. Over twenty years ago Irwin Hoffman said that a patient has good reason to fear the analyst's susceptibility to countertransference because it holds the danger of repeating the patterns of relationships that they have come to therapy to change (Hoffman 1983: 414)

A therapist, like his patient, might have to endure powerful and dangerous feelings of being lost in the emotional turbulence of transference and countertransference, where both feel as 'at risk' as each other until they can recognize to whom the emotional 'stuff' belongs.

Ben had a long history of relationships and therapies where no one was ever 'good enough', and he would constantly berate me for not helping him. For a while his was the last appointment in my working week, and I measured my effectiveness as a practitioner over the whole week by the amount of worthlessness I used to carry when he left for the weekend. One day, when I found myself dreading his arrival, I realized that my fear was the fear that he had but could not express in words. It would be plainly masochistic for a therapist to sit, taking unremitting abuse in session after session, and I was able to engage empathically with this intimidating man when I told him of the effect his behaviour had on me, that he was helping me learn, by using projective identification, what it felt like to be him.

He told me quite emphatically that he didn't want a therapist who felt what he felt! I told him that the difference was that when I was feeling the feelings they did not wash me away, that my feet were on the ground. Much emphasis is placed on the ability of the client to trust the therapist, but the question could be asked: Does the practitioner trust the patient? A therapist's attempt to erect a rigid therapeutic frame might be a defence against their own behavioural 'fault-lines' and their own capacity for 'resistance', 'being difficult', 'acting out', and 'collusion' in relationship, which can be denied by the use of 'stonewalling' silence, to which they can retreat when feeling out of their depth. Since it is the relationship between the analytic pair that heals, each therapeutic alliance becomes a unique experience. It quickly becomes apparent how a person was treated by how they think they can behave towards other people, including me, and how they expect to be treated in return. I often tell clients that we do not get what we deserve in life, we get what we expect.

I found in the early months of practice how exhausting this work was, so that I sometimes had to take naps between patients, rather like a nursing mother. As a colleague remarked: 'They use up the inside of you.' Donald Winnicott described the 'use' that an infant makes of its mother when she digests his primitive feelings of aggression when baby, in fantasy, tests her to destruction and she survives his attack and gives his feelings back as love, without retaliation (Winnicott 1971: 94). Early parental responses to aggressive feelings from an infant can affect the expression of antagonistic feelings thereafter, and therapists will be exposed to hateful and destructive behaviours which are sometimes, surprisingly, their own. Once, when I was experiencing a feeling of mounting exasperation with a patient, and not for the first time, I said to her: 'I wonder why I feel as if I want to strangle you?' She said without a pause: 'That's funny, my mother was always saying that she wanted to strangle me.' The contribution to psychoanalysis of the Kleinian theoretical concepts of countertransference and projective identification has become invaluable to the work of the practitioner. It was not until 1947 that Donald Winnicott addressed the powerful unconscious feelings of hatred that can be evoked in mothers by their infants and in therapists by patients, which, if left unexplored, can become manifest as hostile treatment towards them. In private practice, examples of the therapist's hatred can include arrogance in poor timekeeping without apology or explanation, terminating sessions early and changing breaks or regular meetings without warning. There is much documentation of the abrupt termination of therapy by the therapist for reasons less important than death or illness. Within the transference and countertransference, the analytic pair inhabit together the emotional landscape of the patient's earliest relationship to others which is continually being re-enacted in the present, which Wilfred Bion described as being akin to a 'primitive disaster':

> In the analysis we are confronted not so much with a static situation that permits leisurely study, but with a catastrophe that remains at one and the same moment actively vital and yet incapable of resolution into quiescence.
>
> (Bion 1967: 101)

People in training are often anxious about how they will manage the aggression that will come their way when they work, but sometimes, more disturbing than antagonism, might be the expression of the patient's erotic feelings for the practitioner. The sexual connotations of ordinary happenings – 'Can I put my bike in your hall? Can I put my umbrella in your bath?' – have long been seen in psychotherapy as powerful communications of patients' unconscious desires, evoked in the presence of the therapist. Many ordinary patients are reluctant to express even the gentlest need of the therapist and would not have the slightest intention of sleeping with their therapists in the real world, yet, while they can remain within the bounds of reality, they might still want to feel special in their therapist's eyes.

Sharon playfully expressed the wish that I would display her photograph on the wall, with a sign indicating that she was the favourite patient in my practice. She was able explore this fantasy, knowing that it was a flight of the imagination and that it was safe to do so, without it having to be made real. A patient gave me the valuable insight that, while the 'shrink' has many patients, the patient has only one therapist, so there will always be a disproportionate amount of thought about 'the other' in one half of the pair. Doreen, once told her therapist that she would have a horror of seeing other patients leaving her house, yet she showed up for an appointment fifteen minutes early, and waited outside smoking and drinking coffee. She rang the bell six minutes before her appointed time and said that she had seen the previous patient – 'the bastard who moves the chair' – and had given him a dirty look as he left the house. As the therapist barely had enough time to smooth the cover on the couch and rearrange the room, she says she began the session having the sense of being caught '*in flagrante*' and feeling as if she were in a mild state of '*déshabillé*'.

If we have moved on from the 'cupboard love' notion, inherent in drive theory, that we develop relationships as by-products of our sexual and aggressive drives, and look again from a relational perspective, then sex can be seen as a powerful organizer of our experiences and of our sense of self. The original love relationship of a child and their mother, when it occurs, is deeply passionate, romantic and sensual so that if and when a close relationship forms with the therapist, elements of that early 'love', or their absence, will be reawakened. It is only to be expected that people, reworking developmental 'lost opportunities', will push to be seen and recognized for attachment and connection, not always as sexual 'objects' but as subjects in relationship with another. Mitchell indicated the importance of the sexual body:

> Bodily sensations and sensual pleasures define one's skin, one's outline, one's boundaries; and the dialectics of bodily and sexual intimacies position one in relation to the other: over, under, inside, against, surrounding, controlling, yielding, adored, enraptured, and so on.

> (Mitchell 1988: 103)

That idea that therapy should take place between two reciprocally respectful adults implies a mutuality that is sometimes not apparent in the powerful and primitive feelings that can be evoked on both sides of the room. Many patients learned how to 'do' sex before they knew how to 'be' in relationship, and sex is often confused with intimacy. People who come into therapy may have their own ideas of what it is that will help them, and the expectations that can be projected onto the therapeutic relationship can be profound. They may have come unconsciously expecting to receive emotional compensation for all the disappointments and losses that life has brought.

A man who had formed a strong attachment with a therapist wanted to know if there would be social contact between them after the therapy ended. For a long time he resented that this would not happen and said that he could not begin to trust her if there was going to be nothing beyond the end of the therapy, when he might never see her again. A colleague said that 'sex is a marker of being an equal', so that to be seen as 'just another client' sometimes holds feelings of shame and humiliation.

A therapeutic impasse continued for some time because he felt it was impossible for him to reveal weakness and vulnerability to the woman therapist, upon whom he wanted to make an impression as an attractive and powerful man. He resisted any attempt to talk about his early relationships, seeing this as the therapist's desire to escape the uncomfortable intensity of the moment in the room – and, at one level, he was correct! After all, does the therapist not say that a degree of dependency is necessary for this work to be done? Jody Messler Davies expressed the dilemma of the therapist clearly, when she said:

> Of course; as experienced analysts who have been burned, we learn to hope, and to hope fervently, that the client falls only a little bit in love with her analyst, and does so for what seems a respectable period of time, before moving on.
>
> (Messler Davies 2003: 2)

It can be a delicate balance when a therapist tries to explore the patient's loving and erotic fantasies, but the former can experience increasing guilt when this seems to evoke even more longing and bitter reproaches for the pain that unrequited love can bring. This can make the therapist withdraw to a safe emotional distance, which re-enacts an earlier parental rejection, so a vicious circle is set in motion where the patient will feel betrayed, unloved and unlovable.

A patient who was painfully aware of the doors that were closed to her in my flat, told me that I kept an 'exclusion zone' around me, and that it was a harsh affront to her when she heard someone cooking in my kitchen. She had to come to terms with this evidence that I might have a partner, an insult that took us months to repair. Although it can feel disturbing to a therapist when his or her own private life becomes the focus of the therapy, making calm reflection more difficult, it is important that the patient feels free to explore feelings that may have been foreclosed in earlier life by shaming parents. It becomes essential that the therapist does not treat the patient as invasive and greedy, even when it might feel as if they are!

It becomes understandable that the therapist's early experiences of the transference led to the drives of sex and aggression being 'twinned', because of the perception of the strength of their compulsive power. The pejorative term 'bunny boiler' has entered the vocabulary after reactions to the portrayal of the spurned and desperate woman in the film *Fatal Attraction* revealed a lingering fear in our popular culture of a 'hysterical' woman's unbridled sexual desire turning to murderous aggression.

Under great pressure from erotic desire, the therapeutic alliance can feel tested to its limit when an obsessional patient grasps the therapeutic encounter and the therapist as a drowning person might seize a life preserver. Sometimes an addictive relationship, which can seem all-consuming, is, like all the major addictions, a defence against dependency.

Rosie Alexander describes vividly what can happen when a patient forms an extreme and demanding attachment to her therapist and his responses to her plight seem inadequate to help her work the experience through to a successful conclusion. The patient was not well served by the seemingly sloppy boundaries that Luc, her therapist, maintained. Tantalized by his private life, from which she felt she was agonizingly excluded, she was able to enter other rooms of his apartment, and meet his other patients in his waiting room, because 'he was running late today'. This intelligent and perceptive, but highly disturbed woman put him under enormous pressure to give in to her demands and she could sense his discomfort when he took refuge in the therapist's defence of silence. He seemed to try many approaches, eventually permitting her to sit in his lap, unbuttoning his shirt or touching his genitals with her foot. When he denied the significance of the erection that she had aroused, then it seemed that the frame was almost non-existent and hardly therapeutic at all (Alexander 1995: 106)!

Patients can push the therapist into ways of being that can set them up in 'all or nothing' or 'either or' choices, demanding special treatment where a refusal would lead to inevitable and bitter disappointment. The early fears of transgressive and collusive behaviour that led to a classical austerity do have a basis in reality, and therapists rightly felt they had to protect themselves from powerful temptations. Serious exploitation of trust results when, taking the idea of 'loving care' too far, therapists abandon the therapeutic frame altogether in trying to provide gratification of the patient's desires. But sometimes the therapist, in becoming sexual with them, uses and exploits the patient to meet his or her own needs. Because it is a matter of professional pride that firm boundaries are maintained, the therapeutic frame is most often thought about from the therapist's perspective, with their preoccupations of good management and how they themselves should behave. What can get left behind in these encounters might be the patient's experience and perceptions of the therapist. When hearing of breaches of the therapeutic frame and the latitude some practitioners permit themselves, it is difficult not to judge the therapist and feel concern for the patients and the fate of their therapeutic relationships.

A patient once told me that her previous 'shrink' had gone to a wedding and remained anonymously at the back, so that she could observe the people who populated the narrative that her patient brought. I heard of another woman who had gone to see her boyfriend's therapist, who had discussed him with her, to help her gain a greater understanding of her partner. Someone told me of a practitioner who fed his grown-up patient with a baby's bottle, holding the patient like a baby in his arms, and one creative and dynamic woman was asked to collaborate on a book with the therapist she was seeing. She left the therapy when she felt that the practitioner's needs were becoming more pressing than her own.

A therapist commissioned an artist patient to paint her portrait, in lieu of payment for sessions, and later gave him discounts in her fees for referrals he made to her among his friends. Like horses in the same stable, these friends met regularly and discussed their 'issues' and experiences in therapy; the therapist never discouraged this. The people who gave me these examples were patients who had become disappointed in their therapists, so we must recognize that impingements of the therapeutic frame do not always come from the patient.

Stephen Mitchell has said: 'Clay feet are being exposed in all traditional institutions and psychoanalysis is no exception' (1997: 206). Dissatisfied consumers, who have bad experiences in therapy, are now writing their own accounts of encounters with practitioners, and how they behave towards them. While it might feel tiresome for therapists constantly to defend their trade against seemingly endless attacks from people in the media, important questions are being asked which have to be addressed about how we work and the effectiveness of our work.

We should listen very carefully and be prepared to answer the criticisms of those people with experience of psychotherapy, who have, in their disappointment, become bitter proselytizers against us, without pathologizing those discontented customers. The most common criticism of the therapeutic frame is the rigour and authoritarianism with which some practitioners apply it. I hear complaints about patients' previous therapists who seemed cold, remote and silent and who did not seem to try to engage in a relationship with them. So critics are saying that we should be less severe, more approachable and ethically accountable at the same time.

The patients I meet in therapy do not come with the hysterical symptoms that Freud and the pioneers of analysis often met. Today, many people feel incapable of finding or sustaining meaningful and satisfactory personal relationships across their lives. Somewhere in their relationship history their intrinsic tenderness has been violated, resulting in a damaged sense of self, and what Winnicott described as a 'false self' has adapted to a world that has not met their 'spontaneous gesture'. Fearing true relationship, they have often striven unconsciously to remake and repair their initial unsatisfactory interactions with their parents throughout their relational history.

Conclusion

In the days when psychotherapy required a heavy investment of time and money, the early therapeutic frame was taken too far in its austerity in order to maintain safe and effective practice and to protect the therapist and the patient from sadistic and sexual feelings aroused in the hot-house atmosphere of the therapy room. This model of psychotherapy prevailed unchallenged for half a century, but then began to change.

With the development of object relations and self-psychology in the 1940s and 1950s, people were beginning to question the so-called 'blank screen approach' of classical psychoanalysis. It was easy to feel hostile to a world from which one felt excluded and, in a growing consumerist climate, vast numbers of people renounced the Freudian orthodoxy, voted with their feet, and took their business elsewhere. The advent of 'feminist' and 'queer' thinking in the last three decades of the twentieth century *demanded* that women and gay people be moved from the position of pathological 'objects' to that of 'subjects'.

As an inevitable result of these liberating changes there has been a democratization of training institutes, which has had profound effects on the accessibility to the world of psychotherapy. The integration of the countertransferential experiences of the practitioner has gradually led to a paradigm shift, where the personality and actions of the therapist are understood to have a large impact on what happens in the practice of psychotherapy, leading us to a two-person, 'relational' approach.

Today, Freud might recognize the analytic hour in the same way that Henry Ford would recognize the modern vehicles which have evolved from the Model T of his early invention. The therapeutic frame is still firmly in place, but is slowly changing to a slightly more 'user-friendly' approach to accommodate the growing appetite for the 'talking cure', fed by a culture of daytime television counselling, survivor groups and self-help books. I use e-mail and letters to maintain attachment to patients who have to travel abroad for work, and we have yet to see the effects upon therapy where practitioners have begun to use the Internet. The growing influence in psychotherapy of neurobiology must eventually energize the controversial issue of touch in therapy, where, in the past, this very human need has been distorted, sexualized and treated with suspicion. A major London conference, led by Susie Orbach in 2003,[2] explored the meaning and place in psychotherapy today of touch, the body and its importance in human development.

So, in the light of the changes that have occurred, the question must be asked: Do we, as therapists, need to maintain the therapeutic frame? I would say yes, for reasons made very clear by Stephen Mitchell:

> The main function of the therapist's role is to preserve the relation-ship as analytic in order to protect the inquiry . . . While the analysand's role entails giving oneself over to the experience of the analytic process, the analyst, in addition to the experiential self-monitoring, must also pay attention to holding and protecting the process. The asymmetry of the analytic relationship derives greatly from the necessity for the analyst to bear his responsibility. In some respects the analyst's role is analogous to that of a 'designated driver' at a party.
>
> (Mitchell 1997: 228)

Whilst the idea of a responsive practitioner giving therapy like feeding 'on demand' might be attractive, it is sentimental to imagine that the therapist could create a therapeutic environment where there will be no stress, fear or anxiety for the patient. As they grow, children try to engage with and master difficulty, achieving pride in working through their challenges. Freud observed that his grandson being left alone in throwing a cotton reel away and pulling it back again, whilst shouting 'Fort-Da' ('gone-there'), was creating a game of managing the existential crisis provoked by his mother's coming and goings. A 'developmental line' continues throughout life. We move through conflict to get to more conflict, and all relationships involve taking risks.

Freud became dissatisfied with hypnosis because it was not *powerful* enough to remain effective over time, and the 'talking cure' replaced it. Since we are dealing with powerful processes it is disingenuous to pretend that the role of therapist does not hold power. The patient is a supplicant, asking for help, from someone who is experienced in the business of promoting change. Judith Herman (1992) suggests that this asymmetry of relationship naturally creates an imbalance of power and that the therapist's neutrality becomes important when working with people who may already have suffered from previous abuses of power:

> '*Disinterested*' means that the therapist abstains from using her power over the patient to gratify her personal needs. '*Neutral*' means that the therapist does not take sides in the patient's inner conflicts or try to direct the patient's life decisions. Constantly reminding herself that the patient is in charge of her own life, the therapist refrains from advancing a personal agenda. This disinterested and neutral stance is an ideal to be striven for, never perfectly attained.
>
> (Herman 1992: 135, my italics)

Practitioners are often under great pressure to come up with answers to troubling dilemmas, and a colleague told me that therapists, when trying to hold their own helplessness and desperation at their patient's distress, often feel impelled to 'do something' rather than just 'be with' something. Sometimes, living with 'not knowing' can be a large part of the work we do together. In a public lecture, Joseph Schwartz said that therapists become 'experts in not knowing'. Therapy is not 'skilling', and the patient, like the therapist, does not become 'hardened' to pain. On this journey of discovery that the therapist and patient take together, we might help a person discover the 'gift' of their vulnerability and, in doing so, they will become exposed to the wounded parts of themselves, the 'places in the heart' that were forsaken in order to survive. Through the use of the 'instrument' of the therapeutic frame, and the corrective experience of relationship, the therapist is trying to redress an historical imbalance where an over-indulgent, intrusive or neglectful parental environment has resulted in destructive and self-sabotaging behaviour in the patient. In therapy the movement towards a more self-loving and adult way of being in relationship will 'contain' grief and disappointment, in both senses of the word. The 'fifty-minute hour' already carries a communication that, in therapy, even an hour is not an hour, so the practitioner cannot be 'everything'; they will always disappoint. It is unfortunate but true, that the therapist, like a 'good enough' parent, will fail the patient at times, and pain and fear will be inevitable. What is important is how breakdowns in this new relationship can be managed and repaired. The therapist cannot compensate for what was needed and lost when the patient's birthright was denied. These real-life losses, including those evoked by the therapeutic encounter, can be accepted and mourned within the safe structure that the therapeutic frame provides.

In the long-evolving affiliation between the practitioner and the patient, the frame becomes a continuous, transitional object, held between us, until it is time to let it go. Therapeutic abstinence means that there are also going to be losses for the practitioner in having to forgo the pleasures of closer contact with those people whom we grow to love. Sometimes, invitations to attend landmark occasions in our patients' lives have to be regretfully refused, when it would be personally gratifying to dance at their weddings, to see them at their opening nights and exhibitions, at their children's christenings and their milestone birthdays – not as problem people but as joyous people being effective in the lives which we have been privileged to share for a time.

As the work progresses towards its inevitable conclusion, the therapeutic frame that held a person coming in from a chaotic world can begin to be relaxed, whilst still maintaining and adjusting the firm structure to help contain the grief which therapist and patient will feel when we begin the process of mourning the loss of each other.

Notes

1 I use the generic term 'psychotherapy' to describe the expanding field of 'talking cures' influenced by psychoanalysis to include psychologists, psychotherapists, counsellors, couples and group therapists, the behavioural approaches and short-term dynamic psychotherapy.
2 The Tenth John Bowlby Memorial Conference, 'Touch Attachment and the Body', 10 March 2003, Centre for Attachment-based Psychoanalytic Psychotherapy (CAPP), London.

References

Alexander, R. (1995) *Folie a Deux. An Experience of One to One Therapy*, London: Free Association Books.
Benedek, T. (1953) 'Dynamics of countertransference', *Bulletin of the Menninger Clinic* [New York] 17: 201–8.
Bion, W.R. (1967) 'Attacks on linking', in *Second Thoughts*, London: Heinemann, pp. 93–109.
Bowlby, J. (1969) *Attachment and Loss. Vol. 1: Attachment*, London: Hogarth Press.
Herman, J.L. (1992) *Trauma and Recovery. From Domestic Abuse to Political Terror*, London: Basic Books.

Hoffman, I.Z. (1983) 'The patient as interpreter of the analyst's experience', *Contemporary Psychoanalysis* 19(3): 389–421.

Messler Davies, J. (2003) 'Falling in love with love. Oedipal and post Oedipal manifestations of idealization, mourning and erotic masochism, *Psychoanalytic Dialogues* 13(1): 1–27.

Mitchell, S.A. (1988) *Relational Concepts in Psychoanalysis: An Integration*, Cambridge, Mass.: Harvard University Press.

Mitchell, S.A. (1997) *Influence and Autonomy in Psychoanalysis*, Hillsdale, N.J.: The Analytic Press.

Rogers, C.R. (1951) *Client Centred Therapy*, London: Constable.

Schwartz, J. (1999) *Cassandra's Daughter: A History of Psychoanalysis in Europe and America*, London: Allen Lane.

Wingfield, R. (2002) *CAPP Annual Report 2001–02*, London: Centre for Attachment-based Analytical Psychotherapy.

Winnicott, D.W. (1958) *Through Paediatrics to Psychoanalysis*, London: Tavistock Publications.

Winnicott, D.W. (1971) *Playing and Reality*, London: Tavistock Publications.

Chapter 10

Hospital philosophy

An existential-phenomenological perspective

Greg Madison

Regardless of our orientation to therapeutic practice, few of us can avoid feeling troubled when we are not able to maintain some level of continuity with our clients – meeting at the same time, in the same place, for the same duration, with sessions at set intervals, offering a consistent kind of presence (often comprising at least relative anonymity of the therapist, abstinence of physical contact, etc.), in a confidential relationship, for the benefit of the person seeking our help. Continuity is the mainstay of the frame, versions of which range from the 'flexible frame' (Gray, 1994) to the rigidly defined 'secure frame' (Langs, 1998). In actuality, the frame is a theoretically derived, more or less rigorously applied, *set* of boundaries around the therapeutic setting and relationship. While boundaries can be à la carte, the frame, in any form, is closer to a '*set menu*', set by the theory prescribing it.

In this chapter, I attempt to describe some dilemmas of frame therapy highlighted by psychotherapeutic practice in an acute general hospital setting. In order to do this I will briefly describe the situation in hospitals, some of the needs of clients (patients or relatives), and the obstacles to adopting a frame-based orientation in this setting. Despite the inability to abide by a frame approach, deep therapeutic work is done in hospitals. This raises questions about the necessity of frames, and since frames are the outcome of theory it must also imply questions about the associated therapeutic theory. In response to my experience in hospitals I find myself emphasizing a more philosophical attitude to therapy, implying different responses to frame issues. Delineating alternatives to orthodox frame therapy could prove attractive to those therapists who would like to practise in settings where their usual understanding of psychotherapy is not sustaining.

The hospital

The world of psychotherapy is quite rarefied compared to the glimpsed tragedies and sensory onslaught of daily hospital life. Arriving in hospital itself can generate considerable vulnerability, uncertainty, boredom, in addition to conforming to the routine of a large institution and the subsequent loss of individual choice and privacy. Hospitals are strange and often lonely places, bringing people into contact with the suffering and dying of others, sometimes evoking previous bereavements. As well as issues arising from the environment, patients and families request counselling support for stressors related to physical diagnosis and treatment, such as anxiety regarding invasive procedures, sudden paralysis or loss of a limb, chronic illness, critical or terminal diagnoses, and the inevitable social consequences of having a disease (for other examples, see Spiegel, 1999, 1993, 1994) – all significant crises for which counselling is not routinely provided.[1]

If therapy is to be available to anyone requesting it, practice must be flexible enough to accommodate the physical environment, unplanned procedures, the patient's medical condition, unexpected discharge or death, as well as delayed discharge (when an end to therapy has been planned to coincide with a patient's discharge which is then delayed). Clients who are patients may be at any stage of medical treatment: recovering from a successful operation and looking forward to going home, living with uncertain diagnosis or prognosis, slipping in and out of consciousness, or in the terminal stages of illness and deciding where they would like to die. The hospital environment is very unpredictable, so working there is *unavoidably* as messy as life gets. Listed below are common deviations from frame considerations inherent in working as a psychotherapist in this setting:

1   *Inconsistency of place.* Since many patients are physically unable to leave the ward, sessions might be conducted in patients' rooms, ward managers' offices, day rooms, any available space, and often not the same place twice. For patients who are totally immobile, their sessions take place at their bedsides, sometimes on acute intensive care or high dependency units, and often on busy old-fashioned open wards with just a curtain pulled around the bed.
2   *Inconsistency of session timings.* Understandably, the medical ethos prevails in hospitals, so even if you have a regular time allocated for a client there can often be intrusions. For example, if a long-awaited scan can finally occur at the hour your session is about to start, the

scan almost always takes precedence, usually both from the point of view of the medical staff and the patient/client. If the scan is missed it could mean waiting another week, and thereby prolonging the anxiety of an unconfirmed diagnosis. The therapist soon learns when to avoid scheduling sessions in order to miss busy times (for example ward rounds), thus minimizing this specific collision between therapy practice and medical environment.

3   *Inconsistency of frequency/interval.* The client (patient or relative) can be seen once a week, daily during acute periods of distress, or intermittently upon request. For example, if a family member requests daily contact while the patient is in a critical state it would be difficult to invoke a frame-based rationale for not agreeing to this, knowing that by the next regular session time the patient may be dead and the family member gone. It would mean in effect that therapy could not occur. After discharge, clients (whether patients or relatives) can return for follow-up sessions at the hospital. Due to travelling distances this is not always practical, and those clients wishing to continue in counselling are routinely offered referrals to local agencies or their GP surgery counsellors.

4   *Inconsistency of contract durations.* Therapists find themselves embarking on a contract without always knowing the kind of contract being agreed to. In a sense each session is best viewed as a discreet therapeutic contract since the situation can spontaneously and inadvertently change between the short term, the longer term, and crisis work, and not infrequently therapy is terminated abruptly due to unexpected hospital transfer, discharge, or death.

5   *Inconsistency of session duration.* The patient's physical condition can lead to requests for shorter sessions. Likewise, a relative in distress may request that the therapist remain longer than the normal fifty-minute session, for example until a family member arrives.

6   *Interruptions.* The hospital culture is not rarefied. It is not common practice for staff to pause, knock, and wait for a reply before entering a room. All space is considered fairly public space and staff can interrupt a session for various reasons, to empty a bin, give an injection, or collect a patient for a crucial procedure that's been rescheduled. Often other professionals don't fully appreciate the importance of not disturbing the session.

7   *Anonymity of the therapist, intimacy/distance, and physical touch are challenged.* Therapists may be in a situation in which touch is requested or deemed the most appropriate action. For example, therapists have assisted their clients into wheelchairs, helped to

position them in bed, administered 'suction' to patients who could not swallow rather than have a nurse interrupt the session every five minutes, repeatedly scratched the itchy nose of a paralysed patient, etc. Attending sessions at the client's bedside also introduces an element of intimacy unusual in conventional therapy. Many of our clients have sessions while partially clothed or in pyjamas. And, of course, the fact that the therapist may go to the client rather than the reverse makes it difficult for the client *not* to attend a session. Due to the unusual setting, clients are perhaps more likely to engage in conversation about the person of the therapist, their own life, and not infrequently how the therapist would cope if they were facing the situation the client is in.

8 *Confidentiality and anonymity of the client cannot be guaranteed.* Family members, staff members, other patients, may all know that the client is seeing a therapist. Therapy is not anonymous in that referrals and subsequent session dates for patients must be recorded in their hospital medical notes, but the content of sessions are recorded anonymously in a separate team database. Sessions that take place on open wards also do not meet usual therapist expectations for confidentiality – neighbouring patients and staff can at times partially overhear sessions. Therapists frequently encounter their client's friends and families. Family members and staff who know that the client is having therapy may stop the therapist to ask how the client 'is doing'.

Often our clients have requested counselling or psychotherapy[2] to cope with an immediate medical crisis or related issues. They have come into contact with the therapist because of their association with the hospital – they are medical patients, or relatives, before they are psychotherapy 'clients'. The unique avenue that hospital patients (and their family members) take into a therapeutic relationship may have implications for the appropriateness of working within traditional therapeutic frames.

The frame

After providing some sense of the vicissitudes of a hospital setting I want to outline two frame-based approaches to illustrate how they would be difficult to establish in the situation I have previously outlined. I will assume some familiarity with the concept of therapeutic frames in order to concentrate on highlighting their more theoretical foundations.

Anne Gray's *An Introduction to the Therapeutic Frame* (1994) presents a balanced account of the justification for 'frame therapy'. It boils down to the following argument: our treatment in infancy leads to *predictable* psychological difficulties. The therapist is entrusted with the task of providing the optimal setting that did not exist in early development: 'we should provide a model of care which is consistent, that continuity is ensured, and, like the feeding pattern which is gradually established, a regular period of time set aside just for the client' (Gray, 1994: 10). However, the therapist does not attempt to redress past discrepancies in care:

> We might say then that the frame is both like and extremely unlike the care that parents provide for their children . . . its difference is in the prohibition on action . . . we have to contain our feelings in the service of understanding and at times this can feel cruel . . . The therapist, through an ability to bear feelings rather than act on them, will be experienced as both frustrating and containing. Similarly, the frame becomes the container for the feelings that are paradoxically caused by it.
>
> (Gray, 1994: 15)

The frame therapist forms a practice around the assumptions he or she has about the world of the infant[3] and assumes a causal connection between these surmised childhood experiences and later difficulties, and then acts on these assumptions so as to elicit the earlier parental relationship. Then, no matter how 'cruel' it may feel, the therapist *causes* frustration by not acting (but of course establishing and maintaining the frame is highly orchestrated action!). Frame therapy leads to 'frame feelings', generating a therapy that treats the feelings it has caused, in turn reinforcing and supporting the rationale behind the therapy.

Gray says the frame is not 'written in stone' and that there are settings in which the frame cannot be maintained 'yet useful work can still be done' (1994: 19). This suggests that psychotherapy *can* be done in the setting I have described above, where frame conditions are not possible; but this raises further questions. What makes non-frame therapy 'useful', and does this also function in frame therapy or is it unique to non-frame therapy? If it also functions in frame therapy, is there a question about what *really* makes frame therapy effective[4]? If useful work can be done when the frame is not established, and thus without the primary emphasis on the transference relationship[5], should we question this theory more generally?

Frame therapy assumes that without 'containment', anxiety and chaos prevail. This is a crucial assumption of the theory, suggesting that the only order is an imposed one. Gray concludes that 'Without a framework neither participant in the therapeutic relationship will feel safe enough to experience the complex emotions that are part of all deep and lasting relationships' (1994: 141). This suggests an interesting differentiation between 'frame' and 'framework'. Of course, most 'deep and lasting relationships' do not rely on a 'secure frame', so the secure frame cannot be the only framework. I will suggest later that all human interactions inevitably *imply their own* 'framework', so there may be alternative frameworks for understanding therapy – and life.

Robert Langs' 'communicative psychotherapy' (1997, 1998) presents a variation of frame therapy based upon the idea that the frame *is*, in fact, *the therapy*. The therapist is entrusted primarily with cementing and maintaining the frame so that it can cure the client. According to this theory, the work of the frame is not to make the client feel safe, but quite the opposite: to elicit the client's deepest anxieties regarding death. Langs' view that the frame provides the experience of confinement, the coffin in the grave, and all its so-called 'existential death anxiety', differs from the mainstream analytic view of the frame as providing the safety of the womb, the containment and security of the mother's holding. The intricate contradictions and philosophical quirks of this complex and fascinating theory, and its concomitant technique, have been explored elsewhere (Madison, 2001a). It is significant to notice that adherents of both views see their theories confirmed in their practice. Imagination and perception are intricately woven, and in all our quandaries preconceptions may provide more than a hint of colour to our observations.

Langs points out explicitly that frame therapists attempting to work in medical situations, especially with clients who are facing death, seem to experience 'special problems of technique' (1997: 236). For example, therapists are tempted to become 'human' because of their 'own unmastered death anxieties', and to be 'openly compassionate, non-interpretative, and frame-altering' when their patients are dying. Like conventional psychoanalysis, communicative psychoanalysis maintains a strong prohibition on self-disclosure. According to Langs:

> Inherently, all breaks in relative anonymity unconsciously also place the therapist in the role of patient and ask the patient to assume the role of therapist. Harm is thereby suffered by the patient, and the therapist will suffer from conscious and especially unconscious guilt.
>
> (Langs, 1998: 200)

It is not clear how revealing one's own humanness places the patient in the role of therapist. Isn't it possible that self-disclosure partially deconstructs the polarity of these two roles? What evidence shows that this is harmful? Langs acknowledges the difficulty of performing his therapy in medical clinic settings, where frame breaks are likely and complete confidentiality difficult to insist upon, but suggested ways of reducing these deviations in a clinic setting are entirely unrealistic in an acute general hospital, leaving stark choices for such therapists. Witnessing frame therapists' struggles to abide by or to shed their theory in the face of extremis, suggests that in such situations some of these therapists experience their approach as unacceptable, entailing a narrowing-down of possibilities for interaction.

The clash

Therapists from all orientations have had to adapt their usual way of working to some extent when responding to the unique challenges of a medical setting (see Thomas *et al.*, 2001), and most clearly when working with the terminally ill. Some react to the collision in cultures between counselling and medicine by developing a flexible approach to practice (Logan, 2001: 65–78), including visiting clients on the ward when their illness prevents them from attending a session, and negotiating a different understanding of confidentiality within medical teams[6]. Other therapists have grappled with maintaining their frame approach when working with patients:

> It is generally accepted that secure boundaries are essential to provide containment for the powerful affects experienced in psychodynamic therapy. What is remarkable, given that those who are dying face the loss of all known boundaries, is the fact that the need for a containing therapeutic framework is often neglected in counselling in the hospice setting.
>
> (Birch, 2001: 151)

Birch maintains that some flexibility may be required as a patient's condition deteriorates, but warns that '[c]ounsellors who reduce the duration of sessions from the standard fifty minutes may be motivated by their own unconscious fear of facing death rather than by a need to accommodate the specific requirements of the seriously ill' (2001: 153). She does not explain how *reducing* the session time, rather than sticking to a 'magical' fifty minutes despite compelling circumstances, could indicate an 'unconscious fear of facing death' (perhaps clinging to the frame is as unconsciously death-defying?). Birch is rightly concerned that the counsellor could look for an excuse to truncate the session because of his or her own difficult feelings, but of course there are many ways of avoiding difficult feelings other than leaving, and there are many *legitimate* reasons to shorten a session with a dying patient.

Another frame therapist, Peter Hildebrand, gives an account of working with a gay man dying of AIDS. Hildebrand comes to recognize through his responses to this man that maintaining his frame theory obfuscates a satisfying fuller appreciation of his client's situation: '[psychoanalysts] do not have any real body of experience or practice with dealing with the dying' (1992: 467). He says that when such patients come with their 'existential problems', it is difficult for the analyst to maintain their '*inner standards*' (ibid.; emphasis added)'. When his patient was on his deathbed, Hildebrand shook his hand and told him to 'keep fighting', though it was clear that death was imminent (Hildebrand, ibid.: 466; cf. Madison, 1997: 7). Michele Crossley, a psychologist involved in research with HIV-positive gay men, offers an existential critique of Hildebrand's interaction with this client:

> The negative implications of Hildebrand's inability to conceive of his material in 'terms other than those of object-relations theory', are that he fails to orient to the reality of Matthew's situation; to the fact that Matthew was a person dying who perhaps required nothing more than simple human contact. Because Hildebrand fails to appreciate such possibilities, he succeeds in reducing Matthew's experiences to manifestations of unconscious conflict and Matthew himself to an 'object' of transferential/countertransferential processes . . . The most disturbing evidence of such objectification and dehumanisation is evident in Hildebrand's response to his invitation to Matthew's funeral. He states that: 'I did not go since in my own mind my business with Matthew had been with his inner world which was now dead and his burial was really a matter for his family and friends not for me' (p.446). Surely, Matthew, like all of us, was a person, not an 'inner' or 'outer' world?
>
> (Crossley, 1998: 55–6)

These problems are echoed by Mark Blechner, who says that working with AIDS patients places a burden on analysts because the patient's emotions are 'contagious' and can cause an existential crisis for the analyst and his/her beliefs (1993: 68–70; cf. Madison, 1997: 7). There is an apparent mismatch between orthodox frame techniques, which emphasize *unconscious* anxieties or *fantasized* transferences, and aspects of our human *existence*, 'although psychoanalysis has . . . the theory of the "death drive" . . . psychoanalysis's idea of death has nothing to do with the problems that may be posed for us by our "being toward death"', in other words by our mortality' (Laplanche, 1989: 50; cf. Bauknight and Applebaum, 1997: 92).

Other frame therapists have chosen to abandon their assumptions about practice in order to respond to the reality of their client's situation. Diane Sadowy, a psychoanalyst with an HIV-positive female patient, grasps the opportunity of this relationship to reassess her orientation. She asks herself: 'Where do transference, countertransference, resistance and such have a place when the realities of the situation are so overwhelming?' (1991: 205). Unlike Hildebrand, Sadowy responds by leaving her analytic frame to help in caregiving tasks with her patient.

In the article 'AIDS, Death, and the Analytic Frame', Rebecca Bauknight describes her work as a clinical psychologist working with a man dying of AIDS (Bauknight and Applebaum, 1997). The article is written in a poetic style, consistent with the author's attempts to break what she comes to experience as the punitive restrictions of her theory:

> [the frame's] unmistakeable shatter breaks through the silence as loud as machinegun fire to anyone who listens for the slightest tilting on the edge of the table, the breeze of the disturbed air, the clatter of glass unmistakable to anyone who doesn't question the party line, the analytic lines drawn around the room, the frame . . . I really don't see these lines so clearly . . . Does this mean that I too will meet with death? . . . Will I also find myself crumbling and dying without the sanctity of the frame?
>
> (Bauknight and Applebaum, 1997: 81)

According to Bauknight, the act of 'framing' itself needs analysis – it encapsulates a hint of the paranoid-schizoid in its attempt to 'frame any threats to its own demarcations by stigmatizing them as expressions of "resistance"' (ibid.: 86). 'The frame tells us where to look, and where not to look' (ibid.: 90), it is an attempt to contain what could never be contained without the tacit agreement, or collusion, of the participants.

In therapy, two (or more) people form an interaction which always exceeds the frame and which can be referred to from within the frame and from outside it. Outside the sessions, client and therapist dream about their encounters, think about each other, prepare for their meetings. As

Bauknight points out, the frame is always open (ibid.: 90–1). Yet, the metaphor of the frame encourages the illusion of a sterile Petri dish form of therapy, purely isolated from the contamination of the world outside. *Even the so-called 'secure frame' is more a membrane than a solid container.*

It is clear from the diverse attitudes toward maintaining the frame that stirrings within individual frame practitioners can override theoretical restrictions as to which possibilities of engagement with others are permitted or important. Especially in the face of imminent death, many frame therapists feel compelled to reach out in a gesture of human connectedness. But if this is possible when faced with death, why not in other situations? Where do we draw the line in terms of seeing an outstretched hand as humane, thus excusable, or as 'failure'? How flexible can a frame approach become and still be a frame approach – focused on generating 'frame feelings' (transference or death anxiety)?

The shift

The hospital setting often involves working with the severely medically ill, the dying, and their relatives. From the frame deviations outlined in the first section, and the problems encountered by frame therapists in working with the dying generally, it seems clear that a frame approach, and its theoretical emphasis, cannot offer an adequate guide to practitioners wishing to respond to all requests for therapy and counselling in an acute general hospital setting. If such work is to be done, it requires a more appropriate approach, a 'framework' not based upon frames.

In the early days of psychoanalysis, Freud practised in a flexible and variable way, maintaining loose boundaries and dual relationships (Gabbard, 1995: 1115). For example, he practised a style of mutual analysis with his colleague and friend Ferenczi during their voyage to America (ibid.: 1124). Freud also analysed clients while strolling through the streets of Vienna and during summer holidays at the house of a client's brother (ibid.: 1124). From a frame therapy point of view, these are 'violations' of the frame, examples of how our 'impaired colleagues' struggled to 'define the parameters of the analytic relationship' (ibid.: 1117). However, if the aim of therapy is not necessarily assumed to be the archaeology of the unconscious, these early attempts may be viewed quite differently.

Irvin Yalom (2001) comments upon the same early 'violations' mentioned above, arriving at very different conclusions. Yalom presents Freud's early work as 'bold' in that he did not remain aloof but sought encounters with his patients beyond what we now consider to be the orthodox 'frame'. 'He made strong suggestions to them, he intervened on their behalf with family members, he contrived to attend social functions to see his patients in other settings, he instructed a patient to visit the cemetery and meditate upon the tombstone of a dead sibling' (Yalom, 2001: 76). He also admires Ferenczi's experiment with mutual analysis, calling it 'radical':

> A bold experiment in therapist transparency that has long intrigued me was conducted by Sandor Ferenczi (1873–1933) . . . Of all the analysts in the inner circle, it was Sandor Ferenczi who relentlessly and boldly sought out technical innovation.
>
> (Yalom, 2001: 81)

Yalom applauds attempts to 'be human' in therapy. He suggests that therapists should be 'flexible, creative, and individualized' in their practice, incorporating thoughtful self-disclosure and appropriate physical touch. Yalom totally rejects the strictures of frame therapy, especially the rule of therapist anonymity:

> [The Blank Screen] is not now, nor was it ever, a good model for effective therapy. The idea of using current distortions to re-create the past was part of an old, now abandoned, vision of the therapist as archaeologist . . . [these considerations do not merit] the sacrifice of an authentic human encounter in psychotherapy.
>
> (Yalom, 2001: 75)

Yalom does not share the theoretical underpinning of frame assumptions and so is free to take a radically different approach to therapy. He suggests that (any) theory in therapy is an attempt to conceal 'the desolation of a purely capricious existence' (ibid.: 175–6).

The psychoanalyst Steven Gans, consistent with the approach advocated by Yalom, emphasizes the quality of 'therapeutic engagement'. Gans calls his therapy 'ethical analysis', and bases it on the philosophy of Emmanuel Levinas:

> For me psychoanalysis is an ethical practice; it is the practice of just listening . . . I want to propose that the existential psychoanalytic process amounts to a lived ethics, the ethics of putting the other first . . . The other is singular and thus cannot retain its otherness if reduced to the imminence of my own understanding. As soon as

interrogation, investigation, theoretisation, categorisation, exposure and representation occur, proximity (Levinas's term for ethical relatedness) is lost. These are modes of violation of the other, attempts to capture the other and reduce the other to my own mastery and control.

(Gans, 1999: 102–3)

From this point of view, the therapist who starts from a theoretical a priori, as in frame therapy, is displaying a sort of narcissism, not relating on the client's terms but on his own. A less pernicious understanding of frames is offered by Ernesto Spinelli, who suggests:

The frame issues may not be important in themselves, but may rather have the same effect as Dumbo's magic feather. In other words, their importance lies in the fact that *the therapist believes them to be necessary for the 'magic' of therapy to work.*

(Spinelli, 1994: 89)

For clients who share this secure frame superstition, a flexible frame can positively challenge the world-view implied by such beliefs:

The therapy taught me that failure, criticism, and rejection does not automatically ensue from moving boundaries and taking risks, but that in fact flexibility has the opposite effect, as it makes room for other options, options which previously were excluded by rigid, fixed, and hence restrictive boundaries. My life became more open, more forward looking . . .

(Strasser, 1999: 99, 102)

Contrary to rules regarding the need to control extraneous variables strictly in order to achieve the special frame conditions of therapy, Hans Cohn offers a view of therapy that allows for the variations in practice necessitated by a setting like the general hospital:

But we can also see psychotherapy as one of the many possibilities of two or more people meeting each other, but distinguished and defined by its particular aim – to create a therapeutic space for a person in need. In this view, psychotherapy needs boundaries like any other meetings, but they will be more loosely structured and flexible enough to respond to the events and developments taking place within them.

(Cohn, 1998: 113)

Recent attempts to delineate a 'more humane psychotherapy' (humane in terms of more fully accounting for the client's reality, and acknowledging the impetus in the therapist to 'reach out') include replacing the certainty of *one* theory with multiplicity (McNamee, 2003), describing an existential therapy distinct from psychotherapy (Colaizzi, 2002) and challenging the accepted limits of the therapeutic enterprise (Spinelli, 2001). These descriptions, and others, offer an alternative basis for practice in an acute general hospital, and thereby a thoughtful development of therapeutic understanding. What does a model of therapy based upon an alternative to frames look like in a hospital setting?

The development

As we've seen, the hospital offers a radically different practice environment, seemingly requiring an equally radical reworking of our understanding of therapy. The service that I eventually developed in interaction with this environment was called a Psychotherapy Support Team (PST). Faced with the restrictions of the setting in terms of conventional practices, plus the extremes of client issues, an existential-phenomenological approach was adopted in order to maintain maximum openness and flexibility. Working phenomenologically encourages the therapist to bracket preconceptions regarding the constituent elements of psychotherapy, including the necessary frame, boundaries, and 'ground rules', while simultaneously remaining open to the possibility that all aspects of the therapeutic encounter may be equally revelatory.

There is no preconceived view that the transference or unconscious death anxiety must be generated and then addressed, and so there is no insistence on keeping a secure frame around the interaction. If a session is interrupted, these influences from the wider world offer opportunities to explore the client's reactions to others. If the patient is bed-bound, the sounds of other patients and the life of the ward are often overheard and appropriately integrated into the session. The session environment constitutes a shared real-time reality, our reactions to which can reveal fundamental aspects about who we are. The therapist is not a neutral commentator upon a second-hand narrative, but is actually *alongside* his or her client, witnessing and participating in their crises and experiences of institutional routine, offering a reflective and reflexive relationship which itself becomes part of the client's experience as it unfolds.

This approach places greater emphasis on acknowledging that the *wider* context in which therapy occurs may have a significant impact on what occurs *within* therapy. This is in contrast to frame approaches, which rule out the world in order to focus the *treatment*. In the hospital setting an important aspect of the wider context is the way in which power relations, based largely upon medical knowledge, can impact upon the patient and his or her relatives. Therapists working in the hospital setting are likewise affected by a culture that emphasizes hierarchy, competition, and specialized expertise. The 'art' of psychotherapy in such settings can become subservient to its 'corporatization':

> The most serious political consequence resulting from the corporat-
> ization process is that mental health professionals are increasingly
> called upon to use any technique at their disposal in order to sequester
> experience . . ., such that deeply personal existential and political
> questions are primarily addressed through a professional world view.
> For the goal of therapy under managed care and an increasingly
> corporatized health care system is not personal growth or personality
> change, but symptom reduction and behavioural adjustment . . .
>
> (Pingitore, 1997: 117)

The danger is that the therapeutic relationship can become subservient to the therapist's need for professional legitimacy, but also to the demands of the institution, and by implication, the demands of society. The therapist's professional interests and the interests of the institution can congeal in ways that deeply affect the client without being explicit enough for the client to challenge. Putting a frame around therapy does not sequester our clients or us from these outside influences – it just rules out talking about them, labelling such talk as 'resistance' or 'defence'. Two potent qualities of the hospital setting for the therapist to consider are the pervasive way in which 'knowledge' in the form of professional expertise constitutes power over the other and, related to this, the incipient way in which a boundary is maintained between humans designated as 'staff' and humans designated as 'patients'[7].

In the PST model, *the intention* is to prioritize a democratic relationship between the counsellor/psychotherapist and the client. Rather than therapeutic techniques (including attempts to maintain a secure frame), psychometric assessments, categorization and diagnosis, or theory-based interventions, the aim is to develop a relationship to the client's ongoing lived experience, acknowledging that the reality of what is being endured is happening to a specific *historical* individual. There is also an open acknowledgement that the therapist is equally physically vulnerable, and therefore the role of the patient can (and at any moment may) be shared by the therapist. Concerning frames, a transparency is established between the client and therapist so that from the first session the limits of the relationship are explored, negotiated, and then left open to renegotiation. Of course, this allows the possibility that a secure frame might actually be the result of such negotiation with a client. Whether it could be put into practice would depend upon the client's condition and hospital facilities.

Variations of the existential-phenomenological stance have recently been presented by Ernesto Spinelli (2001), Emmy van Deurzen (2002), Hans Cohn (1998, 2002), Freddie Strasser (1999) and Mick Cooper (2003). This approach to therapy utilizes the ordinary language of the world we live in, and the client's own understanding of this world, and thus is perceived by clients and staff as immediately graspable and less 'mysterious' than some other modalities of therapy. It does not hypothesize intra-psychic structures, nor does it pathologize clients' modes of experience. Hospital patients and relatives seem to appreciate this down-to-earth attitude, and the resulting relationship between therapist and client can be unusual in its capability to reveal assumptions, contradictions and sedimented responses to life's contingencies, both the client's and the therapist's. This form of encounter emphasizes the importance of choice while also acknowledging that our human existence is shaped and limited by the situations we encounter, including illness, and we often have little or no possibility to change these, except through the way we respond to them. The following section offers some examples and further discussion of PST practice, with reference to its philosophical underpinning.

The practice

Working existentially acknowledges that as humans we share certain givens, so this approach does not introduce a distinction between therapists and patients in terms of the emotional impact of the hospital environment. Likewise, PST facilitation of staff groups emphasizes the lived experience of all staff working in hospitals, and accordingly the therapists do not hide behind a professional 'blank screen', facilitating others' experience while withholding their own, but instead take a collegiate stance and appropriately disclose their own feelings and experiences. However, this is done within the confines of client confidentiality and these groups are a good reminder that the client as patient (or relative) may be in the midst of many significant relationships, of which the therapeutic is only one and not necessarily the most important or most helpful one.

Without a pre-given therapeutic structure or technique, the therapist is required to be creative and to explore different ways of 'being with' the client. For example, some clients have severely restricted forms of communication, sometimes being unable to speak or unable to remain conscious. A therapist may sit in silence with a client who is passing in and out of consciousness. With an intubated patient in Intensive Care, the session may focus on the mutual frustration of communication, or the ramifications of the patient's total reliance on others. Therapy is an exploration of what happens between the people present, their attempts to connect, understand, engage, the obstacles to this, and how each person then responds to these obstacles. Sometimes we are connected by our stories, sometimes by our silence. This approach to therapy explores the complexities of human ways of being rather than interpreting 'psychic disturbance' expressed in a transference or death anxiety.

The analyst Leslie Farber exemplifies this approach to therapy through his focus 'upon a moral, rather than a technique-dominated, and hence safer, professional engagement with his clients' (Spinelli, 2001: 162). Therapy was not a method practised under controlled conditions; it was not something he 'did' to people, it was his way of being with people. In the hospital this includes being with people in their own room or at their bedside instead of the 'controlled' therapeutic consulting room. Some clients experience their room as their territory, so they have some security while the therapist is a guest, but others experience being in bed as a position of vulnerability in front of the fully clothed therapist. As you can imagine, all sorts of attitudes and issues can emerge from exploring the interaction that arises between two people in this situation.

I recall my first meeting with a man a month after he'd been shot during a bank robbery. He was lying in bed in his single room fully conscious with his wife standing at his bedside. I introduced myself, and entered the room knowing that both he and his wife were eager to meet me. We spoke for about twenty minutes and arranged the first session for the next day. When I arrived the following day, the patient told me that the day before he was in fact on the bedpan under the covers and remained so for our entire introductions. His revelation, and associated embarrassment, opened a whole area of discussion regarding his experience of privacy and dignity in the hospital and established our relationship on an open and frank footing, which we maintained during the subsequent eight months of therapy.

Farber would not acquiesce to the professional scientific impetus that sees people as 'more humanoid than human', artefacts of elegant theorizing with 'just those qualities most distinctively human' omitted (cf.

Spinelli, 2001: 165–6). If meeting is to occur, the obligation is on the
therapist to forsake the profession – this type of meeting is possible
'*despite* . . . inequalities in position, status, background, education or
awareness' (ibid.: 166)

> In his practice with patients, Dr Farber was both far humbler than his
> more conventional colleagues and far bolder: He was humbler
> because he approached his patients as a whole human being, not as
> a semianonymous representative of his profession, and because he
> has abandoned his profession's claims to objectivity and curative
> power . . . It was a brave venture to step from behind the mask of his
> profession, and a dangerous one . . . Many other psychotherapists
> did something similar in the 1960s, of course, often with disastrous
> results.
>
> (Gordon, 2000: 125; cf. Spinelli, 2001: 163–4)

Working as a 'whole human being' raises questions regarding the role
of the therapist, especially in a hospital setting. In the hospital, issues of
the demarcation of therapy are complex and unclear, from the point
of view of the institution, the client, and sometimes the therapist. A
hospital is an excellent environment to explore our attitudes to time, space,
hierarchy and authority. In order to negotiate this kind of flexibility
spontaneously, the therapist must carry 'within' himself or herself a clear
sense of their motivations, an intention to be transparent, and an ethical
stance that prioritizes the relationship with the client. The therapist has
no pre-set rationale for ruling out possible avenues of engagement.

For example, when issues between the client and other hospital staff
become problematic and the therapist could have a beneficial role in
resolving these, the therapist may respond to requests to mediate. This of
course is done with the agreement of the client, and the client's reasons
for making this request and the effect of the therapist taking this role do
not go unexplored. The therapist remains aware of the impact, motivation
and meaning of his or her interactions on behalf of the client and refers
the client's requests to other professionals when this is more appropriate.

Another example is Mr Y, who was referred for counselling by a
physiotherapist who was concerned about his refusal to engage in his
rehabilitation. Mr Y was a retired army sergeant, a large man in his early
seventies, and although his prognosis was excellent, his recovery from
surgery had been unexpectedly slow and he had descended into a mood
of despair. Mr Y agreed that talking might help, and in the first meeting
with the therapist he began to recall the death of his wife two years earlier
and soon found himself weeping openly. In the second session, Mr Y

requested that the therapist take him to the shop so he could buy a paper
and then proceed to the cafeteria, where he wanted to buy the therapist a
coffee. Before embarking, the two of them discussed openly the reasons
for Mr Y's request and whether it was embarrassment from the previous
session or an avoidance of difficult feelings. Mr Y explained that
since his wife's death, and until arriving in hospital, he had always started
his day with a trip to a local café where he would read his morning paper.
It was agreed to continue with the trip to the shop and the cafeteria, where
the two sat at a back table and discussed the previous session, the three
weeks spent in bed, and Mr Y's present mood.

The physiotherapist contacted the therapist the next day to say that the
change in Mr Y's attitude was profound. The therapist met Mr Y for two
more sessions, during which they discussed his change in attitude and
the importance of the therapist agreeing to Mr Y's request. Through this
activity and dialogue Mr Y explained that he was able to recognize himself again and believe in his ability to re-create that routine pre-hospital
world which had sustained him since his wife's death. This belief
encouraged him to engage in his physical rehabilitation. Rather than
'treatment' or personality change, this therapy was about finding the
interaction that allowed the client to believe he could regain some
semblance of his way of being-in-the-world.

Perhaps it is frame therapy's imperative against self-disclosure that
offers the clearest demarcation between frame and non-frame understandings. Mr M, a highly successful and respected businessman, was
referred for therapy by staff who found him increasingly uncooperative
and angry on the ward. Mr M had been recently diagnosed with an
aggressive brain tumour and was told he had only a few months of quality
life ahead. He had agreed to see a therapist, and with some trepidation I
met Mr M at the ward dayroom for our one and only session. Before I had
fully sat down, he announced in an intimidating tone: 'I have one question
for you, what would it be like *for you* to be in this situation instead of
me?' It would be obviously self-protective if I retreated into a professional
role with edicts against self-disclosure, frame-based or otherwise. I had
to take the question seriously and offer a human response, 'I really have
no idea how I would feel if I was in your place right now. I find it very
difficult to even imagine, but I think I would feel devastated.' Hearing
this, Mr M softened, with tears in his eyes he told me about the insensitive
way he'd been given the bad news, how people see him as a strong man
'but in here [gesturing to his chest] I'm just a scared little boy. No one
sees that.' We spent the next twenty minutes talking about his life, his
future, my view of life, and life generally. Both of us acknowledged how

shocking it was for a human being to be suddenly facing death. When the transport team arrived to take him back to his local hospital, we parted with a warm handshake, both of us deeply moved and changed by the encounter. Ernesto Spinelli writes that psychotherapy depends upon the emergence of a relationship that is not only mutually engaging but, in actuality, of mutual benefit (Spinelli, 2003). In fact it may be only when the client sees the therapist's vulnerability, despite the therapist's attempts at concealment, that the client makes a significant shift back into relationship with the world of others.

Rather than a 'secure frame', it may be the sharing of therapist and client uncertainty, confusion and despair that is therapeutic. Therefore, it is paradoxically at the moment when the frame therapist fails to maintain the frame, or unintentionally self-discloses, that they may be most helpful to their client. Perhaps perceptive clients recognize the therapist's attempts to maintain their role and feel compassion for the human being trying to hide and help at the same time. In the hospital setting I've also felt this move towards me when the client, momentarily forgetting their own predicament, looks with concern directly into my eyes, saying something like: 'This must be a very difficult job, how do you do it?' Though this could be interpreted as indicating some failure on my part as a therapist, or as client defence, it can also be seen as compassion in its true sense. For a moment at least, the therapist is pulled back from the sterile two-dimensional world of the 'professional'. According to Farber: 'In therapy the paradox is inescapable that the man who is incapable of arousing pity will find it hard to help another' (Spinelli, 2001: 167).

In the hospital setting such an emphasis is a challenge to the entire professionalization and medicalization of life. On occasions I have witnessed medical consultants prescribing drugs to patients simply because they were distressed. One middle-aged male patient made the mistake of confiding in his consultant that he had not recovered from the death of his wife three years earlier. While describing his bereavement, the patient broke down and wept. The consultant immediately prescribed the patient antidepressants. When questioned about his rationale, the consultant simply replied: 'This is a medical matter, and I have judged this man is depressed.' For whose sake is this man being medicated? For whose sake are we offering therapy as treatment, and treatment of what? Farber has deep misgivings about reducing despair to morbidity or an unhealthy state of mind:

> and thus refusing to conceive it as belonging inescapably in some measure to our lives as human beings – [this] may be more malignant

than the despair itself. (It was Kierkegaard's belief that the worst of
all despairs is that in which one does not know he is in despair.) It
sometimes happens that despair itself provides the very condition of
urgency that brings a man to ask those serious – we might call them
tragic – questions about his life and the meaning and measure of his
particular humanness.

(Farber, 1976: 94)

Farber views therapy as an interaction in which truthfulness is paramount.
Being 'truthful' is not the simple telling of a truth, it is a specific mode
of human interacting. It can require sitting with meaninglessness rather
than running to theoretical content, or retreating into frame repairs or other
techniques. Of course we also shrink from the truths of our existence: 'We
all lie – to ourselves, to others, to the world itself. It is in our nature to
lie, but I think I must add that it is also in our nature not to lie' (Farber,
1976: 219). The lie is not the most significant thing, the *response* to the
inevitable lie, when it comes, is what redeems or damns us.

Despite the significant absence of accepted frames, it eventually
became apparent that deep and effective therapeutic work was occurring
in the hospital. So, rather than continually trying to approximate usual
practice, the importance of the frame and its theory began to be questioned
more generally. While theory is always general, life never is. If specific
circumstances could be taken into account in some cases, then why not
in all cases? Who is in a position to decide which individuals could, due
to the exceptional nature of their predicaments, override the dictates of
frame theory and which individuals remain bound by them? Based upon
experiences in the hospital, the view emerged that the incomprehensibility
of life itself, with its implicit 'existential givens', is the appropriate
'frame' for therapeutic interaction. In this way, therapy develops as a
philosophical practice rather than a 'medical' one, and it seems that in the
hospital environment at least, many possibilities would be lost if we
reduced therapy to 'treatment'.

The conclusion

The frame is a metaphor for the collection of rules that many therapists
need to fulfil the essential criteria of their therapy. *The frame is a
metaphor.* Unlike the frame around a window, the frame of therapy is
meant to refer to more than the concrete walls of the consulting room.
Likewise, interpretation, whether based upon death anxiety or childhood
needs (transference), or existential givens, is also metaphor. *Interpretation*

is not evidence. If an interpretation seems to fit well that does not make it fact. It is still, always, metaphor. But metaphor of what? *Something goes on* that remains more than our understanding or symbolization of it.

Rather than offering yet another theory as a replacement for 'frame therapy', the existential-phenomenological approach tries to stay with this 'something'. The philosopher and psychotherapist Eugene Gendlin (1964, 1992, 1997a, 1997b, 1997c, 2003)[8] has offered explications that point to this bodily felt level of interaction. We know, for example, that the moment someone sits next to us on the bus our bodies are in interaction. This immediately includes living *frameworks.* A *frame* does not need to be added on after, or imposed. If I sit too close, the person's framework regarding personal boundaries, which was implied, is now felt by both of us. In therapy we have the opportunity to reflect upon what is usually left implied and unspoken, including how our ongoing frameworks and lived assumptions interact, and how they create themselves bodily in each new situation. A secure frame is not necessary for us to do this. With or without a secure frame there is already a far more intricate order than we could ever impose or comprehend completely. In fact our efforts to comprehend the situation move the interaction onwards so that our understanding is always exceeded, never comprehensive. We are not lost in some sort of 'chaos' if we don't impose order. We just have to look closely at everyday life to know this. If it is not true that order must be imposed in life, it is not true in therapy.

Frame therapy, in its insistence on either the transference or death anxiety, reduces the full spectrum of possible human interactions down to one. In contrast, the PST model is based upon a more inclusive existential and experiential philosophy that attempts to return to what already 'is' without presupposing which of the possibilities for human interacting should prevail in therapy. In the words of Ludwig Binswanger, an early advocate of the application of Heidegger's philosophy to problems in living,

> Heidegger's phenomenological-philosophical analytic of existence is important for psychiatry [or psychotherapy]. This is so because it does not inquire merely into particular regions of phenomena and fact to be found 'in human beings,' but, rather, inquires into the *being* of *man as a whole.* Such a question is not answerable by scientific methods alone . . . Heidegger's analytic of existence, by inquiring into the being of the whole man, can provide not scientific, but philosophical understanding of this wholeness. Such an understanding can indicate to psychiatry [and technique-oriented

forms of therapy] the limits within which it may inquire and expect an answer and can, as well, indicate the general horizon within which answers, as such, are to be found.

(Binswanger, 1963: 211)

It has been my intention in this chapter to describe working as a therapist in an acute general hospital, to describe the assumptions and dilemmas of frame therapy in this context, and to outline how a more philosophical stance may offer a basis for therapeutic practice in this setting. The philosopher Martin Buber adds a humbling note to help focus our efforts along these lines: 'The essential thing is not that the one makes the other his object, but the fact that he is not fully able to do so and the reason for his failure' (Gordon, 2000: 235).

References

Bauknight, R. and Appelbaum, R. (1997) 'AIDS, death, and the analytic frame', *Free Associations* 7(41): 81–100.

Bingswanger, L. (1963) *Selected Papers of Ludwig Binswanger. Being in the World* (trans. J. Needleman), London: Condor Books/Souvenir Press.

Birch, F. (2001) 'Counselling in the hospice movement', in P. Thomas *et al.* (eds) *Clinical Counselling in Medical Settings*, Hove, East Sussex: Brunner-Routledge.

Blechner, M.J. (1993) 'Psychoanalysis and HIV Disease', *Contemporary Psychoanalysis* 29: 61–80.

Cohn, H.W. (1998) 'Frames for therapies or therapies for frames? An exploration of the relation between setting and aim of psychotherapy', *Journal of the Society for Existential Analysis* 9(2): 108–14.

Cohn, H.W. (2002) *Heidegger and the Roots of Existential Therapy*, London: Continuum Books.

Colaizzi, P.F. (2002) 'Psychotherapy and existential therapy', *Journal of Phenomenological Psychology* 33(1): 73–102.

Cooper, M. (2003) *Existential Therapies*, London: Sage.

Crossley, M. (1998) 'A man dying with AIDS: psychoanalysis or existentialism?', *Journal of the Society For Existential Analysis* 9(2): 35–57.

Farber, L.H. (1976) *Lying, Despair, Jealousy, Envy, Sex, Suicide, Drugs, and the Good Life*, New York: Basic Books.

Foucault, M. (1973) *Madness and Civilisation* (R. Howard trans.), New York: Pantheon Press.

Gabbard, G.O. (1995) 'The early history of boundary violations in psychoanalysis', *Journal of the American Psychoanalytic Association* 43(4): 1115–36.

Gans, S. (1999) 'What is ethical analysis?', *Journal of the Society For Existential Analysis* 10(2): 102–8.

Gendlin, E.T. (1964) 'A theory of personality change', in P. Worchel and D. Byrne (eds) *Personality Change*, New York: John Wiley and Sons.

Gendlin, E.T. (1992) 'Thinking beyond patterns: body, language and situations', in B. den Ouden and M. Moen (eds) *The Presence of Feeling in Thought*, New York: Peter Lang, pp. 25–151.

Gendlin, E.T. (1997a) *Experiencing and the Creation of Meaning*, New York: Free Press.

Gendlin E.T. (1997b) 'The responsive order: a new empiricism', *Man and World* 30: 383–411.

Gendlin, E.T. (1997c) 'How philosophy cannot appeal to experience, and how it can', in D.M. Levin (ed) *Language Beyond Postmodernism: Thinking and Speaking in Gendlin's Philosophy*, Evanston, Ill.: Northwestern University Press.

Gendlin, E.T. (2003) 'Beyond postmodernism: from concepts through experiencing', in Roger Frie (ed) *Understanding Experience: Psychotherapy and Postmodernism*, New York: Routledge.

Gordon, E.F. (2000) *Mockingbird Years. A Life in and out of Therapy*, New York: Basic Books.

Gray, A. (1994) *An Introduction to the Therapeutic Frame*, London: Routledge.

Hildebrand, P.H. (1992) 'A patient dying with AIDS', *International Review of Psychoanalysis* 19: 457–69.

Holmes, R. and Lindley, R. (1998) *The Values of Psychotherapy* (revised edn), London: Karnac Books.

Langs, R. (1997) *Death Anxiety and Clinical Practice*, London: Karnac Books.

Langs, R. (1998) *Ground Rules in Psychotherapy and Counselling*, London: Karnac Books.

Laplanche, J. (1989) *New Foundations for Psycho-analysis*, (D. Macey trans.), Oxford: Basil Blackwell.

Logan, A. (2001) 'Nurse-led counselling in a renal unit', in P. Thomas *et al.* (eds) *Clinical Counselling in Medical Settings*, Hove, East Sussex: Brunner-Routledge.

McNamee, S. (2003) 'Who is the therapist? A social constructionist exploration of the therapeutic relationship', *Psychotherapy Section Newsletter* 34(June): 15–39.

Madison, G. (1997) 'HIV and Human Being', unpublished MA dissertation, Centre for Psychotherapeutic Studies, University of Sheffield.

Madison, G. (2001a) 'Framing death – or, what's so existential about communicative psychotherapy?', *Journal of the Society of Existential Analysis* 12(1): 85–101.

Madison, G. (2001b) 'Focusing, intersubjectivity, and "therapeutic intersubjectivity"', *Review of Existential Psychology and Psychiatry*, XXVI(1): 3–16.

Pingitore, D. (1997) 'The corporatization of psychotherapy: a study in professional transformation', *Free Associations* 7, Part 1: 101–27.

Sadowy, D. (1991) 'Is there a role for the psychoanalytic psychotherapist with a patient dying of AIDS?', *Psychoanalytic Review* 78: 199–207.

Schill, S. and Lebovici, S. (1999) *The Challenge to Psychoanalysis and Psychotherapy. Solutions for the Future*, London: Jessica Kingsley Publishers.

Spiegel, D. (1993) 'Psychosocial intervention in cancer' *Journal of the National Cancer Institute* 85: 1198–1205.

Spiegel, D. (1994) 'Health caring: psychosocial support for patients with cancer', *Cancer* 74 (Suppl.): 1453–7.

Spiegel, D. (ed) (1999) *Efficacy and cost-effectiveness of psychotherapy*, Washington, DC: American Psychiatric Press.

Spinelli, E. (1994) *Demystifying Therapy*, London: Constable and Co. Ltd.

Spinelli, E. (2001) *The Mirror and the Hammer. Challenges to Therapeutic Orthodoxy*, London: Continuum Books.

Spinelli, E. (2003) 'Embracing the world: extending the boundaries of the therapeutic relationship', Address to the BPS Psychotherapy Section, reprinted in *Psychotherapy Section Newsletter* 34 (June): 3–14.

Strasser, F. (1999) *Emotions. Experiences in Existential Psychotherapy and Life*, London: Gerald Duckworth and Co. Ltd.

Thomas, P., Davidson, S. and Rance, C. (eds) (2001) *Clinical Counselling in Medical Settings*, Hove, East Sussex: Brunner-Routledge.

van Deurzen, E. (2002) *Existential Counselling and Psychotherapy in Practice* (2nd Edn), London: Sage.

Williams, M. (2001) 'Counselling in a pain relief clinic', in P. Thomas *et al.* (eds) *Clinical Counselling in Medical Settings*, Hove, East Sussex: Brunner-Routledge.

Yalom, I.D. (2001) *The Gift of Therapy. Reflections on Being a Therapist*, London: Judy Piatkus Ltd.

Notes

1   The therapy model that I will base my comments on is unique within the NHS. Typically, there is no integrated counselling provision that is accessible to all hospital patients and their family members.

2   Although team members were all UKCP registered psychotherapists, I will not make a meaningful distinction between the terms 'counsellor' and 'psychotherapist', and will assume that in this case they refer to the same occupation.

3   This type of epistemological claim has been greeted with much scepticism in philosophy. It amounts to what has been termed 'maze epistemology', the error of ascribing the observer's way of being onto the observed in order to understand the behaviour of the observed. With infants we run the risk of seeing them from our adult understanding, founded upon the language and culture that does not yet fully exist for the infant. We may forget the qualitative difference between life before language and life after language.

For example, we do not know that an infant experiences a separate mother at all, or can distinguish between self-sensations and the touch of another.

4 If the response is that non-frame therapy is useful but not as useful as frame therapy, there should be empirical evidence to substantiate this, but as far as I know this has not been substantiated by research.

5 Fascinating questions regarding the transference remain unanswered, for example, is it a universal phenomenon or a deformed interaction induced by certain styles of therapy? If the transference occurs everywhere, why do we need to induce it in therapy, surely we can investigate it anywhere? See Schill and Lebovici, 1999: 266 for more questions.

6 Though Logan decided to keep details of sessions in her own notes and not share them with the medical team, others have taken the view that they work as part of a team and that relevant information will be shared with other staff (for example, Williams, 2001:138).

7 See Michel Foucault's *Madness and Civilisation* (1973) for a detailed discussion of these themes. Also, Holmes and Lindley (1998) for a discussion of what defines a profession and the specific problems this raises for psychotherapy. It is worth mentioning that for professional reasons therapeutic provision in the NHS has loosely mimicked medical specialisations, for example, epilepsy counsellors, oncology counsellors, rehabilitation counsellors, HIV counsellors, renal counsellors. While dividing medical science into disease processes or body parts makes sense when treating physical illnesses, does it make sense from a psychotherapeutic point of view to form similar specialist divisions, and what effect does this have on therapeutic relationships, if any?

8 I have attempted to describe how Gendlin's philosophical method of Focusing is useful therapeutically and how it offers an intersubjective reconceptualisation of therapy (Madison, 2001b).

Chapter 11

Boundaries of timelessness

Some thoughts about the temporal dimension of the psychoanalytic space

Andrea Sabbadini

The psychoanalytic situation can be usefully observed from the perspective of its specific temporal structure, consisting of a complex interconnection of different temporalities. I stress the importance of interpreting the mental events happening around the temporal boundaries between the analyst's consulting room and the outside world. Time plays a key role in psychoanalysis – a process which is always terminated, while being intrinsically interminable – because bringing about change is one of its fundamental therapeutic functions and because the transference operates according to temporally determined mechanisms, such as regression and repetition, involving the actualization of aspects of the past in the present. I use the expression 'contrast of temporalities' to describe a fruitful and therapeutic conflict between the strict time limitations imposed upon the setting by analytic technique, on the one hand, and, on the other, the atmosphere of timelessness so often characterizing the experience of psychoanalysis, both as a whole and within individual sessions. I trace the roots of this timelessness to the original experience of unidimensional time ('infantile omnipresent'), which is in turn related to the timeless quality of our unconscious life.

All psychoanalytic relationships – like human life itself, chess games and most worldly things – have a beginning and an end. 'And time, that takes survey of all the world,/Must have a stop', says Hotspur in his monologue before dying (Shakespeare, *1 Henry IV*, v. iv 82).

The player might checkmate his opponent, lose, accept a draw, get bored with the game and quit, or kick the board to the floor in a fit of rage. Either or both participants in the analytic encounter might give it up, emigrate abroad, agree to terminate their meetings, or die. And yet, what Freud (1900: 297) had to say about the analysis of a single dream ('It is in fact never possible to be sure that a dream has been completely interpreted') also applies to psychoanalysis as a whole: however far you go, you can go further; however 'deep', you can go deeper. In this sense, then, psychoanalysis is ultimately interminable, and can only be interrupted; it must be considered as 'interminable within a terminable psychoanalytical treatment' (Berenstein, 1987: 30). If we extended this paradoxical statement about the nature of the analytic relationship to other human relationships too – from the one to the primary object onwards – we might gain some further understanding about the causes of much emotional suffering.

Several authors have published their views on various aspects of time in psychoanalysis, but with the exception of Arlow (1984, 1986) and Hartocollis (1972, 1974, 1975, 1983) no one has explored these themes systematically or offered original perspectives about their significance. In this chapter I shall give a contribution to the studies on time by focusing on the temporal structure of psychoanalysis.

As to the psychoanalytic space (in its concrete meaning), we know that our work takes place within the walls of the analyst's consulting room, where the analyst sits in a chair and the analysand usually lies on a couch. Issues that can arise in relation to the analytic space include intrusions into the consulting room from the outside – such as another analysand, a bumble-bee or a voice – and concerns about those transitional areas that surround the therapist's room: its entrance and exit door, the waiting room, the house, the street, etc. The importance, and often the difficulty, of analysing what happens in such grey territories – in the space between the inside and the outside of the consulting room, in the time between a session and what immediately precedes or follows it – cannot be overemphasized. To know a country, you must become acquainted with its boundaries.

Certainly the perspective and the focus of attention constantly shift, so that for instance an analyst might emphasize, in the course of the interpretation of a dream, that one of its elements is a reference to his own country of origin; or he might stress that the dream itself has taken place on the night preceding the analysand's birthday. Both the reference to space and that to time might be true and relevant, but the interpretation of that dream will be centred more around one than the other, as a consequence of the analysand's associations and the analyst's choice.

However, much as a clear demarcation between inside and outside is not always possible, it is often impossible to differentiate spatial elements from temporal ones. For instance, when we speak about the waiting room we are referring to the space of a room but also to the time of waiting; when we try to describe the experience of the analysand walking across the threshold of the consulting room at the end of a session, we are emphasizing both where that experience takes place and when. The fact that the analysand is on the way out of the analyst's room is as crucial to the understanding of its meaning as the fact that this happens after the analyst has announced that their session is over.

Often, then, the two dimensions of space and time can and must be considered together. Let me give you some brief clinical vignettes as illustration:

> At the end of her last session before a Christmas break, Miss A gets up from the couch and, on her way to my door, stumbles and falls down. She swiftly picks herself up and, looking most embarrassed, leaves my room without saying a word about what has just happened.

> Upon her return after the holiday, I try to relate Miss A's fall to her anxiety about separating from me for the Christmas break. Falling down in my room was her way of letting me know that she wanted to stay there for the following two weeks too, that she needed my help, that she wished me to have some physical contact with her, and so on.

> The spatial and temporal dimensions could not be isolated one from the other: had Miss A fallen down on the same day in her bathroom, or in the same place at a different time in her analysis, the meaning of that accident, and my understanding and interpretation of it, would have been different.

> On leaving my consulting room for the last time after eight years of therapy, Mr B closed the door behind his back. He had never done that before, not even once. I believe that Mr B had shut my door as an unconscious enactment of the fantasy of locking me into my consulting room forever. In there, where he was not allowing himself to come anymore to see me, no one else would have been able to reach me either, and I would have been imprisoned in solitary confinement for a timeless eternity.

> The cellist Mrs C never replied to my saying 'Hallo' when I met her in the waiting room, nor to my 'Good-byes' at the end of sessions. For her, doing so would have meant acknowledging the existence of an empty time between her sessions and of a gap between her and me; and also the existence of a real relationship between us.

Her analysis was, in her experience, an uninterrupted piece of music that could not tolerate breaks in its performance, or composition, without coming to a premature end. The 'real' breaks that exist in it – the transitional space between waiting and consulting room, between the door and the couch and the door again – like the intervals between feeds in the experience of the baby, undergo magical denial: timelessness is allowed to have no boundaries.

'I am in hell', Mrs C once told me, 'I come here, then you tell me it is time to stop, then it is hell again.' Between 'here' and 'hell' – between timelessness and time – there is no intermediate region.

This brings me closer to what I consider to be a central aspect in the temporal dimension of psychoanalysis: the peculiar admixture of strict adherence to the precise, though hopefully not obsessionally enforced, rules about time in the analytic setting on the one hand, and on the other the indeterminate, timeless atmosphere of the analytic encounter itself. This atmosphere 'is created by a deliberately relaxed unconcern with the passage of time and by a calculated seeming disregard for the duration of the treatment' (Namnum, 1972: 743).

The formal time boundaries in psychoanalysis are normally set and controlled by the analyst, who – being in charge of deciding upon the duration of sessions and the dates of holidays, and of announcing the beginning and the end of each meeting – can be seen as the true 'master of time': at this level at least, the analytic relationship follows the pace dictated by the analyst's clock and by his calendar.

H.D. (Hilda Doolittle), in her 1956 account of her analysis with Freud, describes how he saw himself as having responsibility for time within the session: 'The other day the Professor had reproached me for jerking out my arm and looking at my watch. He had said, "I keep an eye on the time. I will tell you when the session is over. You need not keep looking at the time, as if you were in a hurry to get away"' ([1956] 1985: 17).

Here is some clinical material:

When Mr D left his session, he believed I had deprived him of three minutes of his time: he was furious with me and felt that I was exploiting him. On his way home, though, he realized that in fact I had kept him for 52 minutes, instead of the usual 50. He would not have been caught unprepared by my announcing him the end of the session, had he calculated the time correctly during it; he could have decided to stop talking at the right time, as he always does, thus getting control of terminating the session himself and not having to feel rejected by me.

Mr D arrived at the next session without wearing his wristwatch. He explained that, as an experiment, he had left it outside in the waiting room, in his coat pocket. But now, without it, he felt very anxious as he had to rely entirely upon me. Later in the session Mr D suddenly felt like turning around, grabbing my arm and looking at my watch; not to know the time, he said was almost unbearable for him, be it in his kitchen, in the street or in my consulting room.

About half an hour into this session, he reported a dream from the previous night. While telling me this dream, Mr D became overwhelmed with anxiety and asked me whether there was enough time left for him to continue with it. The dream was as follows:

> Mr D is in Barbara's car; she is driving and he is not wearing the safety seat belt. He is frightened that they might have an accident and get hurt, or that the police might stop them and punish him with imprisonment for an indefinite term. He feels entirely in Barbara's hands. She is now trying to park the car, and there is a lorry coming towards them. He wakes up in a state of fear.

His associations link the car seat belt to his wristwatch: being without wearing either is dangerous. I am Barbara, in whose hands he has unwittingly placed himself, thus becoming exposed to danger and vulnerable. The lorry is the overwhelming anxiety that could reach him and destroy him, finding him unprepared to cope; the police is his internal persecutor – both his rigid father and myself in the transference – punishing him for his unacceptable wishes by keeping him indefinitely in prison: an indefinitely long (or short) session with me.

One of the meanings of Mr D's relationship to time became evident a few months later, when he described how his mother perceived him as growing thinner every time she saw him. Before he leaves her to go back home, she always provides him with chocolate bars and crisps, which he experiences ambivalently, as both a caring gesture and a way of infantilizing him.

Having told me this, he then felt silent. When I asked him what he was thinking about, Mr D replied that he wanted me to take over in these last minutes of the session, to feed him with nice analytic food so that I would remove from him the anxiety of starving himself with silence; at that moment he felt that he could not be an independent adult capable of looking after himself properly without growing too thin, because suddenly, at the end of the 50-minute-long analytic meal, he would be asked to leave the table.

Underlying this anxiety, Mr D also expressed the fear that if he started talking he would become unable to stop, he would be going overtime and be swamped by greed and eventually guilt. My taking over with my words would then have relieved him of the anxiety pertaining to both sides of the oral coin: starvation and greed.

By the way, Mr D has never worn a watch again in a session. His internal clock tells him more or less when his time is coming to the end, which means that, not unlike before, he still remains quiet for the last three or four minutes of each session.

Antinucci-Mark (1986: 15), following in McDougall's (1982) footsteps, compares the analytic scenario to what happens in the theatre: 'The opening of the door', she writes, 'is analogous to raising the curtains which reveal the theatre, its boundaries and its contents . . . What we define as the theatrical event is rigidly delimited by the duration of the performance and the space of the stage. The phenomenon which occurs in the consulting-room has strict temporal boundaries and follows quite closely the concept of unity of time, place and action which classical theory borrowed from Aristotle's poetic conceptions. Precisely because of these fixed norms a multiplicity of experiences can be represented' (Antinucci-Mark, 1986: 15).

The timeless quality of the content of analysis is determined by, and in constant interaction with, such formal time arrangements, set by the analyst and altered only under exceptional circumstances. It is this *contrast of temporalities* that shapes the analytic encounter, modulating its rhythm and punctuating its discourse. Each of these temporalities is unthinkable without the other.

Their paradoxical coexistence can be exemplified by the tale of 'The Sleeping Beauty': the universe of timelessness, of the frozen breath, of the eternal indistinctness between life and death, can only emerge from the background of nature and reality, of movement and 'normal' time surrounding the boundaries of the spell-bound castle. What is most interesting to us is not one world or the other, but the fine edge separating them: the kiss of the handsome prince, the first smile of our beauty awakening to sexuality (Bettelheim, 1975: 225), the initial effort of the clocks of time to start moving again after their rusty centennial paralysis.

Within the safe temporality of the 50 minutes, of the five weekly sessions, of the consistency, continuity and repetitiveness of the analytic process and its rituals, regression to a more primitive timelessness is facilitated. Unstructured representations related to primary-process logic and to unconscious functioning can thus emerge: these take the shape of free associations, where the 'freedom' we require (and never fully obtain) from our analysands is mostly freedom from the exacting bonds of time.

It is because of the coexistence of different temporalities that we can come across those rare, but exciting moments of insight and enlightenment in the course of the psychoanalytic process; and some of the most intense moments in our existence – giving birth to a baby, falling in love, the heights of sexual, mystical or aesthetic pleasure, probably the transition to death itself – share with the analytic experience features of its specific temporality, including the sense of timelessness: their main phenomenological features are a partial loss of the sense of identity, an 'oceanic' fusion with the object, and a momentary slackening of the bonds of time involving a regression to a more primitive temporality.

Freud has pointed out that the temporal laws that govern our relationship with the external world do not operate in the unconscious: 'The processes of the system Ucs.', he wrote, 'are timeless; i.e. they are not ordered temporally, are not altered by the passage of time; they have no reference to time at all' (1915: 187).

Evidence of the 'timelessness' of the unconscious can be found not only in the structure of dreams and in their manifest content, but also in the still undifferentiated experience of time in early infancy, when the instinctual need and its gratification form a magically inseparable unit (Sabbadini, 1979). For the baby, time is not yet organized around a three-dimensional structure, but is experienced instead as *omnipresent*. This is an eternal present that transcends the boundaries of time: it is related on the one hand to the pleasure principle and to primary narcissistic omnipotence, whereby needs and wishes are magically satisfied without delay, before the establishment of a past dimension (memory) and a future one (expectation), and on the other hand to a lack of clear differentiation of the self from the outside world, before the establishment of object and self-constancy, of whole object-relationships, and of the sense of identity (Sabbadini, 1988, 1989).

The spatio-temporal components of the analytic setting have for the analysand a structuring function similar, in many respects, to the supportive (holding, containing, facilitating) environment provided to the growing child by good-enough parenting. In fact, the experience of time during psychoanalysis is often not intrinsically different from that of the young child.

The analytic regression also manifests itself – and most specifically – in this respect. The weakening of the ego defences and of secondary-process functioning – facilitated by the structure itself of the analytic setting, and in particular by its temporal arrangements – gives way not only to a freer expression of unconscious material but also to a more primitive experience of time and relationship to it. The analyst, in a state of free-floating attention, has to accomplish the 'impossible' task of loosening control over his ego in order to listen to the analysand's internal world while at the same time preserving the capacity for secondary-process activities in order to reflect upon it, understand it and interpret it; he has to read the words of a text, while at the same time reading through its lines; he has to listen with his 'third ear', while also listening with the other two.

Within safe analytic boundaries the temporal sequence of events becomes irrelevant to a large extent, the chrono/logic of everyday life gives way to a different timeless reality; what belongs to the past is fused with the *hic et nunc* of the transference; memories of old gratifications and frustrations get mixed up with wishes and fears of future ones; the 50 minutes of a session can seem to last a brief minute or an eternity; a dream-like atmosphere can pervade the analytic space and time; a rigid sense of identity and clear-cut demarcation in the relationship between the two participants in the process, facilitated by the paradoxical predicament of the analysand on the couch who does not know whether he is talking to himself or to his analyst, gives way to a more regressed state of undifferentiation between self and object. Within this temporality, sessions unfold according to unevenly rhythmical patterns – of utterances and silences, monologues and dialogues, sighs, pauses and encouraging noises, associations, reconstructions and interpretations – that bear little resemblance to the time structures of the normal extra-analytical interactions among adults.

This, of course, only applies to some analysands and for brief periods of time; analysands often resist relinquishing their hold over their more habitual temporality, unconsciously fearing that a regressive attitude to time would lead to loss of ego identity and to an excessive dependence upon their analyst.

> Miss E was usually withdrawn and detached from me in her sessions, as indeed she found it most difficult to express any warmth towards her mother, for whom she had most ambivalent feelings. But occasionally she would indulge in the fantasy of meeting me outside the consulting room in order to go for romantic walks in the woods;

or of soon terminating her analysis so that there would be no more formal obstacles to us getting married.

In my interpretations, I tried to bring Miss E's fantasies back (spatially and temporally) to the here-and-now of the transference. I suggested that her wish to have a closer relationship with me – which she had safely moved outside and after her analysis – was in fact a dis-placed and dis-timed wish to have such an intimacy with me inside my consulting room and in the present.

When analysands allow themselves to experience the more timeless reality in their analysis, referred to above, this has to be understood and interpreted in the context of the transference. Its main psychodynamic mechanisms are regression and repetition, both of which are characterized by a temporal component: regression inasmuch as the transference involves the abandonment of the current mental organization and a restructuring of the internal world according to previous and only partially overcome ways of functioning and of object-relating; repetition in so far as it draws its power from unresolved conflicts, forgotten traumata and repressed memories rooted in the past.

Thus, in the here-and-now of the transference, childhood experiences, family romances and scenarios, screen and traumatic events and whole object-relations patterns, are sometimes reactivated and actualized with the same emotional qualities and intensity as their original models.

The transference, in its relation to time, emerges then as the theatre of a paradoxical situation: within it, and through it, we analyse the past in order to give meaning to the present, and at the same time we interpret the present in order to recover the past. Remembering is a creative activity that takes place in the present. The 'essence [of the psychoanalytic process] is the constant and repeated interaction of past with present and present with past, activating each other, as if, in effect, time was transcended' (Namnum, 1972: 740). The transference – with all its past reverberations and echoes – is still a new relationship.

But psychoanalysis does not simply consist of an interplay between the past and present temporal dimensions: inasmuch as its two participants embark upon it in the hope of bringing about new life rather than digging out old corpses, of bringing about some change in the organization of the internal world of one of them – though sometimes they have to accept the impossibility of it – the psychoanalytic experience is an endeavour fundamentally projected towards the future; without this dimension, creative timelessness would turn into sterile repetitiveness and analysis would get embedded into the meaningless impasse which is so typical of analysands with conditions characterized by autistic, 'disaffective' or borderline connotations (Innes-Smith, 1987).

I have so far referred to the whole therapeutic process of psychoanalysis, and to each single psychoanalytic session. It is interesting to note how the temporal structure of the latter reflects and repeats that of the former, and is in turn reflected and repeated in it:

> A middle-aged analysand, Mr F, always arrived obsessionally on time for his sessions. As a result of some analytic work, we discovered his punctuality to be a defensive reaction formation against coming to terms with his sense of hopelessness for having arrived to psychoanalysis too late in his life.

Without stretching the similarities too far, it might be useful to compare the first session of a long analysis (where some of the main themes are first introduced) with the 'opening' of each single session, often suggestive of the atmosphere of the rest of the session itself. Like the listener of the overture of an opera, the analyst is faced with a sort of initial concentration or recapitulation of themes which will then be referred to, repeated, developed and worked through in the course of the following forty or so minutes, and of the following weeks, months or years.

Furthermore, the passage from the 'real' time in the outside world to the timeless atmosphere of analysis, and then back to a time-bound external reality, again applies both to analysis as a whole and to each individual session. Some analysts might prepare their analysands for termination by gradually introducing elements of reality into the relationship and replacing some of their original transference interpretations with more reality-oriented ones; analogously, most analysts tend not to leave their analysands with an excessive amount of unworked-through anxiety between their meetings, by trying to avoid 'deeper' interpretations in the last few minutes of each session, or in the last session before a weekend or a holiday.

The integrity of the ego functions, allowing the analysand to move in and out of regressive states – in and out of the session – is an important condition for analysability. Greenson writes:

> In order to approximate free association, the patient must be able to regress in his thinking, to let things come up passively, to give up control of his thoughts and feelings, and to partially renounce his reality testing. Yet we also expect the patient to understand us when we communicate to him, to do some analytic work on his own, to

control his actions and feelings after the hour, and to be in contact with reality . . . [We] require the patient to possess the capacity to regress and rebound from it.

(Greenson, 1967: 54)

I remember a rule-of-thumb I was taught at art classes many years ago: the darkest and the lightest areas of shading should never be at the edges of a drawing. Something similar would apply to the 'edges' of psychoanalysis and analytic sessions alike, to their beginnings and their ends. Here the so-called 'tact' of the analyst, the timing of his interpretations, his awareness of how the analysand will experience them and be capable of tolerating the resulting anxiety, are all issues of crucial technical importance.

Certain events, experiences and relationships are fixed in duration, and consequently their length is predictable.

We know that our babies are likely to be born about nine months after conception and that a psychoanalytic session lasts 50 minutes; we know that a summer love affair is likely to be over at the end of the holiday or that the chess battle is reaching its conclusion when the white king is surrounded by black pieces checking him from all around the board.

Other events, experiences and relationships – most of them perhaps – are more open in time, and their conclusions are to a large extent unpredictable. A young child does not know when his absent mother is likely to come back, if at all; a major source of distress during wartime is not knowing when the war is going to finish; we might ignore how long an illness is going to last, or when an analysis or a chess game is going to end; even if we have the conscious knowledge that we are going to die, we do not know when. And, of course, we adopt all available psychological defence mechanisms, such as denial and rationalization, to deal with the anxieties aroused in us by such uncertainty: a new drug will make me promptly recover; the war will be over by Christmas.

'Three days and nights of awful suffering and then death. Why, it might happen to me, all of a sudden, at any moment,' he thought, and for an instant he was terrified. But immediately, he could not have explained how, there came to his support the old reflection that this thing had befallen Ivan Ilyich and not him, and that it ought not and could not happen to him . . . After which reflection Piotr Ivanovich cheered up and began to ask with interest about the details of Ivan Ilyich's end, as though death were some mischance to which only Ivan Ilyich was liable, but he himself was not.

(Tolstoy, [1886] 1960:107–8)

My schematic differentiation of experiences according to their temporal predictability is valuable in so far as our knowledge – or lack of it – about the termination of a given event or relationship deeply affects how we perceive it. Our appreciation of the psychoanalytic relationship would be quite different if we were to know how much of it was left: indeed, after a decision about termination has been reached analysis becomes different to what it was before. In the rare occasions when a human being knows when he is going to die (the case of a man sentenced to death by a court of law or by a terminal illness with a predictable course), our experience of life, our attitude towards ourselves and others, our priorities and values and beliefs, inevitably undergo dramatic changes.

Whatever structural similarities one may identify, a crucial feature in the psychoanalytic encounter remains the difference between the temporal dimension of each individual session (known, regular, predictable) and that of the analytic relationship as a whole (unknown, varying, unpredictable). If our technique is such that it does not aim towards the preservation of this vitally important contrast of temporalities, the essence and spirit of the analytic process itself undergo major alterations.

Such a contrast of temporalities can be upset in at least two different ways. The first one, devised by Lacan and supported by his followers, consists of the explicit introduction in the analytic contract of a rule according to which the therapist can arbitrarily decide to cut a session short if he feels that not much is to be achieved by letting it continue for the normal 50 minutes. Perhaps some analysands might be stimulated to 'work harder' (whatever that means) by the fear of having their sessions suddenly curtailed; but I remain opposed to such a gross distortion of the analytic atmosphere and to this persecutory manipulation of the analysand's freedom.

The second way in which we can disturb the contrast of analytic temporalities is by imposing an artificial date for termination of psychoanalysis. This can be the result either of a particular choice of treatment, such as brief or focal therapy or crisis intervention, or of pressures from external circumstances, or of the analyst's conscious decision to put an ultimatum to an analysand in order, for instance, to achieve 'quicker' results. This, as is well known, is what Freud himself did with some of his analysands, including the Wolf Man, and later regretted having done. 'This blackmailing device', he wrote, '. . . cannot guarantee to accomplish the task completely. On the contrary, we may be sure that, while part of the material will become accessible under the pressure of the threat, another part will be kept back and thus become buried, as it were, and lost to our therapeutic efforts' (1937: 218).

We are all familiar with the oft-repeated objection to psychoanalysis as being too lengthy a form of treatment. Freud (1913: 130) described the wish to shorten analytic treatment as 'justifiable', but he added that 'unfortunately, it is opposed by . . . the slowness with which deep-going changes in the mind are accomplished – in the long resort, no doubt, the "timelessness" of our unconscious processes'. There are still no short cuts available, much as there is generally no easy route to checkmating a masterful opponent in chess.

We have thus come back to the somewhat rhetorical question about whether psychoanalysis is *endliche* or *unendliche*; I would like to dodge it by answering that it is always lengthy. Analyst and analysand alike commit themselves to share the same space for a regular and limited period of time – say 50 minutes a day, five days a week – over an unlimited number of years. Such a commitment, and what derives from it, lies at the core of the psychoanalytic process.

References

Antinucci-Mark, G. (1986) 'Some thoughts on the similarities between psychotherapy and theatre scenarios', *British Journal of Psychotherapy* 3: 14–19.

Arlow, J.A. (1984) 'Disturbances of the sense of time with special reference to the experience of timelessness', *Psychoanalytic Quarterly* 53: 13–37.

Arlow, J.A. (1986) 'Psychoanalysis and time', *Journal of the American Psychoanalytic Association* 34: 507–28.

Berenstein, I. (1987) 'Analysis terminable and interminable, fifty years on', *International Journal of Psychoanalysis* 68: 21–35.

Bettelheim, B. (1975) *The Uses of Enchantment: The Meaning and Importance of Fairy Tales*, Harmondsworth: Penguin Books.

Freud, S. (1900) *The Interpretation of Dreams*, *SE*, 4, London: Hogarth Press.

Freud, S. (1913) 'On beginning the treatment', *SE*, 12, London: Hogarth Press.

Freud, S. (1915) 'The Unconscious', *SE*, 14, London: Hogarth Press.

Freud, S. (1937) 'Analysis terminable and interminable', *SE*, 23, London: Hogarth Press.

Greenson, R.R. (1967) *The Technique and Practice of Psychoanalysis*, London: Hogarth Press.

Hartocollis, P. (1972) 'Time as a dimention of affects', *Journal of the American Psychoanalytic Association* 20: 92–108.

Hartocollis, P. (1974) 'Origins of time: a reconstruction of the ontogenetic development of the sense of time based on object-relations theory', *Psychoanalytic Quarterly* 43: 243–61.

Hartocollis, P. (1975) 'Time and affect in psychopathology', *Journal of the American Psychoanalytic Association* 23: 383–95.

Hartocollis, P. (1983) *Time and Timelessness or the Varieties of Temporal Experience*, New York: International Universities Press.

H.D. ([1956] 1985) *Tribute to Freud*, Manchester: Carcanet.

Innes-Smith, J. (1987) 'Time and terminability in the psychoanalytic process', unpublished paper.

McDougall, J. (1982) *Théâtre du Je*, Paris: Gallimard.

Namnum, A. (1972) 'Time in psychoanalytic technique', *Journal of the American Psychoanalytic Association* 20: 736–50.

Sabbadini, A. (ed.) (1979) *Il Tempo in Psicoanalisi*, Milano: Feltrinelli.

Sabbadini, A. (1988) 'Tempo e identità: alcune considerazioni psicoanalitiche', in P. Reale (ed.) *Tempo e Identità*, Milano: Franco Angeli, pp. 116–27.

Sabbadini, A. (1989) 'How the infant develops a sense of time', *British Journal of Psychotherapy* 5(4): 475–84.

Tolstoy, L.N. ([1886] 1960). 'The Death of Ivan Ilyich', in *The Cossacks and Other Stories*, Harmondsworth: Penguin Books.

Index

Page entries in **bold** type represent whole chapters devoted to that topic